A NEGOTIATED WORLD:

*Three Centuries of Change in a
French Alpine Community*

HARRIET G. ROSENBERG

A Negotiated World:

*Three Centuries of Change in a
French Alpine Community*

FOREWORD BY ERIC R. WOLF

UNIVERSITY OF TORONTO PRESS
Toronto Buffalo London

© University of Toronto Press 1988
Toronto Buffalo London
Printed in Canada

ISBN 0-8020-2640-0

Canadian Cataloguing in Publication Data

Rosenberg, Harriet
  A negotiated world

  Includes index.
  ISBN 0-8020-2640-0

  1. Abriès (France) – Social conditions.   2. Abriès
  (France) – History.   3. Villages – France – Abriès –
  Case studies.   I. Title.

  HN438.A28R67 1988   944'.48   C87-094717-6

To the memory of Leibel Rosenberg and Alex Lee

FRONTISPIECE: Eighteenth-century carved door with sunbursts and
grapevine borders, characteristic Queyrassin motifs

'These words shall go where tears cannot reach.'
Louise Michel 1882

Contents

Illustrations

Foreword

Books have a history, and this book has a historical context of its own. Harriet Rosenberg studied history and anthropology at the Universities of Toronto and Michigan during the tumultuous 'sixties and 'seventies, a time when social historians, political economists, and students of peasantry began to define common problems and to converge in working towards their solution. Investigators who turned to the study of rural France could draw on the exemplary legacy of Marc Bloch, embodied and expanded in the years after World War II in the journal *Annales*. Innovative French historians of rural life such as Georges Duby and Emmanuel Le Roy Ladurie were joined by scholars from this side of the Atlantic, such as Charles Tilly, Laurence Wylie, and Natalie Davis. Simultaneously, the ferment of the stormy 'sixties brought on a rethinking of the nature of class, society, and the state, as well as efforts to comprehend the workings of capitalism, imperialism, colonialism, and neo-colonial dependency. Nor did this questioning remain on the level of abstract concepts. There was much concern with how one might live one's life in a world not of one's own making, but a concern also with how the concrete social lives of men and women, past and present, could be recorded and better understood when placed against the background of economy, society, and polity.

A major challenge faced during this period turned on a re-examination of 'modernization theory,' then the dominant paradigm of received opinion in the social sciences. Modernization theory envisaged the world as set on a trajectory from adherence to 'tradition' towards a rational innovative 'modernity.' Yet when both tradition and modernity were re-examined against the background of shifting political and economic forces with variable outcomes for social classes and regions, tradition came to be seen as often less traditional and more congruent with change, and modernization more subject to failures and reversals, than predicted by linear models of progress. Thus the period opened a search for new models, new ways of conceptualizing more heterogeneous and complex realities.

This book takes up that challenge. Harriet Rosenberg takes us to a village in the Hautes-Alps. There we find ourselves in one of the many 'ancient nations on a small scale' (Fernand Braudel) that have gone into the making of France. It has, as she demonstrates, its own history of changing and ever re-'negotiated' positions in the political and economic arrangements that successively constituted French polity and society.

We learn of the autonomous political institutions and subsistence skills of the area during the Old Regime; its contradictory stance during the Revolution; its subjection to the centralizing politics and intensified capital accumulation during the 19th century; its uncertain future. The focus is simultaneously on the changing demands brought to bear on the community from outside, and on the ways through which villagers sought to cope with these impositions. We meet salient notables who mediated between the village and the world beyond, but also ordinary folk whose lives are captured in archival documents, in genealogies, and in contemporary comment and recall. At the same time, Harriet Rosenberg shows us how the import of these transactions and negotiations, alignments and realignments, extends well beyond the confines of locality. They form the warp and woof of 'another' France, another French reality, different from other Frances and sometimes in contradiction with them. We are thus also enabled to change our thinking about France herself, to see her processually as an ensemble of diverse elements – sometimes consonant and at other times dissonant – periodically re-orchestrated over time, rather than as the unitary and unchanging exemplification of an archetypical myth. And in this there is a large gain.

ERIC R. WOLF
Herbert Lehman College and Graduate Center,
City University of New York

Preface

In the late 1960s I began my graduate work in anthropology and French history at the University of Michigan. Around me swirled the student protests against the war in Vietnam in which peasants suddenly became key actors in world politics. I became intellectually and politically committed to understanding more about peasant societies and found myself drawn to the works of French social historians and to social anthropologists who were interested in peasant societies.

It was a time when an enormous number of grants seemed to be available to graduate students. I was able to tour French and Swiss archives one summer through the generosity of the Ford Foundation and later install myself in France for two years of field-work and archival research with the support of the Canada Council and the Ford Foundation. From 1972 to 1974, I worked primarily in Abriès, a village in the Department of the Hautes-Alpes. (The local pronunciation of the name is ab-ree-ez.)

I loved living in France and was amused when my anthropologist colleagues who worked in more exotic locales asked about my time in the 'bush'. I would bravely attempt to match their stories of hardship by pointing out that 'my village' was more than twenty-four hours away from the nearest three-star restaurant. In fact, having come to rural France directly from life as a North American student, my standard of living actually improved in the field.

My first few weeks in the region were spent touring various villages trying to select an appropriate field site. I was also able to spend time with Rayna Rapp, Randy Reiter, and Susan Harding who were then doing field-work in southern Europe and to discuss my odyssey with them. By a stroke of good fortune, Robert Burns, who had done pioneering field-work in the Queyrassin village of Saint Véran, was visiting the area and was kind enough to share his insights with me and show me around the region.

The first stages of field-work were both frightening and exciting. Since I did not know how to drive, I hitch-hiked from village to village on school buses, milk trucks, and fruit and vegetable vans. (Village mayors and priests arranged most of the rides for me.) The participants in these travel arrangements often had interesting comments to make about the positive features of their village compared to the negative features of a neighbouring commune. On the whole, drivers from the lowlands tended to dismiss alpine village life in its entirety, while alpine residents had a more refined sense of discrimination about the merits of individual villages.

Many of the villages in the Briançonnais had excellent archival sources but were so depopulated that the prospect of living there as a field-worker was quite unappealing. Some had fewer than fifty people in them, and many seemed like ghost towns. Wherever I settled, I was going to be living for an extended period of time, and I did not want to run out of people to talk with.

Eventually I chose Abriès. It had a population of about two hundred, and a preliminary search of its archival resources suggested they were quite impressive. Furthermore, the village appeared to be engaged in sorting out a variety of interesting political, economic, and social problems. Admittedly, the driver of the van that first took me to Abriès told me that he and his sister had decided that it would be terrible for a stranger like myself to live alone among such 'savages'. Speaking as a lowlander, he was certain that the Abrièsois were so close-mouthed and tight-fisted that they would never speak to me or help me in any way. I don't think he believed that they would actually harm me, but he was concerned that I might perish from loneliness.

Despite this well-intentioned advice – or maybe because of it – I decided to live in Abriès. The room I rented had a bed, a kitchenette, a work-table, an indoor washroom, and a wood-burning stove for heating. In retrospect I realize that it was a very small space but at the time it seemed quite large in comparison to the places I had lived in as a student.

I soon began mapping residence patterns, learning local pronunciations, attending church, going on processions and pilgrimages, working on corvées (communally organized work parties) to clear avalanche debris, collecting life histories, counting sheep, cattle, and tourists, and reading municipal council reports, parish registers, diaries, and letters. The villagers were a little wary at first, I thought, but hardly 'savage'. I later learned that they were simply puzzling over what a young girl was doing alone in their village. Eventually, someone took me aside and asked me if my mother knew where I was. I explained that I just looked very young for my age and produced pictures of my family.

As friends who were doing field-work in Europe began to come through the village and as my French improved, I'm sure I began to seem more three-dimensional and less like a lost child to the villagers. Within a few weeks, my explanation that I was in Abriès to study its history and way of life found general acceptance. After that, all doors were open to me and I was invited everywhere. It was not uncommon for someone to say to me in the course of a casual conversation, 'Write this down, Mlle Harriet. This is important.'

Archival research took me to the mayor's office for local records, to Gap, which is the departmental capital, and to Paris, where I consulted the National Archives and the marvellous military archives at Vincennes. In addition many people in the region shared private letters and documents with me. Whenever I left the village to go to the Paris archives, there was much joking about whether I was going to abandon the village for the bright lights of the city, and when I did indeed return many people had rather visible expressions of pleasure.

The villagers proved fascinated by and knowledgeable about genealogy and local history – often family history for them. As I worked my way through dowries, wills, marriage contracts, court cases, cadasters (land survey registers), ledger books, the deliberations of the escartons, memoirs of army engineers, the correspondence of intendants, prefects, and sub-prefects, accounts of pastoral visitations, records of army recruits, censuses, tax rolls, agricultural questionnaires, newspapers, and local histories, I shared my findings with villagers. They always seemed to be interested in what I was learning. Often they fleshed out my research, even discussing events hundreds of years in the past; some people still knew precisely which fields had been owned and abandoned by Protestants fleeing the village during the wars of religion in the seventeenth century.

The Abrièsois were keen on uncovering migration patterns and added much oral history to the gaps and inconsistencies in the written record. Villagers also explained to me the methods used for outwitting customs officials, border police, and tax assessors in the nineteenth and twentieth centuries. They pointed out inaccuracies in census figures and explained why and on which records it was politic to be vague or confusing. I learned the concrete lesson to which historians often pay lip service: not to believe everything one reads.

This system of moving back and forth between the village and the archives was both a source of inspiration and a check on flights of fancy. Grounding ethnography in history and history in ethnography provided me with a sense of what was plausible and what far-fetched in both fields. Many villagers had wonderful senses of humour and were quite capable of pulling a researcher's leg. But it is precisely such tall tales that are the pleasure of field-work. They also offer another important lesson: not to believe everything one hears. How well I have achieved the balance I aimed for is up to the reader to decide.

Funding for my field research was generously provided by the Canada Council and the Ford Foundation's Foreign Area Fellowship Program. This book has been published with the help of a grant from the Social Science Federation of Canada, using funds provided by the Social Sciences and Humanities Council of Canada.

I gratefully acknowledge the support and efforts on my behalf by M. Playoust and Mlle Robert, archivist and assistant archivist of the Hautes-Alpes departmental archives in the 1970s. Many other French scholars and administrators also contributed time and effort to this project, and I especially wish to thank M. Pons of Gap, Mme Dürreleman of Briançon, the staff of the Direction Départementale d'Agriculture in Gap, and an anonymous sous-archiviste at the military archives in Paris who performed a miracle of red-tape cutting. My warm thanks also to Michelle and Gérard Quiblier for giving generously of their time, energy, and friendship. For assistance in research and translation, I extend appreciation to Sheryl Adam, Leslie Silver, Lorna Weir, and Mariana Valverde.

I would also like to express my appreciation for the unflagging support of my editor, Rik Davidson, and the wise and literate suggestions of my copy-editor, Lenore d'Anjou.

To my teachers – Robert Burns, Natalie Davis, Emmanuel Le Roy Ladurie, Charles Tilly, and Eric Wolf – I express thanks for teaching me about peasants, mountains, and interdisciplinary research.

In this long project I have cherished the support of my sisters, Maureen FitzGerald, Meg Luxton, Rayna Rapp, Ester Reiter. To

Richard Lee and our daughter, Miriam, and to David Lee, your encouragement, kindness, and good humour have meant more to me
than you can imagine.

And finally I acknowledge the graciousness and warmth of the
people of Abriès who shared their memories, their insights, their work.
Thank you, dear friends.

The gorges of the Guil River in the valley of the Queyras: the 'Tournequet'

Sundial on church in central Abriès. Inscription reads: 'It is later than you think.'

Transhumant flock in a high alpine meadow

A cultivator trying to catch a lamb that has become separated from the flock during the assembly of the collective herd in the spring

A young cultivator descending into the village with a load of hay

A family of three generations haying. In the background a tourist boutique is being built.

Man pausing on a corvée to clear
avalanche debris

Garde champêtre calling villagers to
a corvée

Villagers and tourists in a religious procession in the abandoned hamlet of
Valpréveyre

A villager and ex-villager meet at a procession.

Mother and daughter enjoying a sunny day

Hay cart traversing the central *place* of Abriès during the tourist season

Tourist accommodations under construction

1

A Cautionary Tale

Abriès is an alpine commune of fewer than two hundred people in a southwestern region of France called the Briançonnais. The overnight train from Paris stops a few miles west of Gap, the capital of the Department of the Hautes-Alpes. From there, a local bus winds slowly up the steep and rugged valley of the Queyras. It is the highest inhabited valley in Europe. At the top of the valley, ringed by mountains dotted with abandoned hamlets, sits Abriès (see Map 1).

Lowlanders call the montagnards 'renfermés' – a word meaning both 'closed in' and 'musty with age.' They wonder why anyone would go to so isolated a place except perhaps for a little camping or skiing. Public officials describe the valley as dead – 'un pays mort.' They dismiss the whole area as a backward region inhabited by a remnant population who subsist on government handouts. Some do, however, argue that tourism may – perhaps – revitalize the area and staunch the flow of out-migration. The Briançonnais is, after all, a breathtakingly beautiful spot.

Today's visitors to Abriès would be surprised to learn that two hundred years ago the village supported a population of close to two thousand people. It was an active market centre connected with famous local and regional fairs. In the seventeenth and eighteenth centuries, the Abrièsois were regarded as well-educated and very enterprising peasant-traders. The Briançonnais region as a whole was renowned throughout France for its high literacy rate. Peasants hired locally trained schoolteachers to instruct their children in French, Latin, and arithmetic during the long alpine winters.

Abriès was also known to French officials, lay and ecclesiastical. From the fourteenth century, Abriès, as part of an ancient regional confederation of fifty-one villages pursued trials through French

MAP 1 Location of Abriès

courts. Sometimes the peasants engaged in decades-long litigation, using village funds to hire lawyers and lobbyists to plead their cases. They fought new taxes and tithes and tax increases, they resisted disadvantageous jurisdictional changes, they opposed conscription into the French army, and they demanded payment for provisions supplied and for war damages. Frequently they won. Litigation in the Briançonnais was more than a political/legal affair; it was a form of art and theatre.

Famous as shrewd negotiators, the inhabitants of the Briançonnais had successfully resisted seigneurial rule and the region was sometimes called 'the little republic.' Some government officials openly admired the area's peasants. Others were alarmed by their independent spirit and, as one put it, their 'vanité insupportable' (insufferable vanity), fearing that their loyalty to the French state was questionable.

Prominent in this dynamic system stood the far-from-isolated town of Abriès and its thriving hamlets. In the seventeenth and eighteenth centuries Abriès did not look or behave like a 'traditional' peasant community, if 'traditional' is taken to mean illiterate, passive, isolated, and poor.

Thus, in order to conceptualize the changes which unfolded in Abriès, I begin by eliminating the notion that rural people are 'traditionally' poor or apolitical. Peasant poverty or wealth, political mobilization or passivity, are not givens. Rather, they are aspects of peasant society requiring historically contextualized explanations.

The theoretical underpinnings of this book owe most to the works of those scholars who have adopted a political economy approach combined with a detailed analysis of change. Analysts such as Bloch (1961; 1966), Slicher van Bath (1963), Le Roy Ladurie (1966; 1975), and Wolf (1969; 1982) represent a pattern of scholarship in ethnohistory which is based on a non-teleological view of change rather than a model in which a negatively valued traditional life is inevitably succeeded by a positively valued one.

Implicit in the concept of modernization is a marching-to-glory metaphor embedded in the ideology of capitalist progress which discounts local-level resistance as being simply characteristic of peasant ignorance. Some marxist works on the sociology of development, while deconstructing hallelujah theories of change, have also tended to undervalue action at the local level.

The aim of this case study is to put agency in the forefront by documenting the complex negotiations through which Abrièsois constructed their history.

HISTORY AND ANTHROPOLOGY

I approached the study of this village as both a historian and an anthropologist. Anthropological studies of communities in complex societies have changed in recent years, acknowledging the need to analyse the wider context in which the community is embedded. In complex societies the local system is no longer seen as a representative sample of the total culture and society. For many anthropologists, it is the patterns of articulation among the several levels in a society which provides the basis for inquiry (Leeds 1973; Netting 1981).

The historical dimensions of state formation and its role in local life are also increasingly being integrated into ethnographies to explain contemporary social formations, especially in studies of complex societies. Such studies explore local social organization and ecology, and they also analyse the connection between local life and large-scale transformations. For example, in a comparative study of two Tyrolese villages of differing ethnicity, Cole and Wolf (1974) consider the villages' differing adaptive strategies within similar ecological niches and the context of a long history of state formation in the region. The authors cite mountain living as putting important constraints on agriculture and housing, but they also emphasize that 'the rise of the state introduces into the ecological set a specifically political element that transforms problems of ecological limitation into decisions of political economy' (1974: 285).

Other anthropologists have tackled the problem of 'transition' by pointing out that the development of industrial capitalism did not obliterate peasant agriculture. European states and capitalist entrepreneurs tried to remodel agriculture along industrial lines; they developed policies to break up communal lands and promote large private holdings on the assumption that economies of scale would work in agriculture as they had in industry. Yet European landholding has never been very concentrated, and is not so today.[1] (The exception is areas of cereal production.) Smallholding persists for a variety of complex

1 As of 1970, 65.5 per cent of all farms in France were fewer than 20 hectares in area and only 8.5 per cent were more than 50 hectares. By contrast, the United Kingdom had 23.3 per cent of its farms in holdings of more than 50 hectares and 52.4 per cent of its farmlands in holdings of fewer than 20 hectares. At the other extreme, close to 95 per cent of Italian farms were fewer than 20 hectares and only 1.7 per cent were concentrated in holdings of more than 50 hectares (Goodman and Redclift 1981: 17).

reasons including splits in the structure of the agricultural market, the limits of capital investment, and the highly skilled nature of animal husbandry, as well as political resistance. The continued existence of significant peasant production in Europe is not an archaic hold-over but part of the development of capitalism itself (Goodman and Redclift 1981; Servolin 1972).

Historians, particularly French historians, have also found a political economy approach useful in historical ethnographies. Le Roy Ladurie, following in the footsteps of scholars of the Annales school, has been influential in this regard. His classic study of Languedoc from the fifteenth to the eighteenth century (1966) and his village ethnography *Montaillou* (1975) have provided models for exploring the political economy of peasant life with a long-term perspective. My own book echoes the issues and problems of these works: the tracing of trends in class formation, subsistence patterns, market conditions, tax systems, and demographic cycles as well as the investigation of aspects of power-holding, gender roles, and production.

Le Roy Ladurie's work on Languedoc is also significant to my work because it grapples with the question of reverse development in a peasant society that was relatively well-off in the 1400s but impoverished a few centuries later. Although Le Roy Ladurie analysed Languedoc only up to the eighteenth century, he concluded his book with the suggestion that one could usefully study such change into the modern period, an approach which is adopted in this book.

Other historians working in France have concentrated on the transformation of peasant societies in the nineteenth and twentieth centuries. Weber (1976; 1982) describes a process of modernization and the reluctant integration of apolitical peasantry into the mainstream. Other historians (Judt 1979; Margadant 1980; Vigier 1963; Berger 1972) argue that both political mobilization and demobilization were features of peasant politics in the nineteenth and twentieth centuries. Their data, interpreted without the model of unidirectional modernization employed by Weber, present a view of the peasantry in which some people are radicalized and others conservatized during the course of the nineteenth century.

Anthropologists also often describe contradictory and complex patterns of power-holding transformations. The work of Wolf in *Europe and the People without History* (1982) is an important contribution to the analysis of agency and the multiple levels of connections in which local change is embedded. I have also found that anthropological enquiries into patron-client systems provide useful insights into local-level processes and articulations with larger systems. (Kenny 1960; Foster 1965; Wolf 1966a; 1966b; Campbell 1964; Boissevain 1966; 1969; 1974; Pitt-Rivers 1954; Paine 1971; Silverman 1968; 1974; Bailey 1969; Mayer 1966; 1967; Eidheim 1963; Bee 1974). Some theorists of patronage argue that personalistic politics is an eminently 'modern' part of political life, not a traditional lag from pre-existing political cultures' unused to present-day institutional forms. For example, ethnographies of local politics (such as Blok 1974; Eidheim 1963; Mus 1952; Tilly 1964) demonstrate that modern bureaucracies do not necessarily function to eliminate local tyrants; sometimes, in fact, they create them. The political boss and the political favour are just as much a part of today's politics as is the vote and the party. And like people in Chicago, Montreal, and Paris, Abrièsois take these aspects of political life in their stride.

For the three hundred years covered in this book, the villagers of Abriès farmed, fought, formed alliances, traded, plotted, organized, resisted, and acquiesced. They seized some opportunities, and lost others. They were real people who lived through real historical transformations. And they are still there. The village continues to change as it struggles with the problems of tourism, agriculture, and the finding of suitable marriage partners for its young people.

Abriès is not a microcosm of peasant life. In many ways it is unique. It was a market centre. Its region had an unusually high and early literacy rate. And it is unlike peasant villages in other countries because it is French and therefore obsessed with record-keeping. But Abriès does not have to be completely representative in order to be significant. The history of this village is important because it is interesting in and of itself, because the survival of abundant documentation makes it possible to recount its story, and because it reveals the complexity of social change. The history of Abriès is a cautionary tale warning us not to accept stereotyped myths about peasant societies.

The Abrièsois themselves are quite confident that their story is worth telling. When I arrived in the village, I said I had come to study not the history of kings, governments, and wars but the history of the villagers. 'Of course,' said an elderly peasant, 'of course. We are important too.'

2

The Village during the Old Regime

The village of Abriès is situated in the sunny, dry, intra-alpine zone of the southern French Alps in the upper valley of the Guil River, a tributary of the Durance (see Map 1). The seven communities of the Guil now compose the canton of Aiguilles and constitute a subregion called the Queyras (see Map 2), the highest inhabited valley of western Europe. The centre of the village is at an altitude of 1550 metres, and its hamlets range as high as 2400 metres. The whole region of the Queyras has a rugged, seemingly impenetrable aspect. It is ringed by mountains, and the narrow gorges of the lower Guil enforce the impression that the valley is a cul-de-sac. In fact, however, the Queyras is penetrated by numerous passes which integrate the region into its surroundings and connect it to Italy. Most medieval and early modern travel funnelled through these passes, rather than along the river valley.

During the ancien régime, the Queyras was part of a larger geopolitical unit of five major valleys called the Briançonnais or the Republic of the Escartons (see Map 3). The regional, political, and economic capital was the alpine city of Briançon, the highest city in Europe (1326 metres). Each escarton functioned originally as a medieval tax-sharing unit, but they soon developed into a system of deliberative assemblies that gained semi-autonomous political status within the Dauphiné region and later within France. The term 'republic' was applied to the valleys because the population was principally peasant smallholders who also held a great deal of land in common. Manorialism never took root in the Briançonnais, and there were very few aristocrats in the region. The Briançonnais escartons were structurally akin to the semi-independent peasant coalitions of the Basque and Tyrol

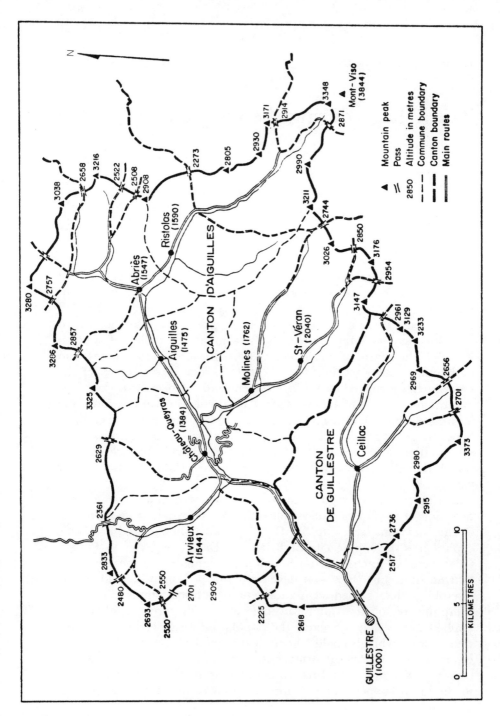

MAP 2 Valley of the Queyras

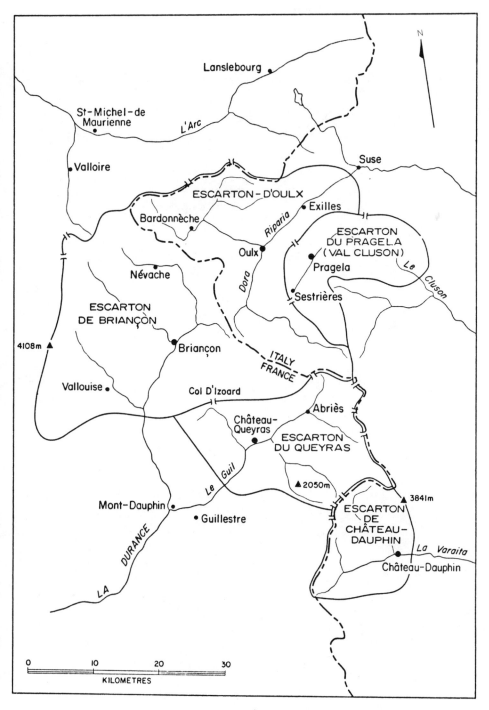

MAP 3 The five escartons of the Briançonnais

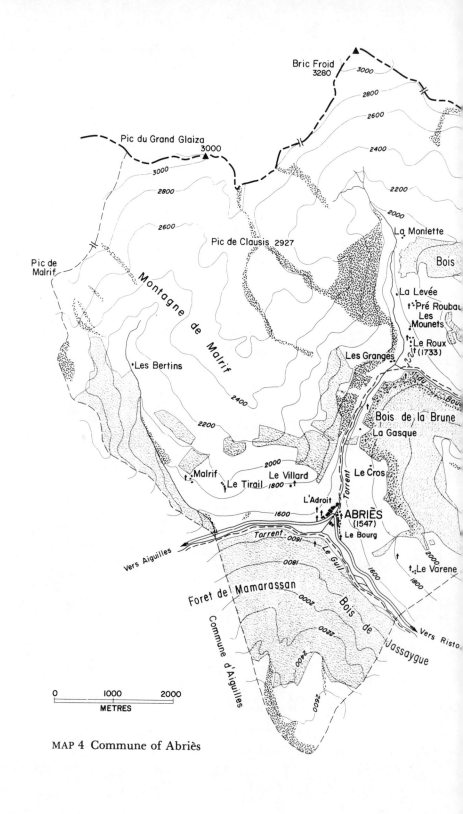

Bric Froid
3280
3000
2800
2600
2400
2200
2000

Pic du Grand Glaiza
3000
3000
2800
2600

La Monlette

Pic de Clausis 2927

Bois

Pic de
Malrif

La Levée
† Pré Roubau
Les
Mounets

Montagne de Malrif

Le Roux
(1733)

Les Granges

Les Bertins

2400

Bois de la Brune

2200

La Gasque

2000

Le Cros

Malrif
Le Tirail

Le Villard
1800

Torrent

L'Adroit

1600

ABRIÈS
(1547)

2000

Le Bourg

1800

Vers Aiguilles

Torrent

0091

0081

Le Guil

1600

† Le Varene

Foret de Mamarassan

2000

Bois de Jassaygue

Vers Risto

2200

Commune d'Aiguilles

2400

2000

2600

0   1000   2000
METRES

MAP 4 Commune of Abriès

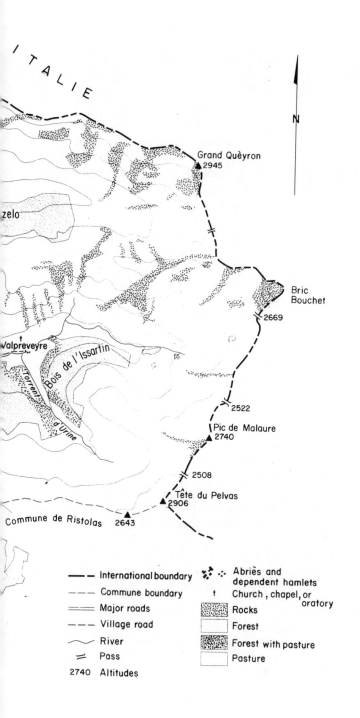

I T A L I E

Grand Quèyron
▲ 2945

zelo

Bric
Bouchet

⊁ 2669

Valpreveyre †

Bois de l'Issartin

Torrent d'Urine

2522

Pic de Malaure
▲ 2740

⊁ 2508

Tête du Pelvas
▲ 2906

Commune de Ristolas   ▲ 2643

N

—— International boundary
--- Commune boundary
=== Major roads
--- Village road
~~~ River
⇒ Pass
2740 Altitudes

✷ ⁝ Abriès and
     dependent hamlets
†   Church, chapel, or
     oratory
▨   Rocks
□   Forest
▨   Forest with pasture
□   Pasture

regions, the Swedish frontier, Iceland, Switzerland, and many woodland regions of Scotland, Holland, and Belgium.

In 1713, the Treaty of Utrecht ceded the three eastern valleys of the Escarton union to Piedmont. Thereafter the term 'Briançonnais' referred to the two remaining French valleys.

In the seventeenth and eighteenth centuries, the community of Abriès comprised a large central agglomeration called Abriès and a principal hamlet called Le Roux, each surrounded by satellite hamlets (see Map 4). The most significant hamlets near the central village were Le Villard, Le Tirail, Malrif, Varenq, and Le Clot, while those dependent on Le Roux were Les Granges, Les Traverses, Praroubaud, Monteite, Allevay or La Levey, L'Eymounet, and Valpréveyre.[1] All these hamlets are now abandoned, while Le Roux has a population of about twelve people. Abriès was the marketing centre for these hamlets and for the villages and hamlets of Ristolas and Aiguilles nearby on the Upper Guil. It was also a trade centre for neighbouring Piedmontese villages and articulated with the larger Briançonnais trade network.

The centrality of Abriès was expressed in its solid stone architecture, which contrasted with the primarily wooden buildings found in much of the Queyras. Houses of the central quarter, Le Bourg, were three-or four-storey stone buildings. The weekly Wednesday market was conducted under the stone arches of Les Halles. The central village also contained a large Catholic church and two smaller chapels, which were destroyed and rebuilt in the seventeenth century, and a Protestant church, which was destroyed and never rebuilt after the Revocation of the Edict of Nantes in 1685. Le Roux also had a large church and in the early eighteenth century was considered populous enough to be designated an auxiliary parish served by its own clergy.

In short, contemporary observers of old regime Abriès thought of it as a substantial, virtually urban centre. It contained an important market and was the religious and administrative focus for the Upper Guil.

During the seventeenth and eighteenth centuries, the economy of the Briançonnais was disrupted by wars and migrations and influenced by political decisions made in Paris. Nevertheless, some patterns and

---

1 Most of these hamlets, with some variation in spelling, are shown on Map 4. Some of the other hamlets it shows, such as Les Bertins, were used only in the summer. Those listed above had substantial periods of year-round occupation well into the nineteenth century.

strategies remained constant over the years. The Briançonnais had been part of the Roman Empire. In the Middle Ages it was part of the Dauphiné and came under the direct rule of the Dauphin, political facts that affected the municipal organization of its towns and villages. The presence of the popes in Avignon involved the population in lucrative transalpine trade. The plague epidemics of the fourteenth century devastated village populations. Population recovery after the Black Death led to a reorganization of production methods – a move into labour-intensive canal irrigation, for example – which raised productivity. The people evolved a strategy of winter migrations for male labour, and this pattern also went through various changes (Blanchard 1950: 951–9).

Thus, when considering the Briançonnais economy in the seventeenth and eighteenth centuries, we must see it as an evolving and adaptive system that had been integrated into the wider society for centuries. To view it as an isolated peasant economy endlessly going through unchanging rhythms would be erroneous.

AGRICULTURE

During the old regime, the Queyras was famous for its highly productive agro-pastoral economy. For example, de la Blottière, a military engineer stationed nearby, commented in 1708: 'There is hardly a region whose lands produce more than these mountains' (in de Rochas 1882: 140).[2] Military observers and administrative officials agreed that the population lived in comfort and viewed the causes of this 'aisance' as both moral and ecological: the economizing spirit and hard work of the people and the high quality and abundance of pastureland which permitted sheep-raising. Neither seasonal migration nor intensive labour input during the agricultural season was seen as an indicator of hardship or poverty. Even during the worst years of the religious wars, when the economy was often disrupted, observers expressed the belief that agriculture was productive and could meet the needs of the population once hostilities had ended. There was no sense of complete des-

---

2 De la Blottière was a military engineer stationed in the Queyras. A report he wrote in 1708 was eventually published as part of a descriptive historical article, 'Le Briançonnais au commencement du XVIIIe siècle,' edited by Albert de Rochas (1882). We shall encounter de la Blottière and his report in more detail in Chapter 3.

peration or of living on the edge of famine; warfare produced intermittent crises but not sustained disaster.

Adequate production levels were maintained by combining intensive irrigation and fertilization with cultivation to the highest feasible altitudes. There were two major crops, hay and grains, and small gardens. The hayfields or meadows were natural prairies, which were not planted but were irrigated at all altitudes. The Abriès hamlet of Malrif, at 2400 metres, still has visible traces of a canal system whose maintenance required enormous labour.

The natural hayfields were of three kinds: flat bottomland, which produced long hay; a middle zone, which produced short hay; and high-altitude fields. The long-hay fields, which were the most heavily fertilized and irrigated, were cut in July and September, while the others were cut only once a year. The high-altitude fields provided little in quantity, but they did yield a high-quality product. All these resources were exploited because the hay harvest had to provide fodder for stock that wintered indoors for seven to eight months, even though as many animals as possible were sent to the Po valley for the winter (Blanchard 1950: 909-12).

Grain was also grown for both animal and human consumption; here too the altitude and irregularity of terrain were of major importance. The soil was good and light, so heavy plows were not needed; however, the sloping fields required terracing – another labour-intensive operation. In some places the angles were so great that the topsoil tended to slip down to the bottom of the fields; every few years it was carted up by the basket-load and redistributed. Fertilizer was distributed in a similar manner; brought up to the fields on muleback or in cart-loads when possible. Brunet tells us that the grain fields were also irrigated (in Guillemin 1892: 333).[3]

The grain fields were rotated from fallow to rye and then to barley or oats. The altitude precluded growing much wheat, and what little was planted was often harvested green; but the hardier grains, especially rye, did very well. No fruit-trees or vines grew in the Queyras. De la Blottière noted that wine was an especially important trading item with Piedmont (in de Rochas, 1882: 40-3).

3 Jean Brunet (1700-55) was born in Cervières, a Briançonnais village, and became seigneur of L'Argentière, a non-Briançonnais village in the Durance valley. Guillemin published the first chapter of Brunet's *Mémoires historiques sur le Briançonnais* in 1892.

The agricultural season began in April, sometimes before the snow had completely melted. Grain fields were ploughed (using cows as draught animals), barley or oats was planted, and gardens were prepared. In June the villagers cut wood in the communal forest, laying in their winter supply of firewood. In July the haying began and continued into September. August and September were the heaviest work months: the hay and grains were cut and the rye for the next season planted. De la Blottière said of this period: 'During these two months, the men and women work like slaves, night and day' (ibid. 43). In October fertilizer was spread on the fields.

Although the labour needs for this agriculture were high, they were all met from within the village, without bringing in workers from elsewhere.

Sheep-Raising

In the seventeenth and eighteenth centuries the villages raised much stock for local uses as well as for trade. Pigs, cows, and mules were kept, but the most important animals in the region were sheep. Abriès was famous for the quality of its pastures and the large number of sheep they supported. In 1694 Ricord, an army engineer stationed in Abriès, wrote: 'Abriès is the richest and most prosperous community of this valley ... Before the war this community alone maintained more than forty thousand ewes each year a thing which might appear incredible if it were not known throughout the Briançonnais' (DGFV), carton 1, art. 8, sec. 1, no. 7). Ricord was also impressed by the handsome profit the Abrièsois turned by trading sheep and selling ewes' milk, butter, and cheese in the Briançonnais and Piedmont.

The 40,000 sheep Ricord spoke of were a mixture of locally owned animals and flocks brought up from the plains of Provence and Piedmont to pass the summer in high pastures leased from the montagnards (Crubellier 1948: 265). In the autumn the Provençal sheep returned to the lowlands, and many of the village flocks were left to winter in the Piedmontese valleys, only a two- to three-day walk away. This pattern of transhumance (summer in the Alps) and inverse transhumance (winter in the Piedmontese valleys) was a semi-nomadic adaptation that was very ancient, probably dating from the Neolithic Age (Blanchard 1950: 916). It involved the Queyras villages in far-flung networks and important contractual obligations with people from the lowland areas. The diplomacy required to maintain these networks over centuries served to develop political skills of non-violent negotiation. Even during the wars of the seventeenth century many Queyrassins wintered with their flocks in the Piedmont (ADHA E531).

The Abbé Albert, writing three-quarters of a century after Ricord, reaffirmed the importance of sheep-raising in Abriès:

> The inhabitants of Abriès are much engaged in commerce ... involving ewes. Several individuals have considerable flocks of ewes, which are sent to spend the winter in Piedmont and the summer on the mountains of the Queyras. Everything about these animals, which are the symbols of sweetness and innocence, is productive. The wool, although considerably rougher than that produced elsewhere, is excellent for making thick sheets that last a long time and mattresses. The milk results in quantities of butter which are retailed in the Embrunois region [on the Durance River a day or two away on muleback]. The lambs are sold to the inhabitants of the Queyras, who buy them in order to replace the ewes that have been sold to the same shepherds. (1783: 191–2)

Thus, sheep, important for trade and for immediate local use, were a symbol of the wealth of the area.

COLLECTIVE INSTITUTIONS

Important factors in creating the wealth of the Queyras were its mixture of communal and private ownership of land, collective labour inputs, and seasonal labour migration.

The Abrièsois held a majority of the community's land in common. In the Middle Ages, the whole Dauphiné had a form of communal holding: groups of families, sometimes so large that they incorporated whole hamlets, joined together to work holdings collectively and to share tax burdens. Undivided property was passed on to groups of relatives. Marriage contracts and wills were constructed to avoid the partition of property and to forestall as many sources of friction as possible. Peasants made contracts with detailed instructions for ploughing, sowing, and threshing as well as for the arbitration of disputes by groups of friends. This 'communal working of land, derived from communal inheritance' was a common practice in the Dauphiné until 'the push of individualism that happened during the Reformation' (Chomel 1970: 315–16).

By the seventeenth and eighteenth centuries the Abrièsois owned fields and flocks individually, but the forests, waters, and pastures – more than 80 per cent of the surface area of the 7000-hectare community – were still held collectively. The village derived many advantages from this arrangement. Use of the pastures was leased to transhumant flocks; thus the commons were an important money-making resource for the village, the revenues being used to pay taxes and the salaries of community schoolteachers and municipal officers. Some of this money was even invested (ADHA E400). Communal ownership also provided a form of security for the poor of the village since no one could be denied access to important resources necessary for making a living.

In return for their communal benefits, all villagers were required to work in corvées (work gangs) to maintain roads, paths, and canals. Some regulations governing these work routines in the Briançonnais were written down in the Middle Ages and have survived (Fauché-Prunelle 1857: II, 243–311; Routier ca 1970: 56–63; Burns 1963: Blanchard 1950: 950–9; de la Blottière 1708 in de Rochas 1882: 41).[4]

Building and maintaining the canals and distributing the water were organized by unions of irrigation sharers. Each spring those who shared the irrigation system convoked a meeting to discuss the work. Men who failed to attend this meeting were fined. Here the group elected men to supervise the repair of canals and the dispersal of water. They also chose a canal keeper who would determine the irrigation schedule. Because of the importance of his task, the canal keeper swore an oath before the elected head of the village, pledging to fulfil his duties without favouritism. He received a wage paid by the village as well as half of any fines levied against delinquent users of the system – those who did not participate in repairing canals or did not draw their water correctly. Supervisors and canal keepers kept detailed scheduling records and registers of payments and fines.

This system of elections, scheduling, and fines was replicated in forest management. As with canal regulation, each community developed its own rules, but they were remarkably similar from village to village in the Briançonnais. Slash-and-burn encroachments, times of pasturing animals in the woods, cutting times, and the distribution of firewood were regulated with great care to protect villages against avalanches, erosion, and flooding. Village-elected forest guards could impose severe fines for infringements. In 1769 a group of Briançonnais communities described their system of communal forest management in a brief to the king: 'guarding the forests has always been the work of

4 The organization described here is based on the countryside near Briançon but is representative of the Queyras as well.

municipal officers in each community ... The surveillance of the forest is not thereby less rigorous, and the conservation of the forests depends on this severity. Each person becomes his neighbour's spy, and denounces him as soon as the sound of the falling branch reaches his ear' (in Fauché-Prunelle 1857: II, 299).

This rigour and degree of collective organization were the hallmarks of agriculture and forest management in the Briançonnais. High alpine pastures were managed in a similar fashion.

Such collective patterns were common in France in the middle ages (Bloch 1966: 167–89). The unusual feature of Abriès and the Briançonnais was the extent of communal ownership which survived to the early modern era (and even to the present). One reason for this survival can be found in the political system, in which power was not wedded to agriculture or land ownership. There was no landholding seigneurial elite with an interest in breaking up the commons to further its own position. Moreover, the poor, who might have benefited from encroaching on the commons at times of population pressure, did not have enough political power to break up the system. As Bloch has said, the bonds created by collective ownership and supported by collective obligations in cultivation were incredibly strong (1966: 180).

In Abriès and the Briançonnais these obligations had the weight of both custom and legal authority behind them. (As we shall see in Chapter 3, the regulations became part of a charter granted to the Briançonnais by the Dauphin in 1343.) In addition, although flocks were owned individually, they were pastured collectively. In the spring and autumn, sheep roamed freely over the stubble of everyone's arable fields - the right of vaine pâture - depositing much-needed fertilizer.

This method of fertilization, like canal irrigation, was essential to the success of cultivation and tied the individual holding inextricably to the collective system. Given the short growing season in the mountains, extensive fertilization was necessary to enhance soil fertility. The practice of vaine pâture benefited all cultivators, but it was especially important for those with small flocks. The fierceness with which this ancient pattern has been defended throughout the history of Abriès signals the community's continued acceptance of collective responsibility for its poor.

The labour needs of households varied greatly by season. In the summer every villager was required to work long hours, but in the winter labour requirements were slight. Most men migrated out of the village at the end of September, after the feast of St Michael (29 September), which also marked the major fall animal fair, and went to work as hemp combers in Piedmont.

The migrants returned in May; Brunet said their employment brought them 30 to 40 livres each in 1754 (in Guillemin 1892: 335), earnings useful for paying taxes, purchasing stock to be fattened in the summer, and accumulating wealth for dowry payments. De la Blottière said of Queyras villages in 1721 that the system of seasonal migration served the region well; it reduced the demands on food consumption, brought in income to pay the taille (direct royal tax) and other taxes, and 'meant that there were few paupers begging' (in de Rochas 1882: 104n). De la Blottière's observation is worth stressing because it emphasizes seasonal migration as a way of combating poverty, not as a consequence of poverty. He thought of the region as wealthy, as did his predecessor, Ricord, and attributed this wealth to the fertility of the well-fertilized and well-irrigated lands, the large flocks, and the economizing spirit of the peasantry.

TRADE AND COMMERCE

The economy of Abriès was neither closed nor self-sufficient. Trade and the circulation of money were an integral part of it. Sheep, around which the agricultural system revolved, were important for their 'liquidity' – the ease with which the conversion from sheep to money to sheep could be made (Guillaume 1901: 170). The necessity for this conversion was rooted in the ecology of the region. The length and harshness of the winter season made it impossible to pasture animals out of doors year-round, and only a small number of sheep could be kept in the stables. Some flocks were wintered in Piedmont, but many animals were sold at Abriès's autumn fair. Replacements were purchased the next spring, fattened in the alpine pastures during the summer, and sold in their turn in autumn.

We do not have market price lists for eighteenth-century Abriès so we cannot estimate the volume of trade or profit. In 1694 Ricord estimated, however, that the Abrièsois made a profit of 3 to 4 livres per head on sheep purchased at the spring fair and sold at the autumn one, creating jealousy among neighbouring villages (DGFV, carton 1, art. 8, sec. 1, no. 7). Thus, part of the profit made on autumn sales was used to replenish stock in the following year. Other uses for cash were to finance seasonal migration expeditions, which produced profits in their turn.

From the thirteenth century to 1944, Abriès had a weekly market (a French translation of the 1259 charter is reproduced in Abbé Berge's manuscript, ca 1920). Every Wednesday, winter and summer, were traded not only animals but also grains, wines, oil, and rice. Many of these items came through the passes from Piedmont. Even during wartime and after the Treaty of Utrecht (1713) put a border along the crest of the mountains, Piedmont continued as an important trading partner with the Queyras.

As part of the Queyras, Abriès was also part of the Briançonnais trade network. During the residence of the popes at Avignon, the Briançonnais had been at the centre of a very lucrative trade between Avignon and Italy. Merchants from Milan, Genoa, Florence, Germany, and Flanders as well as from the Dauphiné, Provence, and other parts of France criss-crossed the Briançonnais. By the fifteenth century Briançon's fourteen-day fall fair was one of the great exchange markets of the Alps. Naturally, sheep were important in this trade – and Piedmont was one of the chief buyers. Other trade items included nuts, oil, wine, hemp, small hardware, iron, fine wool cloth from Provence, local cheeses, rough cloth, leathers, and furs, as well as silk, gold cloth, and linen from Languedoc, arms from Milan, bonnets and ribbons from Lyons, and pewter, bronzeware, and tapestries (Blanchard 1950: 951-71).

The return of the popes to Italy in addition to endemic warfare in the sixteenth, seventeenth, and eighteenth centuries reduced the volume and diversity of trade. Commerce with Piedmont became increasingly difficult, and the more exotic items of international trade tended to disappear from the Briançonnais network. Grains, leathers, cheeses, and animals continued to be exchanged, although the volume of the first three items was much reduced (ibid. 961). In the middle of the seventeenth century, the consul (municipal leader) of Briançon appeared in Turin to give personal assurance of safety for Piedmontese traders (Chabrand 1888: 202).

During the eighteenth century trade with southern France became increasingly important for Abriès and the Briançonnais. A substantial source of revenue for the region continued to be trade in animals, which grew rapidly through the century as mules, donkeys, horses, and cows entered the market.

The Abrièsois also sold butter and cheese made from ewe's milk within their own region and in Provence (Brunet 1754, in Guillemin 1892: 333), an occupation that became increasingly more important to their economy throughout the eighteenth century as the Piedmontese began encouraging their own textile industry and discouraging French migrants from working there in the winters (ibid., 350–1; Roux-La-Croix 1747, in Roman 1892: 355). Later, peddling in southern France became a very lucrative replacement for hemp-combing in Italy.

Throughout these centuries, the image of the Briançonnais peasant as a shrewd trader was part of the mythology of the region (Blanchard 1950: 951). Some observers thought that dishonesty went along with shrewdness. In 1708 de la Blottière noted, 'They know how to deceive people, even repeatedly' (in de Rochas 1882: 104). In 1754 Jean Brunet offered: 'The peasants are sober, robust, and tireless in their work, honest in commerce ... they are in some places very stubborn in haggling' (in Guillemin 1892: 344).

COMMUNALISM AND WEALTH

Despite the communal aspects of its economy, Abriès was not a completely homogeneous community. Its people differed in wealth, status, power, and occupation. These differences were not, however, hardened into a class structure.

The key to social organization in Abriès and the Briançonnais was the fact that the villages had neither aristocrats who held large amounts of land and controlled the labour power of other families nor, apparently, a group of landless, dependent labourers. Abriès did include people whom contemporary record-keepers called journaliers/journalières, terms which in the nineteenth century came to mean day-labourers. In the eighteenth century, however, journaliers/journalières were not a propertyless rural proletariat. In Abriès, Ristolas, and Aiguilles these people married, acquired wealth, and made wills.[5] In 1748 one Abriès journalier, for example, left a will bequeathing sums of money ranging from 9 livres to 80 livres to several sons, daughters, and grandchildren. The total estate was not small, and it is interesting to note that both female and male heirs benefited. No surviving

5 The *Table Alphabétique des Extraits des Sépultures* (ADHA II C Abriès, no. 1, vol. 1, 1754–78) lists the occupations of people who died in that twenty-five-year period leaving some taxable property destined to go to collateral relatives. (These descendants represented about 46 per cent of the village's total deaths in that period.) The largest category was journalier/journalière, which included 174 people or 63 per cent of those recorded.

records or descriptive accounts give any indication of a pauperized propertyless class in the village, and there is no mention of formal sharecropping (although informal undocumented arrangements may have existed). It seems fair to conclude that in a region committed to detailed recordkeeping and contracts, the existence of a class of dependent agricultural labourers would have been recorded. Instead, we find a roughly egalitarian property system embedded in complex inheritance and dowry arrangements.[6]

The genius of the system was its very complexity. An individual might receive property or goods from a parent at one time, from an uncle at another, from a sibling, cousin, or grandparent at still other times. The disposition of inheritances was often spread out over a lifetime or even through more than one generation. People could never be sure exactly how much they would get in their own lifetimes. All they knew was that they would get something eventually and that they would leave something. Family fortunes undoubtedly varied, but the underlying principle clearly provided something for everyone within the larger communal system of joint forest and pasture ownership and management.

Complexity operating as a levelling mechanism can be seen in the ways in which resources were distributed. Peasants' wills and marriage contracts describe the dispersion of resources among many people through time. Responsibility for the disposition of property and wealth was often carried through several generations. For example, in 1744 a peasant named Charles Toye left a will naming his cousin as principal heir, but specifying many more transactions. Toye stipulated that his two uncles and a male cousin each be paid 400 livres owed them from their grandfather's will. An additional 30 livres was owed a female cousin from the same grandfather for her dowry. Finally, Toye's two brothers and a sister were owed portions from their mother's estate.

Dowry arrangements operated in similar ways. Women accumulated

---

6 The Abriès vital statistics registry shows that making marriage contracts and wills was a universal practice among the peasants. The data here are based on my analysis of thirty wills and twenty-two marriage contracts for the years 1737–8 and 1744–8. ADHA series E 1E3953 and 1E3954 are the notarial archives of Claude Berthelot, one of several regional notaries. In addition, I used the registry of these acts in Sous-Sène IIC 5–6 (1737–8) and IIC 10–14, 'Registre des formalités' (1744–8), and series Q, uninventoried, 'Tables des contrats de mariages Canton d'Aiguilles,' vol. 1, 1780–2.

dowries from a variety of sources, including parents, other relatives, and their own resources. Marriage contracts usually specified that dowries were to be paid to husbands in instalments, with annual interest payments; some of these contracts stretched out as long as fifteen years.

The logic of instalment dowering and inheritance worked on many fascinating levels. It probably took most smallholders considerable time to accumulate adequate dowries, and they were not willing to delay marriage until the full sums were assembled. Instalment payments also meant that resources had to be kept track of carefully, involving peasants in complex record-keeping and legal institutions.

The institution also operated as a labour-holding device for an area in which male seasonal migration was common. When men left each winter to work in Italy or southern France, what guarantee was there that they would return in the spring? Instalment payments of inheritance and dowry operated as insurance for their return. Most marriage contracts specified that the father-in-law would pay in the summer; to get the money, a son-in-law had to return to the village.[7]

The pattern of inheritance and dowering also made it difficult for a single person or family to accumulate large tracts of land at the expense of others. No one could expect to receive or pass on a single estate intact. This pattern was reinforced by mountain ecology. A viable farmstead required several kinds of land – fields, meadows, and access to communal forest and high pasture land. Slight differences in altitude, slope, exposure to the sun, and quality of irrigation made great differences in the quality and productivity of land. Small fields were also convenient units to distribute in wills. The best strategy was to diversify and hence spread the risks with small, scattered holdings.

Egalitarianism
The inheritance system, the pattern of collective labour, the election of office-holders and record-keepers, and the system of vast communal holdings all contributed to an ideology of communal egalitarianism in the village, an ideology that was a reflection of reality.

7 A small percentage of contracts indicate a fall payment date – 29 September, the time of major annual markets and just before the winter snows. There was money about, and some seasonal workers may have needed it at that time. And some sons-in-law may have wanted to ensure that their fathers-in-law would not skip out with the money.

One indication of this levelling of lifestyles is a phrase that recurs in wills. Abrièsois who remained in the village over the winter, no matter how rich they were, moved their households into the stables to economize on scarce fuel by profiting from the heat of the animals. 'In bed, in the stable,' appears over and over again in reference to will makers on their deathbeds (ADHA 1E3953, 1737–9; ADHA 1E3954, 1744–9).

Marriage contracts also reveal a great deal about the distinctions in wealth among the people of Abriès. Most marriages in the district were preceded by contracts, which were made out by notaries and registered in Abriès. A 1744–8 record that has survived (ADHA IIC10–14, 1744–8, Abriès 'Contrôle') frequently distinguishes between the value of a trousseau – a woman's personal property of bed, chest, and linens, and so on – and the dowry wealth she planned to bring into the marriage. (Although men, too, brought wealth into marriages, these amounts were rarely recorded.)

A woman's dowry was pieced together from various sources: shares from parental estates, sums received or expected from the estates of other relatives, property or cash she had mobilized by her own efforts. Thus the amount of wealth a woman brought into marriage signified the resources available within a family network.

Of the fifty-one dowries for which we have complete information in the years 1744–8, the average was approximately 280 livres. This figure excludes a 1650-livre dowry belonging to a member of the elite Berthelots, then Abriès's outstanding family, whose wealth came from practising law.[8] For peasants, amounts were much lower and the difference between the richest and the poorest was small. In terms of amounts mobilized for doweries, the top 20 per cent of peasants were only about four times as wealthy as the poorest (see Table 1). Even if one includes the Berthelot dowry, the ratio is 4.87, a very minor difference in comparison to the spread of dowries in Abriès in the nineteenth century (see Chapter 6, Figure 6).

The levelling ideology also discouraged conspicuous displays of wealth. Thus the registration records of the marriage contracts discussed above indicate a consistency in the amount women spent on trousseaus, no matter what the size of their dowries. In 1747, for

8 Similarly, the records for 1738 show Jeanne Berthelot bringing a dowry of 5000 livres into a marriage with a notary from a distant Briançonnais village (ADHA IIC6, 1738, Abriès 'Contrôle').

TABLE 1
Peasant dowries, Abriès, 1744–8

	No. of cases	Total value (livres)	Mean value	% of value
All cases	51	14,262	279	100.00
Highest 20%	10	5,781	578.1	40.53
Lowest 20%	10	1,469	146.9	10.30

Ratio of highest 20% to lowest 20% = 3.93

Note: Non-peasant dowry of 1650 livres (Berthelot family) excluded.
Source: AHDA II C10-14, 1744–8, Abriès

TABLE 2
Dowry and trousseau values, Abriès, 1747

Dowry (livres)	Trousseau (livres)	total value (livres)
140	60	200
120	55	175
200	112	312
150	80	230
90	85	175
240	90	330
130	80	210

Average trousseau = 80 livres

Source: ADHA II C10, 1747

example, the average trousseau was valued at only 80 livres, and few went above this mark (see Table 2). Even the wealthy Berthelot woman had a trousseau valued at only 150 livres.

In short, the whole socio-economic system of eighteenth-century Abriès contained wealth and status differences within a range that was rather small, especially compared to the enormous differences that occurred in the nineteenth century.

GENDER AND PROPERTY

Flexibility and non-restrictive access to property was also found in gender relationships. Several scholars claim that the old-regime property arrangements in the Briançonnais were patriarchal, based on rights of the eldest son and the power of 'masculinité' (see Pecaut 1907; Tivollier 1938: II, 253; Guillaume 1968; Burns 1963). These scholars argue that the Briançonnais region was characterized by single male inheritance which was maintained clandestinely after 1791, when the Revolutionary Constituent Assembly decreed equal partible inheritance. The claim is that men naturally attempted to keep patrimonies intact through generations because constantly dividing estates would have been uneconomical. This thinking applies the logic of nineteenth-century capitalism to a highly communalistic eighteenth-century peasant economy.

In fact, estates were constantly divided. Men and women inherited and bequeathed wealth. Neither dowered nor non-dowered women were excluded from succession as Pecaut (1907) argues; women could and did accumulate a variety of resources. If the aim had been to provide a single patrimony for a male heir, female universal heirs would presumably not have existed and provisions would have been made to bring in an acceptable male over the heads of the daughters. But in examining thirty wills made in 1737 and 1738 and 1744 through 1748 (ADHA 1E3953; ADHA 1E3954), I found no case of the substitution of a nephew or a son-in-law for immediate female descendants. (For son-in-law substitution in Ireland, see Arensberg and Kimball [1940].) Furthermore, testators frequently enjoined lesser heirs, both male and female, to remain silent and content with their shares of inheritances to prevent costly litigation.

In the thirty wills I studied, men dominated as major heirs but women were constantly involved in property management even when they did not inherit the bulk of an estate. If an underage son was named as an heir, his mother was always named as estate administrator; male relatives were never interposed. In most cases the widow was given sole responsibility for the management of the property, was exempted from having to provide an inventory of holdings when the inheritance was eventually turned over to the main heir or heirs, and was permitted to sell property up to a specified amount (200 to 400 livres) at her discretion. Very often the woman retained use rights over the entire estate, not just until the heir grew up but for her whole life.

Women, particularly widows managing property, also had the right to speak and participate in village assemblies (Tivollier 1938: II, 293-300).

All this information is extremely important. It indicates that women played an active decision-making role in family economic enterprises and were expected to know about agricultural matters. That is, the Alps had no sexual segregation of labour which said that farming was a masculine concern and women were to occupy themselves exclusively with household matters. In the Mediterranean region, in contrast, strong ideological splits between a female/domestic/private realm and a male/agricultural/public realm have been documented (Schneider 1971; Reiter 1975). In the south, even when women worked the land, their activities were devalued and considered just helping out. In the Alps, however, women's agricultural work was not culturally disclaimed; in fact, it was written directly into the legal system. Women were property owners and estate managers. They had control over resource distribution, which is considered an indicator of high status (Duley and Edwards 1986). Even their dowries were not controlled by their spouses, who had only use rights. Dowered property could not be alienated by husbands; it was seen as a trust fund for women in their old age and was supposed to be used, according to the standard phrase of contemporary marriage contracts, to 'feed and maintain' widows.

As a consequence of this power base, neither virginity nor submissiveness was highly valued in Abriès, as both were in the Mediterranean (Peristiany 1965; Campbell 1964; Schneider 1971). Male control of female behaviour was limited because most men were gone in the winters. For six months of the year women were responsible for the care of animals, property, and much of the village business. Perhaps this is why virginity does not seem to have been an important behavioural code for women. No marriage contract ever mentions it as a prerequisite for the bride, and there is no evidence of anything like a demand for virginity tests or public deflorations on the wedding night (Schneider 1971: 21). In all likelihood, given a labour-intensive economy with few alternative sources of labour recruitment, the proof of fertility may have been more important than virginity. (See Anderson and Anderson 1964: 128-30 for a discussion of premarital sex in Scandinavian villages.)

Women's social strength was reinforced by the practice of marrying within the village and its hamlets. Endogamous marriage meant women did not have to break family and friendship ties and move away where they might be without support, dependent on the goodwill of their in-laws. (See Friedl [1959] for a discussion of exogamy and the problems of separation for modern Greek women.)

In Abriès women's networks were very strong. Women worked in teams in the summer to produce the dairy products that men marketed in the winter. While in the high pasturelands engaged in cheese production, women frequently visited and exchanged meals. In the winter, this productive labour was praised in evening story-telling as old women described their skills in manufacturing 'beautiful and good butters and cheeses which were fat and tasty' (Guillaume 1901: 252).

In addition, the rhythm of the economic system resulted in an interesting fertility pattern which probably also contributed to female solidarity. A study of birth months for the first part of the nineteenth century (when seasonal migration patterns were identical with those of the eighteenth century) shows that most babies were born in January, February, and March.[9] Because so many men were gone in the winter, a high proportion of conceptions occurred in the summer. One can imagine the district with large numbers of women due to give birth at about the same time. Midwives hurried from house to house offering advice and aid. Immediately after parturition, relatives, friends, and neighbours delivered gifts, especially eggs, to the new mothers. Later, new mothers offered bread and special cheese to the people whom they encountered when they left the house for the first time (Tivollier 1938: I, 258). The symbolism of exchanging eggs and cheese – reproduction and production – is striking.

In considering the areas in which women had power and status, we must not forget, however, that the total system was not equal. Men still had certain advantages and controls over women. Although men did not attempt to control unmarried women in terms of virginity, they did specify in wills that no widow was entitled to a pension unless she led a chaste life. (How – or whether – this injunction was enforced, we do not know.) Again, although Abriès women could participate in village meetings, they could not hold public office. Thus there was a real gap between their actual activity in the public sphere in relation to agriculture and their potential for overt political power.

---

9 This evidence, drawn from ADHA 204M, état civil, Abriès, is presented in Chapter 6, Table 7. The text there discusses the pattern described here as well as the change later in the nineteenth century when seasonal migration stopped.

DAILY LIFE AND EDUCATION

As already mentioned, the Briançonnais montagnards spent their winters in their stables with their animals, a practice which continued in Abriès until the 1950s. Weber (1976: 278–9) describes this living situation in extremely negative terms. His unnamed nineteenth-century sources were apparently disgusted by animal stench, fetid air, and mucky floors. Present-day Briançonnais peasants speak differently of what they considered an ingenious solution to fuel shortage. Housewives were proud of the cleanliness and order in their homes. The six months of living in the stables was certainly not a gloomy imprisonment. The Queyras often has dry winter days in which many activities can be carried on comfortably out of doors (Blanchard 1950: 682–726). Furthermore, since more than half the population was gone during the winter months, those who remained were not crowded in the small winter quarters. In the summer months, when the migrants returned, two or more bedrooms under the haylofts were used.

Another feature of life in the Queyras which has been much discussed was the communal baking bread only once a year, a custom which continued until the 1880s when the first commercial baker arrived in Abriès town. (In other parts of the Queyras communal bread-baking continued well into the twentieth century.) This too was a fuel-economizing strategy. Every autumn the collectively owned ovens were stoked for two or three days, and the villagers brought prepared rye doughs to bake for twenty-four hours. The bread was then stored in the upper haylofts, where it was kept away from rodents and exposed to the dry, cold mountain air. The bread did not spoil but became rock-hard as the year progressed, and special axes or guillotine-like blades were used to break it up. Many Queyras households still have such devices.

The shattered bread was used in soups, usually made with a barley base, which were the mainstay of the diet. The peasants also ate meat since game was plentiful in the mountains and there were no feudal restrictions on hunting. Smoked or salted goat meat and some beef or pork were also part of the diet, as were beans and dairy products, especially cheeses. Wine and fruits were scarce, but the most significant dietary lack was iodized sea salt. Goitre was a common disease in the Alps. Yet a contemporary observer was generally impressed by the healthiness and longevity of the montagnards. 'People live very long and I have seen several old people over 100 years old,' said Brunet in 1754 (in Guillemin 1892: 334).

The writings of Abbé Albert (1783) have much to tell us of the clothing styles worn by mid-eighteenth-century Queyrassins. He noted that
they wore much better-looking and finer-quality clothing than the peasants of the Auvergne, where he had served previously. Albert's
descriptions are so detailed that they could be used as the point of
departure for a whole monograph on clothing styles of eighteenth-
century peasants. One of the small points that struck him was that
almost all peasants in the valley used buttons and buttonholes and
wore cravats and clean hats. Only in a few remote hamlets 'cravats are
not used at all and instead of buttons, clothes have little hooks made of
brass' (1783). It is clear from his description that the villagers were
aware of the latest fashions – a visible sign of their integration into a
larger society.

Amusements and Games

Social life was very lively in the Queyras. 'The youth were never bored
in the Queyras in the olden days; they did not resent the winter seclu-
sion nor the hard work of summer, they were full of lively activities,'
says the folklorist Tivollier describing ancien régime village life (1938:
I, 277). He describes veillées (evening get-togethers) at which women
knitted, men played cards, and young people could easily organize a
dance, a dramatic or farcical presentation, or a debate. In the winter
the dances and choral entertainments took place in the stables, and in
the summers they often moved out of doors. A medieval stringed
instrument was used to accompany the singers and dancers.

Apparently Queyrassin youngsters were famous for their love of
practical jokes. A favourite summer activity was stealing the laundered
clothes of young women and older housewives from their courtyards
and scattering them in the fields or high up in the trees for all to see.
The next day brought 'general hilarity as people watched the young
people looking for their things' (ibid., 275).

Children's activities were plentiful. Youngsters played a game
similar to croquet in the summer and enjoyed sledding in the winter.
In the springtime they used their slingshots to hunt game birds and
went into the forests to find wood for carving whistles. The Queyrassins
were excellent wood carvers and often made wooden toys for their
children.

Education

Perhaps the most famous example of well-being in the Queyras was the
ancient practice of communities' hiring lay schoolteachers. Evidence

for the paid communal teacher, called recteur or regent, dates from the fifteenth century: in 1458 Abriès hired 'Giraudus Marcellini, rector scolarium' (ADI B2750). This practice continued until the national education reforms of the nineteenth century.

The schools were held in stables. French, Latin, writing, arithmetic, and catechism were taught; girls also learned sewing and embroidery. The schools were *free*; the teachers were paid by the community. A 1790 Abriès tax roll earmarked 200 livres for 'les gages de Maître d'Ecole' (the wages of the School Master) that amount being about a third of what the parish priest received (ADHA F2725). Salaries were low, but teachers worked for only the six months of the winter. The high literacy rate of Briançonnais and their taste for education were considered remarkable by contemporaries; both the seventeenth-century intendant Bouchu (Blet, Esmonin, and Letonnelier 1936: 260) and the early-nineteenth-century prefect Bonnaire lamented the lack of education in the lowlands and praised the zeal of the montagnards. Bonnaire said: 'In order to find a desire to learn, and even a certain amount of real education, it is necessary to climb up into the Briançonnais, penetrate deep and narrow valleys in hidden places ... which appear to be inhabitable only by hordes of savages. It is there one feels the value of education, where everyone, without exception, devotes their youth to it. It is rare for a child to not know how to read, write, and even do some arithmetic' (in ibid. 268).[10]

These views by contemporary observers are substantiated by statistical information. Goubert (1969: 259) has examined literacy rates across France for 1686–90, using the ability to sign the marriage act as a criterion of literacy, and found the highest rate in the Hautes-Alpes.

10 Bonnaire attributes this aptitude for learning to the seasonal winter migration patterns. One of the trades widely plied in the Briançonnais, especially at the end of the eighteenth century, was schoolteaching in the lowland valleys. Just as certain regions of the northern Alps became famous for clock-making or gem-cutting or masonry (Allix 1928), so the Briançonnais specialty became school-teaching. This fact does not, of course, explain why the specialties were distributed in such a fashion. Burns (1961) connects the penchant for education to the legalistic tradition of the escarton system and to the democratic rotation within the villages of various tasks, such as supervision of irrigation. Every man was pre-adapted to be a record-keeper and a functionary. In addition one may hypothesize that the early appearance of the Vaudois heresy, which relied on colporteurs to spread its message through books, may have been influential. (The rise of the Vaudois, a populist movement that began in the twelfth century, is discussed in Chapter 3.) Perhaps the best explanation is the cumulative impact of all these factors.

TABLE 3
Ability to sign marriage contract registration or marriage act

	Total	Signers		Non-signers		Ambiguous cases
		N	%	N	%	
Abriès[a]						
Men		80	90.91	8	9.09	15
Women		24	27.90	62	72.09	17
All France	344,220[b]		55.55		73.12	

[a] 1744-8
[b] 1686-90
Sources: For Abriès: ADHA II C10-14; Abriès parish register; for France: Goubert 1969: 259

When I looked at the 1744-8 records for Abriès, I used the ability to sign registration of a marriage contract (ADHA IIC Abriès *Contrôle* 10-14), and I also turned to the parish register for evidence from those couples who did not make contracts. I found a sizeable number of ambiguous cases, but in the instances that were clear, 91 per cent of the men could sign (see Table 3). It seems likely that Abriès had at least one literate person in every household in the eighteenth century.

Queyrassins felt that literacy was important. In 1766 a montagnard penned the following verse in the margins of an escarton proceeding:

> To my children
> Learn if you are wise
> Because knowledge is more important than inheritance
> You may lack an inheritance
> And knowledge will nourish you
> Learn from wise people and teach the ignorant and
>   God will give you recompense.
>
> (ADHA E372; in Tivollier 1938: I, 335)

School-teaching as a winter employment for Queyrassins was described by Victor Hugo in *Les Misérables*. Teachers seeking employment would go to lowland fairs. One feather in their hats signified that they could teach reading, two feathers reading and arithmetic, and three feathers reading, writing, and Latin. Often these teachers were quite young – fifteen to eighteen – and their salaries low, especially if they were without experience. There is evidence from the old regime that some of the migrant teachers were women. In 1724 'Agnez de Queyras' taught a girls' school in Guillestre for the sum of 30 livres; in 1741 Pierre Berthelot taught in the same town and was paid 150 livres (Tivollier 1938: I, 342).

DEATH AND DISASTER

Like other French villages, Abriès suffered from the wars and epidemic diseases of the seventeenth and eighteenth centuries as well as from high infant mortality – features we associate with old-regime demography. The seventeenth century was an especially difficult time for Abriès, as it was for much of France and Europe (Aston 1967). The Wars of Religion loomed large in the Dauphiné and the Queyras, which had a large Protestant population.[11] Abriès was unlike many pre-industrial villages, however, in that it was not dependent on a single crop and, therefore, was less subject to price fluctuations or famine resulting from crop failure (see Goubert 1952; 1960).

Bouchu, the intendant of the Dauphiné, compiled figures about population size in 1687. His data indicate that Abriès had a population of 2000 minus 226 migrants (probably refugees from other villages) for a total of 1774 (AN TT243). It is difficult to know how accurate these figures were, although we can assume that some effort was made towards accuracy because the readjusted population figures were to serve as a basis for revised taxation rates. Clearly, Abriès had the highest population in the Queyras at the time.

Epidemics
Demographic data raise questions about how people viewed life – or rather, death – in a pre-industrial community. Fourastié describes a typical life cycle at the end of the seventeenth century and compares it to that of an average Frenchman born in 1909. In his description the seventeenth-century person is beset by disease, poverty, and poor

---

11 We do not know the exact effect of the Revocation of the Edict of Nantes in 1685. Figures for resulting out-migration from the Dauphiné vary from 10,000 to 40,000, and figures from the high-Alpine region are equally variable (Geisendorf 1961: 245-64). We do know, however, that Abriès was not an important Protestant centre and thus probably did not suffer as much as Molines or Arvieux.

medical care. In summarizing his grim findings, Fourastié argues: 'In the traditionalist era, death was the centre of life, just as the cemetery was the centre of the village.' For the modern French person, however, 'death, poverty and physical pain have retreated' ([1959] 1972: 34).

It is certainly true that infant mortality rates have declined and life expectancy is longer. But it would be hard to argue that death and pain are any less at the centre of life in the twentieth century than they were in the seventeenth century. A French person born in 1909 and age fifty in 1959 would have lived through two devastating world wars and a foreign occupation, a major world-wide influenza epidemic in 1918, and prolonged economic hardship resulting from depressions – none of which Fourastié mentions.

Fourastié also implies that 'traditional' people could do very little about the disasters that befell them, perhaps because 'traditional humanity was vegetal, with its intellectual faculties fallow' (ibid. 36). However, the people of Abriès and the villages of the Briançonnais were far from passive in the face of disease, warfare and poor harvests.

The major epidemics of the ancien régime were smallpox and plague. Soldiers brought smallpox into the Queyras in 1630, and the combination of war and disease was devastating. Ceillac lost 120 people, and the Queyras village of Arvieux was said to have lost two-thirds of its population (Estienne 1970). Smallpox hit Abriès again in 1704 and once again in 1776 to 1780. In the winter of 1778/9 forty-eight children under the age of twelve died (Blanchard 1933: 85; Abriès parish register). Until the introduction of the smallpox vaccine, discovered by Jenner in 1796, very little was effective in controlling the disease.

Against the plague, however, the villagers were able to organize effective public health measures. In 1720 the news reached the Dauphiné that 'the plague is in Marseilles, and measures have been taken, in all towns in Provence and Languedoc, to prevent as far as possible, the spread of this evil' (ADHA E390). In the Queyras the issue was immediately considered by the escarton, which established guards at the mouth of the valley to prohibit entrance and exit to people without health certificates. Not happy with the diligence of the guards, the escarton soon established a health council composed of notables of the Queyras (including a doctor) with orders and full powers to do all that they thought 'reasonable to preserve the valley.' This council immediately promulgated eighteen articles of protective measures, including fortifying the entry guards, prohibiting hunting in the valley, inquiring whether the disease could be spread by merchandise imported into the valley, and determining alternative ways of acquiring 'the variety of things necessary for life.' In addition, it ordered prayers (ibid.).

During the council's tenure it constantly supervised guard activities; for example, a valley notable received a stiff fine for absenting himself from guard duty to go to a fair and another man was punished for permitting a person without a health certificate to enter the valley. The *Délibérations* of the escarton note that although the 'contagious malady' was making progress in Provence, Languedoc, and Avignon, it made no headway in the Queyras (ibid.). The danger was finally judged past in 1723; after three years of effort, the health council was disbanded and its members thanked for their efforts on behalf of the valley (ibid.).

Warfare
Similar organizational efforts were expended to cope with the passage of troops through the region, with the requisition of food and supplies during wartime, and with the devastation caused by warfare. The next chapter describes these communal efforts; here, for an individual perspective, we turn to a notebook kept for two centuries by a Queyrassin peasant family.[12] Among the brief entries describing such events as the arrival of Italian entertainers displaying a dancing bear and winter misadventures in alpine passes are accounts of battles and the movements of troops in the seventeenth and eighteenth centuries. The notations are concise and dispassionate even when they describe astounding events. In 1651, for example, French soldiers tormented residents of the neighbouring valley of Château-Dauphin. The peasants, according to Pierre Ebren, 'were obliged and constrained [to hire] ... 300 bandits who came and killed more than 60 soldiers and disarmed the rest.' When the authorities heard what had happened

12 The 'Transitions de Molines-en-Queyras: Mémoires of Pierre Ebren de Font-gillarde (1577–1775)' was published in the late nineteenth century (Guillaume 1890). 'Transitions' were notebooks kept to sketch rural roads and paths used at harvest time so that the least damage possible would be inflicted on the fields. The original manuscript of thirty sheets is incomplete; Guillaume complained that it was torn and incredibly dirty and had obviously been handled by unclean hands in the stable.

Since even the extant pages are clearly the work of several individuals from successive generations of the Ebren family, it is not clear why Guillaume decided to use only Pierre Ebren's name in the title.

and came to inspect the village, they could find only two bodies hidden in a church (Guillaume 1890: 404–5). Pierre Ebren recounts this stunning story in a matter-of-fact manner. He obviously sympathized with his neighbours in Château-Dauphin and found it totally unremarkable that they should have organized such an extreme action and gotten away with it.

The Ebren family recounted many more incidents of conflict between peasants and soldiers. Sometimes, as in 1654, the peasants were able to buy soldiers off; at other times, such as 1665, nothing could be done to prevent the massacre of villagers. All these accounts are noteworthy for their absence of fatalism or resignation. Nowhere is God's name invoked to explain such disasters. They are not presented as inexplicable events but rather as part of life – something to be recorded accurately and remembered. In 1743 'Dom Philip, son of the King of Spain and his army ... in the number of fifty thousand men began to pass through this place of Molines, to go to Italy.' Daniel Ebren recorded their confiscations, the stripping of wood off roofs and doors, the sick soldiers left behind, and the deaths and hardship all this meant in the village. Yet even with these disasters occurring in his home village, Ebren did not express the belief that the villagers were the targets of uncontrollable fate. His attitude was rather that they were caught up in a political event which could be understood and analysed. The political world was unpleasant, but it was not a mystery to this peasant family.

Crop Failures

Poor harvests were also a threat to Abriès during the ancien régime, but they never reduced people to eating bark or grass (in contrast, see Wrigley [1969: 66] on Norwegian famine years of the early 1740s). The mixed agro-pastoral economy of Abriès served as a cushion in times of poor harvests; the villagers did not depend on one crop or on the purchase of grain for survival. The situation of Abriès can be compared to that of the Beauvaisis parish of Auneuil, one of three parishes studied by Goubert (1952; 1960). During the crisis years of 1692–5 there was great suffering in the neighbouring parishes of Breteuil, whose economy was based on cereal monoculture, and of Mouy, a textile centre with a large grain-buying proletariat. In the peak crisis year of 1694, when the price of wheat was at its highest, the three Beauvaisis parishes varied widely in the number of burials recorded; Breteuil had 229, Mouy had 262, but Auneuil had only 97 (Wrigley 1969: 67, tables 3:1 and 3:2). The diversified agro-pastoral economy of Auneuil protected it from devastating dependence on a suddenly scarce single crop.

Similar diversification in Abriès's economy protected the village from prolonged disaster in times of crisis. The years 1760 to 1766 were considered years of poor harvest in the Queyras: 'une misère incroyable par la manque de récolte' (an incredible misery because of harvest shortfalls) (ADHA E490). Yet even during these seven lean years, the mortality rate in Abriès was not staggeringly high. Only 1766 (seventy-two burials) and 1768 (eighty-two burials) can be considered true crises. If the population had been weakened by poor nutrition from a scarcity of food, one would expect sustained high levels of mortality.[13]

At issue is not the productive capacity of old-regime communities but the effects of dependence on a monocrop and the operation of the market. It was the high cost of grain coupled with a lack of alternative food sources which intensified the demographic crisis in Breteuil and especially in industrial Mouy. Thus it would be inaccurate to characterize all old-regime populations as living on the margin, automatically responding to the movement of grain prices. The nature of the economy of a village and its relation to the market must be considered before one can make a generalization such as 'the price of grain almost always constitutes a true demographic barometer' (Goubert 1952: 468).

Politics must also be considered in regard to the old-regime food supply. In areas where manorialism or sharecropping was the rule, peasants could not control the food-distribution process. But in the alpine villages of independent smallholders food went directly to the primary producers; nothing was skimmed off to a non-productive landholding elite. Furthermore, in the non-feudalized Briançonnais, peasants had the right to bear arms, and to hunt to supplement their food supply.

13 The Abriès parish registers for 1660 to 1760 show an average of thirty-one burials per year. The mortality rate was much more influenced by epidemics than by subsistence crises. Peak burial rates coincided with regional outbreaks of plague and smallpox: 1735 (83 burials), 1747 (110 burials), and 1749 (74 burials).

CONCLUSION

The ancient altar of the church in Abriès is festooned with carvings of wheat sheaves and grape clusters. These symbols may be inaccurate reflections of the crops actually grown in the village, but they signify both the wish for bountiful production and the reality of an agricultural base which generally supported villagers in comfort.

During the old regime, Abriès's agro-pastoral system was sustained by collective institutions which discouraged stratification and individual accumulation of resources. Productive capital passed through the community and through generations within limits which no one could fall below or rise above. Within these boundaries variations existed, but the logic of the social relations or production inhibited class formation.

The Abrièsois were enthusiastic about education, loved practical jokes, fought epidemics, and struggled with the great religious controversies of the seventeenth and eighteenth centuries. And as we shall see in the next chapter, these far from passive peasants also engaged in a wide variety of political activities.

3

'An Insufferable Degree of Vanity':
Institutions, Politics, and Power-Holders

In 1343 the five valleys of the Briançonnais purchased a charter from
Humbert II, the dauphin (ADHA E357, French version of the charter,
prepared in 1788). Elected representatives of fifty-one communities
negotiated with Humbert II and his council, bishops, and court notables. The agreement was that the communities would collectively
make an annual tribute payment, in exchange for exemption from
future taxes and various rights, which were specified in the charter.

Five years later the Dauphiné became part of France. The charter,
which was ratified by successive French monarchs, became the region's
political underpinning, so significant that three and a half centuries
later Ricord, the army engineer, could write:

One could say with Truth that these people govern themselves like Repub-
licans not recognizing any leader among Them nor having or suffering any
nobility having made them flee 300 years ago by their Vexations and as a
Consequence having generally acquired all Seigneurial rights as is apparent in
transactions passed with the Authority of the prince Dauphin Humbert de
Viennois, which has rendered in them always an insufferable degree of
Vanity. (DGFV, Art. 8, sec. 1, carton 1, no. 7)

To understand the political system of seventeenth- and eighteenth-
century Abriès, it is important to understand the terms of the charter
and the larger political structures which it recognized and guaranteed.

The charter was a political agreement between peasants and a weak
central authority; both sides gained advantages by the agreement. In
the long run the chief outcome of the charter was to set the political
system of the region within a legal context, so that village dealings with

the state were negotiated through the courts. Lawyers became the chief power-brokers within the Briançonnais villages by virtue of their legal expertise.

The charter recognized and legitimized local elective government, a system of yearly deliberative assemblies (the escarton system), and a five-valley territorial alliance. This alliance had been preceded earlier in the century by smaller-scale coalitions among various hamlets and villages; there was, for example, a three-community league of Bardonèsche, Béollard, and Rochemolle in the beginning of the fourteenth century. As the charter of these groups, registered in the Dauphiné, puts it: 'Fecerunt ... inter se pacto expresso vallaverunt uniones, pacta, convertiones, confederationes et legas' (they made among themselves unions, pacts, coalitions, confederations, and leagues) (in Fauché-Prunelle 1857: II, 324). These alliances were constructed for defence and for the sharing-out of tax obligations.

By the middle of the fourteenth century, these peasant coalitions, enriched by transalpine trade,[1] were wealthy enough to consider buying a charter in much the same way that medieval towns had bought their freedoms. When the villages went to deal with the dauphin, they acted as if they were just continuing local immemorial customs, but they actually went much further, creating more substantial institutions and claiming a wider variety of rights, privileges, and exemptions. Alliances were completely self-organized and not created by any overlord (ibid. 324-6).

Such coalitions were not uncommon in French history. They were part of the struggle that rural communities fought to gain recognition of their rights from the state. Community coalitions were rooted in collective activities such as communal husbandry and cultivation, communal decisions on matters such as harvest dates, and the performance of collective service for the benefit of the group as a whole, such as road

---

1 The town of Briançon, located near the major transalpine pass of Montgenèvre, was the major beneficiary of this trade, but its effects spilled out into the whole Briançonnais region. Article 32 of the charter deals with the trade of animals and merchandise between the Briançonnais and the city of Avignon. Blanchard, in concluding his description of this trade, observes: 'The wealth acquired through trade has allowed the Briançonnais people to buy their liberties with gold in 1343; the republic of the five escartons is the daughter of commerce' (1950: 954).

maintenance, as well as collective ownership. They were often replicated in community political and religious associations. These linkages
were expressed by villages when they called themselves 'voisins,' 'communes,' 'consulats,' 'syndicats,' or 'universités,' and formed leagues
among themselves when dealing with a common enemy, usually a
seigneur (Bloch 1966: 166–70).

Medieval villages were anti-seigneurial and often successfully so,
either through disregard of seigneurial jurisdictions and appointment
of their own officials or by collective violence. Moreover, like towns,
village communities were eager for legal recognition. Both these considerations are important to an understanding of the Briançonnais
valley assemblies – the escartons – and to an awareness that they were
not an aberration but well within the political culture of their times.
But, like other corporate groups, the escartons, once they had been
legitimized, found themselves caught in the contradiction of having a
vested interest in the existing legal/political system. Like other groups,
they 'subjected themselves to some fairly narrow limitations. This was
the price they had to pay for full membership in the honourable society
of bodies corporate' (Bloch 1966: 180).

For Abriès, corporate status meant that its political life was closely
associated with escarton politics. Politics came to revolve around using
the charter in disputes with other villages or the state. It meant rarely
resorting to collective violence. Finally, it meant the rise of a legal
oligarchy that could process cases through the complex legal system of
medieval and ancien régime France. Within those limits there was a
great deal of manoeuvrability in the political arena.

The 1343 charter supported the anti-seigneurial rights of the dauphin and the villages. The rights of the nobility were already restricted
in the Briançonnais in that they held their lands jointly with the dauphin. The castles belonged to the dauphin and were used by him to
garrison troops. By the thirteenth century only three seigneuries were
left in the Briançonnais. After a series of manoeuvrings in the following century, Humbert II became the exclusive seigneur of the Briançonnais with the exception of some restricted territory in the community of Névache (Routier ca 1970: 40).

The dauphin, chronically in need of money, enjoyed the compact
jurisdiction, which gave him convenient tax and fee-collecting powers,
forcing out local aristocrats. The villages too received important benefits from the charter. By legitimizing local self-government, it bol-

stered their capacity to resist aristocratic claims.[2] Having a single seigneur in the person of the dauphin meant they did not have to deal with the maze of jurisdictional problems which often dispersed the energies of peasant communities.[3] Furthermore, in dealing with the dauphin, the Briançonnais developed the habit of going straight to the top – a habit which persisted into the seventeenth and eighteenth centuries, after the Dauphiné had been incorporated into France and succeeding French kings administered the Briançonnais charter.

Ancien régime observers were struck by the republican or anti-seigneurial nature of the Briançonnais (Ricord 1694, DGFV, art. 8, sec. 1, carton 1, no. 7; de la Blottière, in de Rochas 1882). The 1343 charter had reduced status distinctions between commoner and noble. Article 35 recognized the Briançonnais peasants as francs-bourgeois (freemen). They were, for example, not required to kneel and kiss the dauphin's thumb at audience; rather, they could kiss his ring or hand – a sign of men 'francs et libres.' With this free status the Briançonnais obtained some rights hitherto reserved to seigneurs. For example, men and women could transmit their lands by inheritance (Article 1). Property transactions could be made without the consent of superiors (Article 16). Before 1343, wastelands, pastures, forests, and water were held by the dauphin with peasant usufruct; after that date, such property was held in common by each community and was subject to its municipal regulations (Article 22). This arrangement resulted, as we have seen, in a system of collective holdings and labour, the use of elected officials (Article 12 provided for the yearly election of village syndics – later called consuls), and extensive record-keeping in the villages – patterns which made aristocratic penetration difficult. These usages and others described below instilled in the peasants a strong attachment to legal rights; each Briançonnais village built a strong-box to house a copy of the charter. Some of these boxes have survived to the present.

As important to the political life of Briançonnais villages as the anti-

2 Goubert notes that research, especially in central, eastern, and southern France, leads to the 'inescapable (but unanticipated) conclusion that a part of France during the Ancien Régime (and, by definition, the Middle Ages as well) did not undergo the seigneurial system' (1971: 118). And Bloch (1966) demonstrates, as indicated above, that where feudalism did predominate, it did not control all avenues of political expression.
3 A nearby region, for example, had to deal with eighteen co-seigneurs which created immensely complicated jurisdictional problems (Routier ca 1970: 40).

seigneurial aspects of the charter was the establishment of the escartons, assemblies whose original function was to apportion among the communities the annual tribute payment, which totalled 4000 ducats (12,000 florins).[4]

This important right of assembly was phrased in Article 8 of the charter as 'the said Seigneur has wished to grant the said Communities the power and the faculty of taxing themselves and of imposing levies on the Inhabitants and the individuals in those Communities and not outsiders, with freedom to assemble to carry out the common needs and business relative to all that concerns their interest, and other lawful and necessary things' (ADHA E357). This article became the cornerstone of Briançonnais political life and a tradition of self-government that by the seventeenth and eighteenth centuries was viewed with alarm by the central authorities.

When the dauphin signed the charter he was already on the verge of ceding his territories to the king of France. For many years, subsequent French kings found the union of the escartons just as advantageous as had the dauphin and for similar financial reasons. In fact, in the sixteenth century, Henry III blocked an attempt by Vallouise to secede from the escarton system (Fauché-Prunelle 1857: II, 330).

For several centuries the escarton structure remained a convenient system of indirect rule for the king. But by the seventeenth century the region posed a problem to the central authorities. The escarton assemblies operated as a competing power base; peasants were using the system as much to avoid taxes as to pay them. Furthermore, during the seventeenth and eighteenth centuries the Briançonnais was in a crucial position in terms of military strategy. It also had a large Protestant population, so its loyalty was suspect. These facts, coupled with its reputation for being republican, brought it to the attention of the centre.

Moreover, by the end of the seventeenth century the Briançonnais was itself in a paradoxical position. Fourteenth-century arrangements had permitted the region to consolidate its position by exploiting the weakness of the central authority, thus retaining a high degree of independence. But by the eighteenth century the state was in a much stronger position. The strategy of mobilizing political actions through

4 The portion owed by each community was called the escart. The villages referred to their assemblies as escartons because their function was, in local usage, the escartonement (allotment) of the tribute shares (Fauché-Prunelle 1857: II, 327-8).

the court system had inevitably given the Briançonnais a high stake in keeping the existing legal/political structure unchanged; in fact, the villages were pulled towards greater integration into that system. At the same time, their political aims were to preserve autonomy from central authority. The Briançonnais's political infrastructure and aims were now at odds.

QUEYRAS VALLEY POLITICS

An examination of the *Déliberations de la Vallée du Queryas*, the records of the Queyras assembly (ADHA E358-548, 1593-1790), indicates that it was much more than an agency for paying taxes. Like the other escartons, it was a deliberative body that handled a multitude of issues. We have seen its role in the field of public health. In addition, the assembly operated as a lobbying unit, working to reduce or avoid taxes, reduce requisitions made in wartime, and arrange compensations for damages suffered because of war or natural disaster. The assembly also worked to procure grain at times of shortage, regulated market weights, measures, and prices, and directed a series of trials over two and a half centuries disputing the manner of tithe collection in the region.[5]

Queyrassins were involved in so many affairs at so many different

---

5 The Queyras tithe trials evolved in two phases. One was a period when the parish priests and the communities were at odds. The second phase pitted the Chapitre de Notre Dame d'Embrun (archepiscopal centre of Embrun) against the parish priests allied with the communities.

　　The main issue in the first phase was that the parish priests wanted to collect the tithe in kind while the villages wanted to pay cash - a sign of the importance of commerce in the region. The most ancient documents in the dispute are from the 1540s; they increase in the 1630s. The parties reached several temporary accords, such as one in 1652 in which the parish priests agreed to accept a cash settlement and benefits such as a house, garden, furniture, and firewood and exemption from local taxes (ADHA E510). A final accord was agreed to in 1737 (ADHA E526; Tivollier 1938: I, 419-24).

　　Even as this issue was being worked out, the villages made common cause with their parish priests in disputes with the Chapitre d'Embrun. These trials began in 1612 and continued to the Revolution. (See ADHA, ms. 314, 1769, 'Mémoire à Consulter pour La Vallée de Queyras,' written by Queyras parish priests, for an overview of the issues; and ADHA E367, E389, E393-5, E402, E515-16, E525-9 for the costs and the people involved in pursuing these trials).

levels of government that they maintained a network of pensionnaires (paid lobbyists) to protect their interests. The military engineer de la Blottière explained the system in 1708: 'They have a good lobbyist in Paris, someone as qualified as possible; this man is careful to inform them about anything that takes place that concerns them. They always have a person loyal to them near the Intendants; this means that they are kept informed of everything and that they take the proper measures in all affairs' (in de Rochas 1882: 101).

De la Blottière had several other interesting observations about escarton politics. He found much internal fighting, with members often ready to tear each other apart with outrageous insults ('se dechiront par des calomnies outragéants'), but they quickly closed ranks when the public interest was at stake and were therefore often successful with even the thorniest of issues ('qu'il s'agit de l'intérês publicq ... [ils] se réunissent à l'instant et paroisse d'une accorde admirable; cela fait qu'il a très peu d'affaires, quelqu'épineuses qu'elles soient, dont ils ne viennet à bout') (ibid.).

De la Blottière illustrates with an anecdote the Briançonnais method of dealing with an official government inquiry into what the villagers considered a private affair – the information contained in valley archives (which included the deliberations of the escartons).[6] At the

The general issue was that the Chapitre claimed prebendal rights which the Queyras refused to acknowledge. Part of this claim involved paying to the Chapitre a portion of what the village priests were to receive; thus the priests sided with the villagers. The volume and duration of the Queyras tithe trials gave credence to the 1785 complaint by the intendant that something had to be done to rationalize the great number of trials of the Queyrassin communities (ADHA E405).

6 In the seventeenth century, the state was pursuing a policy of integration and control in matters such as taxation. In 1628, the crown created the Bureau d'Election de Gap, a taille office which had authority over the Briançonnais. One of its rights was to verify village tax rolls. The Briançonnais protested not the tax itself but the right of the bureau to inspect village rolls, claiming that Article 8 of the 1343 charter gave them the right to impose local taxes without the authority or permission of crown officials ('mesme d'imposer et lever deniers sur eux sans autorité ny permission d'aucuns officier') (ADHA E357). In 1653, this privilege was upheld by an arrêt of the Dauphiné Parlement. The Bureau d'Election de Gap was permitted to inspect only those rolls pertaining to royal taxes. For the Briançonnais, this ruling meant that – if the villages could make it stick – the centre could be kept in the dark about local resources and wealth (Tivollier 1938: I, 297–311).

end of the seventeenth century Henri Lombard d'Herbigny, marquis de Thibouville and intendant of the Dauphiné, visited the town of Briançon to look into local affairs. The first consul (municipal leader) of Briançon gave a long and elaborate talk, comparing the marquis to famous Roman magistrates and not permitting him to interrupt. The consul was so persuasive in arguing that Briançonnais records were just small details, beneath the great man's dignity to inspect, that the intendant left two days later 'sans en plus sçavoir que le premier' (without knowing anything more than he had at first) (ibid. 101–3).

Village consuls were the representatives to the escarton meetings, and they brought to it many issues of local concern. For example, in 1730 the consul of Molines complained that the tavern-keepers of his village were selling bread, wine, and other goods at too high prices and that their weights and measures were inaccurate. The assembly confirmed the consul in his right to police the local economy by checking weights and measures every six months and fixing the price of commodities within the village (ADHA E391). On another occasion the assembly considered the fact that the Abriès weekly market was using containers for measuring grain that were larger than had been employed previously. The matter was considered quite important since Abriès was the 'only place in the valley where there is a market for the sale of all valley grains.' The meeting delegated the consul of Molines to construct precise measuring barrels that conformed with the standards set by the assembly (ADHA E402, 1773).

Struggling with such issues of local concern and settling disputes over the sharing of responsibilities in intercommunal road and bridge maintenance (see, for example, ADHA E403, 1778) created strong integrative ties among the villages. Everyone knew the other's business. Villages were able to unite on matters of general policy as well as deal with conflicts among themselves, thus building up long years of political experience and networks.

Their sense of the importance of their political business was graphically expressed in the care with which valley archives were guarded. In 1772 the Queyras escarton took steps to have built a 'strongbox or wardrobe, [and] to make for it eight locks with eight different keys' (ADHA E401). One key was given to each of the seven member communities and the eighth to the secretary of the valley. Selected members of the assembly were charged with the job of assembling all relevant documents and creating an inventory of holdings (ADHA E402, 1773). A large, two-doored, handsomely carved cupboard was built and stands to this day in the village of Ville Vieille.

The War of the Spanish Succession (1701–13)
During wartime the assembly had to cope with extraordinary demands as well as with its day-to-day functions. The Queyras Escarton was heavily involved in the War of Spanish Succession (ADHA E389, 1704–17). France was fighting the Austro-Sardes, who had occupied the Briançonnais valleys on the eastern flank of the Alps. The Queyras became a launching area from which the French armies hoped to regain the eastern valleys and press on to Turin. The Austro-Sardinian forces, pushing in the other direction, were able to gain easy access to the Queyras through the many passes into the valley. Both sides demanded tribute payments from the Queyrassins.

In 1705, the *Déliberations* show that the Queyrassins sent 150 men to the French forces and the next month sent barley and fodder to the enemy in Turin. The demands from both sides became enormous. In 1708, the enemy, the Duke of Savoy, levied a 'contribution de guerre' of 3188 ducats against the Queyras. The next year the French forces lodged their troops in the valley for many months and in addition asked for payment of 4800 livres and thousands of measures of hay and straw.

Emissaries from the Queyras were sent to both sides to negotiate reduced tribute payments. Often they were successful. In 1705 the Marquis d'Andourne, leader of the enemy forces in the area, demanded a hundred gold louis but settled for eighty to be paid within forty-eight hours. (Negotiation could be a dangerous job; in 1712 deputies from the Queyras were arrested by an enemy general as they were delivering their payments.)

Sometimes too Queyras representatives were successful in gaining compensation for the fodder and foodstuffs sent to the French forces. In 1712, for example, the valley received a 1200 livre reimbursement from the intendant for supplies that they had provided to troops encamped in Arvieux.

Throughout the war period Queyrassins worked at fostering an image of poverty and the depletion of their resources. In 1705 the intendant had granted the valley an exemption from paying its share of the tax called for in the 1343 charter. The Queyras continued to avoid paying in 1707 and 1708 although French troops were sent to try to force them to do so. The montagnards eventually paid for the expenses of these troops but not the tax (ADHA E389, 1708). In 1712 they sent a delegate to the meeting of the Grand Escarton, the assembly of all the escartons, to choose representatives to carry their briefs 'which contain … the sufferings of the Briançonnais, in order to try to obtain from His

Majesty some relief.' As de la Blottière had pointed out in 1708, when the inhabitants of the Briançonnais had a choice, 'they never fail to address themselves to the most eminent person' (in de Rochas 1882: 101).

Control of Resources

Even in the midst of war conditions the assembly pursued its own interests and made locally based decisions about where to concentrate resources and energies. For example, the Queyras tithe trials continued to dominate the valley's attention during the war period. In 1705, the same year that Queyras declared itself incapable of paying the annual charter tribute taxation, the assembly voted 600 livres to an emissary 'to carry out the continuing legal case brought by the aforesaid valley communities and the parish priests against the chapter of the archdiocese of Embrun.'

In 1707, a representative was sent to pursue the trial at the Parlement in Dijon. Meanwhile, the valley's lobbyist in Paris, the Abbé Morand, had to be paid for his role in the matter – 1484 livres for legal work and 300 livres for expenses. Others too were involved in the case. The total expenses for legal action amounted to 2563 livres in 1707 – the year when the Queyras officially complained that it could not afford to send men, money, or supplies to the French cause because of 'the poverty of this valley' (ADHA E389).

The actions of the Queyras assembly during the War of Spanish Succession indicate that although the valley suffered hardships, the inhabitants did not accept the war fatalistically or as passive victims. Rather they acted in their own interests to reduce suffering and damages. The continuation of activities for the tithe trial shows that the montagnards were able to decide the disposition of their resources even under extreme conditions when the state would have liked to control them for its own ends. (It is very likely that, although the tithe trial was being handled through the French court system, the French military authorities did not know that the villagers were spending large amounts of money to pursue it.[7])

---

7 Recall that, according to de la Blottière, the intendant was unable to gain access to the Briançonnais archives (in de Rochas 1882: 101–3). The presence of crown representatives was not required for escarton meetings. By the end of the seventeenth century the completed deliberations were regularly sent to be initialled by the vibailli in Briançon; however, he was not present at meetings (Tivollier 1938: I, 297–34). The bailli had had important judicial, financial, and military func-

The Queyrassins had evolved a complex, sophisticated strategy. The periphery was manipulating the centre – using the disorganization of the government and the lack of good communication between its branches to serve local interests. The escarton system provided a substantial organizational base from which to pursue such tactics. It was not individual peasants or isolated villages that dealt with the central authority but an alliance of fifty-one strategically important communities. The policy worked for centuries, but it did have hazards for the Briançonnais. As we shall see in the next section, some of them became apparent in the Treaty of Utrecht, which ended the War of Spanish Succession in 1713.

WAR, RELIGION, AND LOYALTY

For the French crown, the loyalty of the Queyras was increasingly in doubt in the ancien régime. In the twelfth century the French Alps had been the centre of the Vaudois movement, a precursor of Protestantism. It was led by Pierre Valdo or Vaud, who originally preached in Lyon but soon moved his base to the eastern Briançonnais valleys of Val Cluson, Germansque, and Val Pellice, which became known as the Vaudois valleys. In the fourteenth and fifteenth centuries there were campaigns against the Vaudois, but Louis XII halted them in 1500.

Soon a new preacher, Guillaume Farel, became known in the Alps, and it is thought that the Vaudois background of the region facilitated his work. He appeared in the Gap in 1522 preaching 'réforme.' By 1560 large parts of the Alps had been converted, and virtual war broke out; in 1574 there was a pitched battle in the Queyras between Catholic troops sent from Briançon and the Protestants of the Queyras. The number of converts to the new religion continued to increase in the Queyras, however. Protestant churches were built in Molines and Abriès. The next decade saw two more battles in the Queyras, one in Abriès in 1583 and another in Château Queyras four years later (Guillaume 1968: 59–86; Leutrat 1966).

The Seventeenth Century
The first half of the seventeenth century was quiet. Consuls, operating in their capacity as escarton delegates, attempted to placate all sides

tions in the Middle Ages. By the seventeenth century, however, the office had been emptied of its functions and was just an honorific (Marion 1969: 31–4). The vibaillis were usually local men, probably sympathetic to local causes.

through the use of diplomacy and strategic gift-giving or bribes, which the assembly paid for. For example, François Berthelot visited various Protestant leaders, the archbishop of Embrun, and military commanders in the region such as the Comte de Sault (ADHA E361).

With the Revocation of the Edict of Nantes in 1685, however, war again broke out. The French military observers on the scene distrusted the Queyrassins' loyalty to the French cause. Richerand, a military engineer who was working on the reconstruction of Fort Queyras in 1692, gave the following picture: 'The ... subjects being of the Protestant Religion in their hearts and Catholics on the surface have no loyalty to France and this is so true that the majority have promised Count Chomberg [leader of the Piedmontese forces] that they would take up arms in the event that he become master of the fortress [Château Queyras]' (DGFV, art. 8, sec. 1, carton 1, no. 4).

Two years later, the engineer Ricord was at work on plans to build a redoubt in Abriès. He too was suspicious of the Queyrassins, their institutions, and their 'insufferable vanity.' In a 1694 brief to Catinat, leader of the French army in the area, Ricord complained that the village assemblies, especially in Abriès and Molines, were dominated by recent converts to Catholicism. Therefore, he argued, the valley acquiesced to enemy demands too readily. Ricord estimated that the Queyras had paid the enemy about 30,000 livres in each of the past four years and supplied so much other material that the annual total in tribute was more than 100,000 livres. In addition, he estimated, the Queyras was paying France 80,000 livres a year in taxes (the gabelle, the taille, and the annual share of charter tribute). The valley was rich, he continued, as shown by the size of the French assessment, the large animal population, and the productivity of the lands. However, the payments to the enemy, in addition to the amounts paid to France, were pushing even this rich valley into poverty. Thus Ricord argued for the construction of military fortifications in Abriès, hoping that a military presence would halt the flow of goods and money to the Piedmontese and remove the pretext that the Queyrassins' 'safety depended on paying tributes to the enemies of the King and Religion' (DGFV art. 8, sec. 1, carton 1, no. 7).

Catinat, Ricord's superior, disagreed with the engineer's estimate of the outlay to the enemy. He felt the total annual figure was closer to 28,000 livres, with only 2000 to 3000 livres as direct bribes to enemy officers. Catinat decided that Abriès could not be fortified effectively and that it was cheaper and easier to let the villagers pay off the enemy than to risk losing villages and hamlets entirely (DGFV, 1695, art. 8, sec. 1, carton 1, no. 10).

The Treaty of Utrecht (1713)
This pattern was repeated during the War of Spanish Succession. Again the authorities found it easier to allow villages to pay off the enemy than to protect them – but again suspicions were raised. In 1710, Du Prat, the subdelegate of the region, demanded that the Queyras give him copies of any treaties made with the enemy about the amounts to be paid. He also asked for receipts ('quittances de payments') 'that have been made, together with an account of all the incidental expenses that the enemy has forced them to pay ... in addition, an account of the grains provided' (ADHA E389).

These incidents, coupled with those described in the previous section, reveal the complex nature of the negotiations going on between state and villages. The army could not adequately defend the Queyras from enemy incursions and so allowed the villages to pay off the enemy. The villages were using the payments to the enemy as a reason for not making tax payments to France. The state tried to exercise some control over the situation by asking for information about the amounts going to the enemy. It attempted to collect money when it could and reluctantly accepted the times when it could not. Villagers perceived the state as having a commitment to reimburse them for losses sustained during the encampment of French troops in their midst and actively pressed these claims at various levels of the state bureaucracy (ADHA E389–91).

What emerges is a picture of constant negotiation and deals in which both sides were politically active, and both made the best of the situation. The state was simply not strong enough to steam-roller its demands over the populace. For manoeuvring in the mountains, it needed the peasants' co-operation in providing men, animals, and supplies.

In the long run, however, the state was more powerful than the region. Negotiation with foreign states, unlike taxation, is not a shared power. Thus in 1713, when France negotiated the Treaty of Utrecht, it was able to trade territory with Piedmont, giving Victor-Amedée, the duke of Savoy, the three eastern escartons (Oulx, Val Cluson, and Château-Dauphin), which contained thirty-two communities, in exchange for the small valley of Barcellonnette. There was nothing the villagers could do about the move. Protests about the destruction of the

escarton system and the contravention of the 1343 charter were completely useless.[8]

Why did France trade away what the French General Berwick called
'such a large and good region' (Guillaume 1968: 96)? I have been
unable to find any primary documents to explain the trade. The secondary literature tends to describe the event as one of the hazards of
diplomacy – the crown arbitrarily created a border, ignoring local
interests (Guillaume 1968: 95–7; Routier ca 1970: 122–4; Crubellier
1948). However, the move could just as easily have been a deliberate
attempt by the French crown to rid itself of a large and disloyal region
which could not easily be controlled and to assert authority over the
remaining valleys: a divide-and-rule policy.

The Queyras had very strong economic ties with Piedmont. The process of integrating the region into France and separating it from the
eastern valleys and Piedmont was a long one. To this day many Queyrassins retain a symbolic separation from France; for example, they
discuss weather in terms of differences between Queyras and France –
an entity to which the valley does not quite belong.

The War of Austrian Succession (1740–8)

During the War of Austrian Succession, France was again at war with
Piedmont, and the Queyras was involved. Again Queyrassins paid tribute to the enemy 'on pain of being burned' and were unable to pay the
full royal tax (ADHA E393, 1745). The valley suffered from the station-
ing of French troops and the passage of Spanish troops, who were allied
with the French at that time (ADHA E393–4).

Once again the question of loyalty to the French cause was raised. In
1747 the military engineers de Monville and de Mureau undertook
military voyages of inspection in the Queyras and the Briançonnais. In
their twenty-five-page brief they reiterated previous enthusiastic
descriptions of the wealth and resources of the region. They noted
especially Abriès's abundant fodder and large sheep herds, but they
were more interested in the fact that Abriès continued to trade with
Piedmont. They suspected that the Queyrassins were still supporting
the enemies of France. They also cited the escarton system as proof of
republican – therefore disloyal – tendencies in the region (DGFV,
art. 8, sec. 1, carton 1, no. 31).

8 The escartons did, however, continue to function on the French side of the
  border. The Grand Escarton became the assembly of the villages of the Queyras,
  the town of Briançon, and the surrounding region.

The French escartons were worried. They had seen the state's power in the dismembering of the union in 1713, and now they were determined to remove the stigma of disloyalty. In 1752 the consuls of the Briançonnais presented a brief to the Marquis de Paulmy, secretary of state and assistant to the minister of war, who was making an inspection of the alpine frontier (Duhamel 1902). The brief was a *tour de force* of rhetoric designed to please and reassure the marquis, to demonstrate the region's loyalty to the crown, and to emphasize the need to confirm the rights and privileges of the 1343 charter.

The consuls began with a pessimistic description of the region's economy, saying that the soil was bad, the crops poor, and the winters long and hard. Only the inhabitant's privileges and exemptions stemming from the royal charter, they claimed, were preventing massive out-migration.

The consuls bolstered their case with a history of the Briançonnais, tracing the legal status and rights of the area. It began with sixth-century Gaul. They pointed out that even the precursors of the dauphins had granted rights and tax exemptions to the villages, and they emphasized the dauphin's special and paternalistic relationship with them, their loyalty to the dauphins, and their ancient hostility to France's enemy, Piedmont. The 1343 charter had been granted, according to the consuls, because of the Briançonnais's loyalty to the dauphin, who wished to rescue villagers from the arbitrariness of previous delphinal tax collectors.

The long brief went on to detail all the charter rights and privileges, clause by clause. These rights, especially the exemptions from feudal dues, had been confirmed over and over again by the kings of France – in 1348 when the Dauphiné became part of France, then in 1481, 1483, 1533, 1547, 1612, 1613, and 1644, and finally in 1727 by Louis XV. Absolutely no mention was made anywhere in the document of the obvious fact that the charter had been violated in 1713 by the transfer of the three eastern escartons to Piedmont. Neither were any of the disputes among escarton members mentioned.

The brief described the escarton system itself as existing primarily to support the crown, a 'union and association in order to share among [the escartons] all the taxes imposed in time of war or in service to the king' (ibid. 197). The consuls assured de Paulmy that the escartons were indispensable to the state since they provided effective security for France in an important border region.

Proof of this support was the region's supposed willingness to pay royal taxes, such as the taille, capitation, and vingtième, and the annual charter tribute. Further proof was offered by recounting the support the region gave French forces during wartime: the peasants of Briançonnais had lodged troops, fed animals, and supplied the army with men and equipment. The consuls estimated that in the border campaigns from 1680 to 1713 the region supported the French cause with 800,000 livres' worth of supplies. Reimbursement, they noted, was slow in coming, yet all obligations had been fulfilled with zeal. The phrase 'zèle des habitants' was repeated over and over in describing the Briançonnais feeling for France.[9] The consuls concluded by saying that their service to the crown would continue as long as the region was maintained in its privileges, for without them villages would be too poor to do their duty.

A supplementary brief, by the military engineer Pierre Joseph Bourcet, whose secretary was Jean Berthelot, an Abrièsois, explained the payments to the enemy as a matter of strict necessity because the many passes into the village made it very hard to defend (ibid. 211–17).

The consuls' brief and its supplement give us an important example of Briançonnais political sophistication. The villages were presenting their case to a government that had demonstrated its overriding power by dividing the escartons. Villages had no comparable power, so they launched an eloquent propaganda campaign in which they minimized the wealth of the region and the significance of the escarton system. Their strategy was to placate the centre and to assure the crown that its border region was in the safe hands of loyal and brave peasants. The escarton, the platform from which Briançonnais peasants had ex-

---

9 We have, of course, already seen considerable evidence which contradicts this claim. We can add the example of the construction of Montdauphin, a Vauban-designed fortress at the entrance to the Queyras. The records (DGFV, art. 8, sec. 1, carton 1, Montdauphin) suggest that from the inception of the project in 1692 until its completion in 1748 peasants were unwilling to work on it. Reports from 1708, 1724, and 1727 show that peasants came to work late, left early, staged work slowdowns, and were quick to demand compensation when their property was affected.

   Golaz says that in 1633–42 peasants near Fort Queyras had also been unwilling to work on its repair and, in fact, wanted the fortress torn down (1971: 34).

   Golaz also notes that during the War of Austrian Succession (1740–8) French attempts to raise troops in the Queyras failed. Many men refused to return from seasonal migrations in Italy for fear of being put in the army (ibid. 85).

tracted so many advantages, was described solely in terms of its capacity to serve the interest of the king.

The document shows that the region was beginning to accept increased integration into the state system. It was in no position to fight back directly; rather, it went to pains to represent itself as a part of that system so that it could manoeuvre from within. Its political aims became to retain the region's right of assembly and tax privileges and to downplay charges of 'vanity' or 'republicanism,' which implied disloyalty.

This propaganda war was entrusted to the consuls of the villages, most of whom were notaries. They had the education and legal experience to carry on this kind of political diplomacy. But this use of their expertise had a price. As we shall see in the next sections, it became increasingly difficult for villagers to control the power ambitions of their own representatives.

VILLAGE POLITICS

The lively politics of Abriès in the seventeenth and eighteenth centuries bears little resemblance to the commonplace notion of 'traditional' old-regime politics. Rather, it was organized around the following factors: the medieval heritage of participatory local government structured into the intervillage escarton system, the selection of community representatives or advocates to lobby on behalf of village and valley interests at all levels of government, the use of the trial as a weapon of political opposition, and the emergence of an oligarchic family – the Berthelots.[10]

In Abriès village assemblies were held in the permanent covered market, 'sous les Halles' (Tivollier 1938: II, 293–300).[11] All adult 'habitants' had the right to attend. The term 'habitant' indicated a household head who held taxable land (ibid.). This property qualification

10 For interesting parallels, see Netting's account of communal institutions in the village of Torbal, Switzerland (1981: chap. 3). Torbal resisted feudalism and later nation-state penetration, managing local resources through similar manipulation of the political/legal arena.
11 I cannot describe the nature of ancien régime politics in Abriès from primary data because most of the records for the seventeenth and eighteenth centuries were destroyed during the Second World War. However, rich data from surrounding villages within the Queyras remain extant.

was not limiting, as were property qualifications for electors under the Empire and the Restoration (Godechot 1968: 518); ownership of *any* amount of land was sufficient, so every household in the village was likely to be represented.[12]

Two consuls were elected yearly, according to Article 12 of the charter. The office was much sought-after, even though it could be held for only one year at a time and successive elections were rare. The numerous functions of a consul included responsibility for village tax obligations. Consuls paid the taille themselves and were reimbursed during the year by the villagers (Roux La Croix, 1774, in Roman 1892: 343–65). This arrangement meant that an office-holder had to be fairly wealthy and may also account for the fact that consuls rarely succeeded themselves in office. Yet the job, in addition to offering prestige, may also have been a source of profit; delinquents paid interest on the amounts owed, which were conceived of as loans from the consul.

Some villages gave their consuls a salary. In 1678 Molines paid its two consuls 60 livres, and Château Ville Vielle set aside fields ('près des Consuls') for theirs. The trips that consuls made on behalf of their village were paid for by internal taxation (Tivollier 1938: II, 309–10).

A 1681 Ville Vieille document announcing an election suggests the following summary of the functions of a consul:

Overseeing internal taxation for village expenses.
Collecting the taille.
Administering village affairs.
Renting pastures.
Representing the village before judges and magistrates, lay and
 ecclesiastic.
Writing official documents.
Notifying villages of government ordinances.
Protecting the poor, widows, and orphans.
Upholding the faith.
Supervising repairs to roads and bridges.

Other consular obligations included policing prices, weights, and measures within the village, settling disputes, and working as a community advocate in dealing with higher levels of government, includ-

12 Recall too from Chapter 2 that qualified women – usually widows who were household heads – could attend assembly meetings, although they were not eligible for election as consuls or councillors (Tivollier 1938: II, 293–30).

ing serving as village representatives to escarton meetings. In short the consular job required wealth, literacy, and legal experience, so it was frequently filled by notaries (Tivollier 1938: II, 300–5).

The fact that the office was elective and that elections were held yearly was crucial in limiting the potentially abusive power of consuls.[13] Even the powerful Berthelot family of Abriès was unable to monopolize the job.[14]

The regulations for consular elections in some Queyras villages have survived. No document indicates how a candidate for election was selected, although it is clear that all male household heads were considered eligible. Tivollier offers the 1727 regulations of the village of Arvieux, which are considered representative of all Queyras villages (1938: II, 300–5). The document begins by stating the participatory nature of the election: 'We shall proceed to the election of two consuls ... The nomination will be made by all the habitants of the community, called for this purpose door to door by the town crier, with a majority of votes, according to ancient custom' (ibid. 306).

The regulations go on to describe the rules of procedure, which suggest the heated and sometimes violent nature of consular elections. Two examples:

Item, that no person undertake to kill, assault, beat, or strike the man or woman beside him or anyone else, under pain of death ...
    Item, that no person undertake to rob, unclothe, or assault his neighbour, on pain of being hanged. (Ibid. 308)

The document goes on at length in this vein, listing quite severe punishments for even minor breaches in decorum, such as swearing. It also notes some of the fines and punishments for those who contravened agricultural regulations.

One reason these elections were so tumultuous was that individual votes were given aloud before a legal representative and the outgoing

13 There were, not surprisingly, tendencies towards self-aggrandizement among those who held the office of consul. By the eighteenth century certain patterns of deference and honorifics accrued to the office – the title of 'sieur,' the wearing of distinctively coloured hoods, and the assignment of special pews in church (Tivollier 1938: II, 305).
14 The significance of these restrictions will become apparent later in the book when we examine the post-Revolution systems of long-term appointment of local officials which led to the emergence of dictatorial mayors.

consuls; the secret ballot did not appear until 1790.[15] Consular elections were said to be ridden by cliques and factions. De Monville and de Mureau, the military engineers on a voyage of inspection in the Briançonnais in 1747, remarked on such tendencies and on the power of notaries in village assemblies: 'Five or six notables who by their insolence or by their wits, or through the office of notary that they hold, become so-to-speak despotic and dominate the office of consul, which they keep for several years or give them over to people belonging to their factions' (DGFV, art. 8, sec. 1, carton 1, no. 31).

We do not know whether these tendencies were typical of earlier periods. I suspect they were not. My guess is that notarial oligarchies began to emerge in the mid-eighteenth century as a part of the general process of state integration. The Berthelots of Abriès, the Laurens of Ristolas, the Jouves of Aiguilles, the Fantins of Arvieux, and others may be taken as representing an emerging class of power-brokers who had begun to disengage themselves from village interests and the village power base and form alliances with each other.

FRIENDS AT COURT: THE BERTHELOTS

The Berthelot family of Abriès was a good example of the rising stratum of mediators and power-brokers in the Briançonnais region. The village's most illustrious people in the sixteenth and seventeenth centuries, they developed networks of articulation that linked them with many levels of government. Their role makes clear the important fact that pre-industrial peasantry were by no means cut off from the centre or unable to influence government decision-making.

The activities of the Berthelots were not completely altruistic. They had a clear intention of doing well by doing good, but whatever their personal motives, they were also of service to the Queyras and the region. As for all mediators, their position was at times precarious: they were subject to attack from both their local constituency and from the supralocal bureaucracy. Their importance to the story of Abriès, however, rests in the way their lives reflect the coming together of the aims of state and village – each a constituency in need of representation to the other.

---

15 The secret ballot did not become generally used in France until 1914.

Acquiring Power: François Berthelot (1579–1660)
The Berthelots, originally inhabitants of Valcluson, one of the eastern escartons, first appeared in Abriès during the fifteenth century. By the early seventeenth century the family was prominent in the village, having produced a notary, a royal notary, and in 1628 a consul (Blanchard 1933: 1–45).

The work of a notary was to draw up acts and contracts (Marion 1969: 400), a very important job in a society that placed great emphasis on legal and contractual arrangements in both the public and private spheres. Marriage contracts, wills, sales of property, agreements of business partnership, and work contracts were prominent features of everyday life. In 1610 Abriès had four notaries; by 1615 there were five, including François Berthelot, who had married into a notarial family (Blanchard 1933: 10–18).

The Career of François Berthelot
François did not remain an ordinary notary. In 1615 he became a royal notary, a venal office (price unknown) which permitted the holder to carry appeal cases within wide jurisdictions (Marion 1969; 400). Royal notaries could specialize in various areas; the Berthelots developed their expertise in 'justice d'exception,' a branch of royal justice that focused on administrative cases such as taxation, rather than on civil and criminal matters (ibid. 314, 318). It became their job to learn the ins and outs of the legal/administrative system of the old regime. This kind of skill and the network of contacts the Berthelots developed were very useful to the escarton system. It is also significant that it was the crown, continuously multiplying the number and variety of notarial offices in search of revenue, that provided a platform for the Berthelots (ibid. 401). Thus the coming together of state aims and local aims was instrumental in launching the Berthelots' careers as mediators.

François was extremely active in valley politics. The *Délibérations* of the Queyras Escarton record that for more than thirty years he was sent on missions for the valley, travelling to Briançon, Embrun, Grenoble, Lyon, Dijon, Turin, and Paris and often dealing with high-ranking officials. For example, in 1615 and again in 1625, he led delegations requesting that the Briançonnais be exempted from providing men for the French army on the grounds that many of the peasants were absent on winter migrations and unavailable for service (ADHA E359, E361). Between 1631 and 1636 he met several times with the Comte du Sault and the comte's son, the Marquis de Tavannes, who had troops in the

Queyras, trying to obtain reimbursement for the damages caused by the army (ADHA E365, E369).

Such missions point up the intervillage nature of many Briançonnais affairs. When, for example, troops were billeted in a village, the costs of supporting them were shared by all fifty-one Briançonnais villages through the escarton system.[16] Thus, when François went out on missions, he was not representing his own village but the region as a whole, and his trips were paid for by either the Queyras Escarton or the Grand Escarton. The payments were much more than tokens. For example, in 1627 François went to Embrun to pursue some matters pertaining to the tithe trial and then to Dijon and Lyon to consult with lawyers on other valley business. He was absent from home for close to two months and was paid 3 livres 4 sols a day for his expenses. He was probably able to profit financially from such trips; in addition, he made contacts which aided his legal career (ADHA E361). The escartons paid for the gifts that were given to important people during these missions. In 1651, for instance, the Grand Escarton sent calves, sheep, trout, and venison as part of a greeting to the Archbishop of Embrun (ADHA E378).

François and the two other Queyras lawyers pursued cases dealing with the salt tax in the Queyras and followed appeals from Grenoble to Paris and finally to the Parlement of Bourgogne in 1635, where a reduction was obtained (ADHA E367).

Finally, François represented the Queyras in the matter of trials against Mathieu Humbert, the valley châtelain.[17] At the end of the six-

---

16 For example, in 1633 François, as consul of Abriès, met with the consul of Vallouise on the issue of the costs of supporting the regiment of Aiguebonne, a charge to be divided among all five escartons (Blanchard 1933: 11).

17 The office of châtelain was a medieval creation which involved military, judicial, and administrative functions. The châtelain, appointed by the dauphin or later by the king of France, was stationed in Fort Queyras in times of war to command local militia. He adjudicated civil cases involving sums of less than 30 sous tournois and criminal cases that carried fines of less than 50 sous (Borel du Bez 1931: 31–2). The châtelain also collected certain dues owed the dauphin and submitted the accounts to delphinal auditors. By the sixteenth century the financial and military aspects of the job had been eliminated by the creation of receveurs des tailles and military governors.

In the fifteenth and sixteenth centuries holders of the office were not Queyrassin in origin; some came from as far away as Scotland, attracted by the profits that could be made from the job's judicial fees (Tivollier 1938: II, 295–6).

teenth century the office of châtelain had become venal and hereditary. In the Queyras, it went first to the Humberts, a local family interested in making a profit from it. Esprit Humbert (held office 1600–14)
and later his son Mathieu (held office 1614–46) claimed the right to be
present at every village assembly of the Queyras and to charge 6 livres
per meeting for attendance (ADHA E361). The Queyras villages were
fiercely opposed to these claims and launched a series of trials against
the Humberts which went on for forty years.

François Berthelot was the most frequent representative of the villages' interests in these trials, working with notaries from Molines and
Arvieux. At one point they were able to buy Mathieu Humbert off with
a lump-sum payment of 2000 écus (ADHA E359). But after a short
interval Humbert again began pressing his claims, expanding on a
1606 decree from the Grenoble Parlement which upheld the
châtelain's claim to be present at village assemblies that elected consuls
(ADHA E428, E431). Over the next several years François made several
trips to Grenoble and Paris on behalf of the valley in the matter. Finally, in 1642, he met with Philippe Meyer, a Briançonnais lobbyist stationed in Paris. Meyer had obtained a decision from the Paris Parlement upholding the villages' right to assemble freely without the
presence or fees of the châtelain except at the election of consuls
(Tivollier 1938: I, 296–311; Blanchard 1933: 13–15).

Something about the office of châtelain must have appealed to François for in 1646 he bought the office from Mathieu Humbert (who was
probably financially exhausted by the cost of the trials), paying 9000
livres – a very large sum of money considering that the office of notary
was worth only 400 livres at that time (Blanchard 1933: 31). François
made the purchase for his middle son, Gaspard, who had just turned
twenty-five and had married the daughter of a Briançon notary. The
hereditary office was destined to remain within François's line until an
absence of male heirs and the coming of the Revolution terminated its
tenure by the Berthelots. (See Figure 1 for the genealogy of Berthelot
châtelains.)

François himself continued to act as a negotiator for the Queyras for
the rest of his life. In 1647 he travelled to Grenoble to try to prevent a
cavalry company from being billeted in Molines (ADHA E376, E437). In
1648 and 1651 he represented the Queyras in joint meetings with the
other escartons. He even continued to pursue the tithe trial on behalf
of the valley. His sons also worked for the valley. For example,
Gaspard, who held the office of châtelain from 1646 until his death in

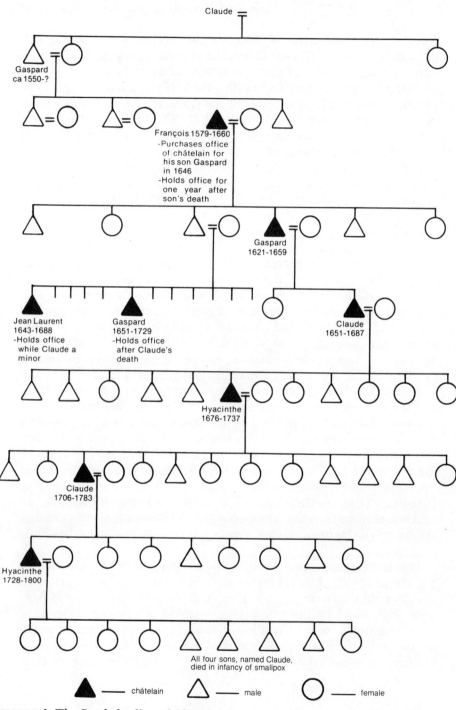

Claude

Gaspard
ca 1550-?

François 1579-1660
-Purchases office
of châtelain for
his son Gaspard
in 1646
-Holds office for
one year after
son's death

Gaspard
1621-1659

Jean Laurent
1643-1688
-Holds office
while Claude a
minor

Gaspard
1651-1729
-Holds office
after Claude's
death

Claude
1651-1687

Hyacinthe
1676-1737

Claude
1706-1783

Hyacinthe
1728-1800

All four sons, named Claude,
died in infancy of smallpox

▲ —— châtelain   △ —— male   ◯ —— female

FIGURE 1 The Berthelot line of Châtelains

1659, served on delegations, represented the valley in trials, and had a term as consul of Abriès (ADHA E377, 1649).

Family Strategy

François's purchase of the office of châtelain raises questions about the nature of power-holding and about his motives. We have no letters or personal accounts of his views, but we can piece together some insights by analysing his will and studying his career and the careers of his children. (See Figure 2.)

Such an analysis makes it clear that obtaining the office of châtelain was not François's only goal in life. Rather than investing solely in one son, François chose to invest in the family as a whole. This strategy makes sense in terms of the demographic realities of the time; in fact, François outlived his son Gaspard, who died in 1659 at the young age of thirty-eight. We can see this strategy at work in François's will (ADHA B223), which shows him to have been a wealthy man with feelings of responsibility towards his large family. He left as principal heirs his two sons and his grandson Claude, child of Gaspard. These three were to divide his estate and carry out François's directions in terms of the lesser heirs. There was no question of primogeniture here nor of support for the holder of the châtelain's office at the expense of others. Neither was there an attempt by François to exercise dictatorial power over the family until his own death. His children received the bulk of their share of the estate at the time of their marriages and only lesser amounts on his death.

François's sons received legal educations and his daughters married into legal families – a pattern that was to be followed through generations. Figure 2 is a genealogy indicating the career and marital patterns of many of François's children and grandchildren. We see the importance of the legal connection and the networks built up among legal families in different towns. We also see that families were often large; a balance had to be struck between producing enough male children to carry on the family legal profession and producing so many offspring that family resources were depleted. (Having large families was not as great a problem for the Berthelots, whose males were expected to work for a living, as it was for contemporary aristocrats.) Daughters were provided for through dowries and by marriages into socially equivalent families. In some cases, male and female Berthelots chose a religious vocation, but overall the law was their preferred profession. The family provided sufficient wealth to educate future lawyers and enough contacts to guarantee suitable marriages.

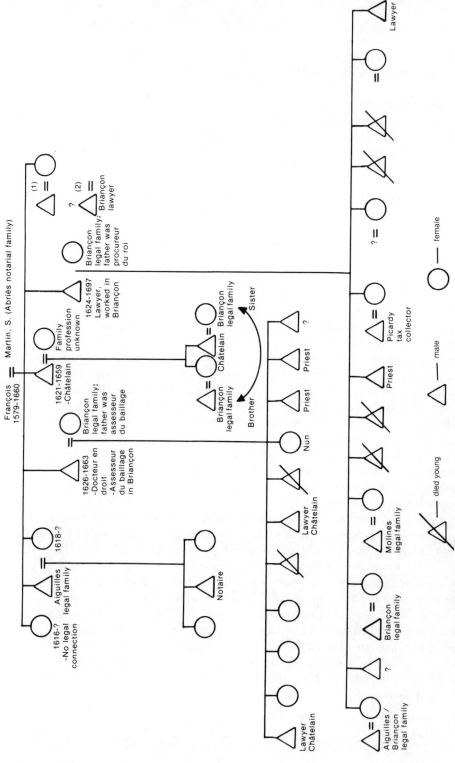

FIGURE 2 Professions of François Berthelot's descendants and in-laws

From the seventeenth century onwards, the Berthelots expanded enormously. The size of the families alone meant that there was always a Berthelot involved in village and escarton legal affairs and politics. François's brother produced lines of notaries and royal notaries. Other Berthelots became important in the religious sphere. From 1643 until the Revolution the majority of Abriès parish priests came from the Berthelot family (Blanchard 1933: 77–87). After the Revocation of the Edict of Nantes, this identification with Catholicism in a region with a large Protestant population probably aided in the Berthelot's political work for the escartons by lending an air of loyalty to the family.

As village notaries, the Berthelots had information about the financial situation of all their clients in the village and the surrounding region. The major life crises, marriage and death, were occasions for property to change hands and required the active presence of a notary. Because the notary had such a central role in drawing up marriage contracts and wills as well as inventories, estate divisions, and work contracts, he was in the position to have a deep understanding of the village, which could be used to recruit loyal clients – when running for consul, for example. Notaries' knowledge of property arrangements within and between families also put them in a position to profit personally, since they had inside information about when to purchase land and houses. The Berthelots followed up such leads and invested their money in the purchase of houses in various hamlets in the upper Queyras and in the town of Briançon.

Consolidation Attempts and Community Opposition

As notaries and escarton representatives the Berthelots were ideal mediators, but by the end of the seventeenth century some important contradictions appeared in their style of power-holding. Their identification with the supralocal system began to increase, and Hyacinthe Berthelot, (1676–1737), who had inherited the office of châtelain, showed some aristocratic pretensions. By 1696 a Berthelot coat of arms appeared in the armorial général (ibid. 55).

Hyacinthe and Claude Berthelot

Nevertheless, Hyacinthe, like his great-grandfather François, worked on behalf of the Queyras escarton. It was Hyacinthe who was active during the War of the Spanish Succession. As châtelain, he was ordered to raise troops, and he led a militia of a hundred men in battle in 1707 (ibid. 67). Hyacinthe negotiated the payments to the enemy

and met with the Intendant d'Angervilliers and the French com-
mander Maréchal Berwick at Briançon and Grenoble to explain the
necessity for these payments. He was also one of the Queyrassins who
went to Paris and worked with the lobbyist Abbé Morand trying to
obtain reimbursement for the food and fodder the valley supplied to
French forces during the war. In addition, Hyacinthe was one of the
chief organizers of the security system against the plague in the 1720s.

Yet everyone did not see all of Hyacinthe's actions as unselfish service to the valley. He had to make a living, and his chief resource was
his office of châtelain.[18] In 1729 the Dauphiné Parlement issued a
regulation granting all châtelains the right to charge a fee of 3 livres to
authorize assemblies; greffiers (registrars) were permitted to charge a
lesser amount. But Hyacinthe charged 24 livres, and his registrar, who
was also his father, charged 12 livres (Tivollier 1938: I, 440; Blanchard
1933: 70). The communities of the Queyras did not accept these high
fees and started legal proceedings, which eventually vindicated the
villages' claim.

Taking legal action against the châtelain was not uncommon in the
valley. This form of opposition was available to all villages; all they
needed were lawyers, time, and money – all of which Queyrassins had.
Thus, when Hyacinthe was lobbying on behalf of the valley during the
War of Spanish Succession, the valley was suing him in an attempt to
prevent his acquiring the post of quartermaster at Fort Queyras (ADHA
E389, 1711). Later, the village of Abriès sued him for constructing a
dike in the L'Adroit quarter which caused the gardens of Le Bourg to
flood during a rainstorm. The village's suit was handled by its consuls
for that year, Chaffrey Berthelot and Claude Berthelot, who were both
lawyers in addition to being Hyacinthe's cousin and son respectively.
Five years later the case was settled in favour of Abriès, and Hyacinthe
paid a fine of 3000 livres plus court costs (Blanchard 1933: 70).

Claude (1706–83) followed in his father's footsteps. In 1738, when he
assumed the office of châtelain, he began to charge high fees to
authorize assemblies: 30 livres to Abriès, 24 livres to Aiguilles, Molines,
Arvieux, and Château Ville Vieille, and 22 livres to Ristolas and St.

18 Like almost all Queyrassins, Hyacinthe held land, but not on a grand scale. In
   1732 he was recorded as owning land in twenty-two parts of Abriès, as having
   paid a capitation tax of 12 livres, and as owning four cows, two mules, and
   twenty-three sheep (ADHA E542; Blanchard 1933: 71–2). Clearly, he was neither
   a great estate-owner nor a large stock-raiser.

Veran (ADHA E392). In addition, Claude appointed his brother as registrar, who charged an additional fee of 12 livres. The communities persisted in their opposition to these fees. Notaries from Abriès and Molines were especially active in their opposition and by 1740 obtained a judgment from the Dauphiné Parlement against the châtelain. He was ordered not to charge more than 9 livres for authorizing consulat elections, and his registrar was limited to 6 livres; in addition, he was forbidden to charge for any other assemblies, which were permitted to meet without his authorization, and he was ordered to make restitution for the excessive fees charged by his father and himself for the preceding twenty-nine years (Tivollier 1938: I, 440–1; Blanchard 1933: 73). Here we see the perils of the middleman role: the state was an uncertain ally and not always subject to manipulation.

This incident was not the end of Claude's legal and financial troubles. In 1745 a Briançon lawyer charged him with falsifying accounts. Forty years later Claude's son was ordered to pay more than 3000 livres in a judgment against his father's misdeeds (Blanchard 1933: 76, 87). Perhaps because of his financial woes, Claude seems to have spent his energy in attempts to make money rather than in the service of the village or the valley.[19]

François Berthelot and Family Size

It was Claude's cousin François (1719–96) who carried on the family tradition of service. François was a royal notary who divided his time among legal duties, municipal service in Abriès, and missions for the Queyras Escarton. François was particularly active during the War of Austrian Succession and often represented Abriès in Queyras assemblies and the Grand Escarton (ADHA E393). He was shrewder than Claude and generally able to avoid litigation.

---

19 In 1773 Claude tried to force the community of Guillestre, a town at the mouth of the Queyras valley but not in the Briançonnais, to pay him thirty years of back fees by virtue of the protection he claimed to have offered the town as châtelain. The records do not show whether he was able to make this claim stick (Blanchard 1933: 84). Earlier, in 1759, he had tried to obtain for his son a road inspector post, which would have involved fees for overseeing repairs. The Queyras Escarton quickly blocked this attempt, claiming that the villages had always repaired intervillage roads by corvée – each village taking its turn – with no fee-taking. Claude's son was denied the commission as road inspector (ADHA E397).

François married twice and had large families with both his wives. He married his cousin Elizabeth Audier-Merle when he was twenty-eight and she was twenty-five. Their first child was born three months later. Within the next fifteen years, Elizabeth bore eleven children; only four of them survived to adulthood, and only two of these were male. Thus, in order to produce a son who could follow in his father's footsteps in the office of royal notary, Elizabeth spent approximately half her married life pregnant. The average birth-spacing was not quite eighteen months, the shortest being only eleven months. Elizabeth died in 1762 at the age of forty shortly after the death of her last-born infant.

Within two years François was remarried, to Marie Audier, and he became a father again nineteen months after the birth of Elizabeth's last son. (We do not have the date of Elizabeth's death or of the marriage to Marie Audier, but if we assume a year of mourning between the death of the first wife and the remarriage, Marie was at least two months' pregnant at her wedding.) Marie followed her predecessor's lead in producing a large number of children in a relatively short period of time. Six of the nine children she bore over nineteen years survived into adulthood. The average birth-spacing between the first eight children was twenty-three months, while nearly six years elapsed between the final two children. François was sixty-four at the time his last child was born. He had fathered twenty children in thirty-six years; of the ten who survived to adulthood, four were males. Two of the sons carried on the family legal tradition. The Berthelot demographic strategy was influenced by the need to produce male heirs to keep the hereditary offices the family held. They enhanced their chances by having large families, encouraging quick remarriage after a spouse's death, and relaxing demands for bridal virginity.

Farming families were smaller. A study of thirty wills recorded in Abriès between 1737 and 1748 by Maître Berthelot (ADHA 1E3953) tells us the number of children in the family of the will maker, which gives us an approximate notion of family size (at least among the people who made wills and sought out Maître Berthelot – there were other notaries in the village at the time, but their records have not survived). Three of the will makers were not married, and six had no children. For the twenty-one families with children, the average number of offspring was 3.3 and only three families had as many as six. Many of these children were minors (under age twenty-five) at the time of their parent's death. We do not know whether they survived into adulthood or whether the surviving parent remarried. (Only a family-reconstitution study could give us exact information on completed family size.)

Doubtless, the phenomenon of seasonal migration, which did not affect the rich Berthelots who stayed in the village year-round, did affect the rest of the population. Since a large percentage of the adult male population was gone for as much as seven months a year and returned to the village only during the peak agricultural season when they worked very long hours, we can assume that the frequency of sexual intercourse was considerably lower in this population than in populations which had year-round access to partners. Seasonal migration can thus be seen as a form of birth control, keeping peasant family sizes small.

DESTRUCTION OF THE BERTHELOT PATTERN OF POWER-HOLDING

The significance of the Berthelots in local government can be most clearly understood by looking at the time when it ceased to be important. The advocacy function of the Berthelots continued past the Revolution, but the new contacts between the village and the new regime were forged not by the Berthelots, the old notarial elite, but by Richard-Calve, a merchant and money-lender (see Chapter 4).

At first Abriès and the Briançonnais welcomed the Revolution because of its anti-aristocratic features. The Briançonnais, who identified strongly with the Parlement at Grenoble and were outraged by its exile, sent representatives to the unauthorized meetings of the three estates at Vizille.

Members of the Berthelot family were active in representing the region in the early stage of the Revolution; a certificate shows that Chaffrey Berthelot even became a Jacobin (ADHA F2052). However, the region was soon caught in the serious contradiction of its own love of the legal system. Its political culture was defined by and dependent on the maintenance of the corporatist system of the old regime: the escartons were corporations like towns or guilds, ratified by charter; the centralized, hierarchical organization of the Revolution destroyed the special-interest-group arrangements of the corporatist system.

When the Constituent Assembly abolished feudal privileges on 4 August 1789, limiting the power of aristocrats, it also abolished the Briançonnais charter and the entire escarton apparatus as part of that 'feudal' system. The region was no longer an escarton political unit but a collection of towns, villages, and hamlets, each of which now had to gain access to the centres of power as best it could. Furthermore, the centuries of political wisdom gained in dealings with the old regime systems were no longer useful, so the value of the Berthelots as brokers was also at an end. The Revolution broke the institutional connection between the region and the supralocal level, and no institutions of equal strength (from the perspective of the village) ever rose to replace them. The strategy of the villages shifted from trying to maintain strong *institutions* to relying on strong *individuals*. This strategy, as we shall see in later chapters, raised its own series of contradictions.

As for the Berthelots, they were by no means destroyed by the Revolution. They had wealth which was not tied to land in Abriès, and for years they had cultivated far-flung contacts with important people. They were able to take up new roles outside the village. Representatives of the Berthelot family continued to live in and serve Abriès, but they never again amassed a concentration of power there.

Pierre Berthelot (1771–1836), for example, continued to live in Abriès. In fact, he served as mayor from 1808 to 1820, he was a notary, and he frequently acted as an intermediary in matters of debt collection between those who had left the village and Abrièsois debtors (ADHA F1490). But Pierre's real business in post-Revolutionary Abriès was as a cheese merchant, supplying local products to his agents in various southern French cities (ibid. 1836). His sons were encouraged to go into law, but they did not have the aspirations of their grandparents. An 1839 New Year's letter to one of these sons from Pierre's brother-in-law summarizes the contemporary situation of the Berthelots who remained in Abriès. The uncle hoped that his nephew would return to the village because 'the Berthelot lineage ... [is] almost extinct; show yourself ... worthy of being able some day to reflect respect on this house which has always enjoyed a great reputation not only in the valley but in the whole Department; you should be proud to belong to such an honourable family' (ADHA F1490).

Under the new regime the real luminaries in the Berthelot family were those who migrated out of the village to larger centres and took up jobs as government funtionaries. They were part of a whole class of administrators who were produced by the new, more centralized regimes of the Revolution and the Restoration. Benoît Jacques Berthelot, for example, was born in Abriès in 1792 and died in Lyon in 1883. At age twenty-five he left Abriès for the town of Guillestre, where he built his career through contacts in the post-Revolutionary government. He served as mayor of Guillestre for more than twenty-two years and was a cantonal councillor for close to fifty. Such long tenure was a common pattern in the nineteenth century and was indicative of new power relations and power-holding patterns which tended to focus on the person and his patronage networks rather than on institutions (Blanchard 1933: 99–105).

By the mid-nineteenth century, the last Berthelot notary migrated out of Abriès and settled in Marseilles. Two and a half centuries of Berthelot notaries in Abriès were over.

4

Integration and Isolation

The pivotal political event of the 1788–1840 era was the French Revolution (1789–1815), which the Abrièsois initially supported because of their anti-aristocratic sympathies. As the revolutionary process unfolded, however, villagers soon found that much of the new regime was not at all to their liking. The Revolution, whatever else it was, was a major step in state consolidation and the centralization of powers in Paris. As the French state became more integrated and more able to impose its control on peripheral regions, the ground rules in village-state relationships were transformed. In Abriès this process was experienced simultaneously as increased assimilation into and control by the new regime's more efficient and expanded bureaucracy and as a decrease in village leverage on the decision-making process at the national level. As villages became integrated into the new, stronger French state, they became less and less able to influence decisions which affected control over their vital resources. This seemingly contradictory process of integration and isolation set the stage for new patterns of village-state dealings and new types of power-holding intermediaries in the village.

THE COMING OF THE REVOLUTION

In the Briançonnais the gathering revolutionary momentum was watched carefully and with approval in 1788. In that year the Parlement of Grenoble met, against royal wishes; finally, its members were 'exiled' by the crown. This move was greeted all over France with outbreaks of popular violence in support of the Parlement members; citizens, angry over the arbitrary royal decree, sent roofing tiles smashing to the streets below. The 'Day of the Tiles' became symbolic of popular displeasure with the king's anti-Parlement stance and of popular determination to allow the three Estates of the Dauphiné to meet. When the Parlementaires pressed ahead to hold an unauthorized assembly in the town of Vizille, the Grand Escarton rushed to meet as well. The group selected four representatives to go to Vizelle on 2 July to represent the interests of the region (ADHA 405). In September 1787 the Dauphiné Estates met again, this time at Romans with royal approval, and again the Grand Escarton sent representatives, including Barthelemy Berthelot, who was paid 324 livres for his expenses in attending. Whenever discussion turned to how the province of the Dauphiné should be organized and administered, Barthelemy spoke persistently in defence of maintaining the 1343 charter rights and privileges (ibid.).

By this time it was clear that Briançonnais privileges were being threatened. The Parlementaires had asked that the escartons select representatives jointly with regional tax collectors. But the escartons did not want their powers diluted, so they refused to co-operate. They proceeded to elect representatives independently, in an atmosphere aggravated by squabbles between Briançon and surrounding villages and between the Queyras and the Briançonnais. (The Queyras representative, Hyacinthe Berthelot, never went to Romans because his selection procedure was discredited.)

By the spring of 1789, the handwriting was on the wall for the 'little Republic of the Escartons.' In the middle of a revolution that was sweeping away custom and legal precedents, the montagnards desperately sought a way to legitimize their rights and privileges. The Grand Escarton met, ostensibly to respond to a questionnaire from the Estates of the Dauphiné. It was never answered (A. Guillaume 1968). Instead, the lawyers of the Grand Escarton drafted statements defending 'the privileges of the constitution and its municipal system' (ADHA E405). In a brilliant stroke of public relations they called the 1343 charter a 'constitution,' catching the drift of radical sentiment that was sweeping France. Representatives from the Grand Escarton went to Grenoble to publish and distribute their position papers, which called for the Estates of the Dauphiné to keep the Briançonnais region administratively distinct, to allow the Briançonnais independent control of the division of tax payments and an autonomous accounting system with no records sent to the provincial estates, to permit local control of road maintenance, and finally to permit independent elections from within the Briançonnais escarton system to the Estates General meeting in Paris.

On 19 July 1789 an assembly of Briançonnais consuls issued orders to celebrate the creation of the National Assembly. They further declared, on 27 July, that they would willingly make sacrifices for the new assembly and would fight against 'ministerial despotism' (ADHA E406). These conciliatory efforts bore no fruit. On the night of 4 August 1789, the National Assembly abolished all privileges and charters of the old regime, including the 1343 charter so dear to the Briançonnais. Still attempting to derive some benefit from the drastic changes, the Briançonnais asked that its 4000-ducat tribute be abolished and turned over as a 'patriotic gift' to the National Assembly. At the same time vigorous protests were sent to the assembly protesting the conversion of local corvée work into paid labour (Tivollier 1938: II, 248–79).

In 1790 the Briançonnais made its last attempt to avoid being swallowed up in the new administrative system. The escartons fired off briefs to the Council of State, the intendant of the Dauphiné, the Estates General, and the king. 'There is no question here,' they said about their charter,

of those abusive privileges which owe their origin to the favour or whim of sovereigns, and which cannot improve the lot of some individual without harming the common interests ... The privileges which they [the Escartons] want to preserve are rights which were legitimately acquired, not just by paying money but also through essential services rendered to the country ... These rights are useful and precious; they guarantee their liberty; they are necessary to their peace and happiness ...

The communities of the Briançonnais have always avoided being subjected to any compulsion whatsoever in their public and private payments or in the use to which their funds might be put. They do not recognize the permission of the King or the Intendant, nor authorization of any court of law, they are not obliged to give such accounts; in a word, in these matters they recognize no administrators or judges other than themselves; and provided that they are exact in paying their share of royal taxes, no-one in the world has the right to trouble them. (Cited in Fauché-Prunelle 1858: II, 704–5)

It was clear that the Briançonnais knew that the issue was power – they did not want to recognize 'administrators or judges other than themselves' – but they did not have the resources to prevail. The French state had moved from a position of weakness, of collecting tribute and negotiating payments, to a position of strength. The era of indirect rule was over.

CHANGES IN LOCAL GOVERNMENT

In November 1789 France began a sweeping administrative reorganization. The country was divided into departments, districts, and cantons. The Briançonnais found itself one of four districts in the newly created Department of the Hautes-Alpes. Abriès became one of the nine cantons of the district until 1800, when it was joined to Ville Vieille as the canton of Aiguilles. Between 1790 and 1795 municipal government was transformed; all pre-existing local offices were abolished and the offices of mayor, adjoint (assistant mayor), and municipal councillors were created.

In large cities this process had wide support since it led to municipal elections, wider enfranchisement, and political participation. In communes of fewer than 3000 people just the opposite occurred. In what has been called 'truly reactionary' legislation (Godechot 1968: 106), most village decision-making was removed from the local level and given to the prefect. People voted for the municipal council, and then the prefect, who was himself an appointed civil servant, selected the mayor and an assistant. Furthermore, municipal officers had six-year terms and could succeed themselves.

Mayors had very strong executive and police powers. Municipal councils were advisory and weak: they were sharply limited to four assemblies a year; any additional meetings had to be approved by the prefect; the prefect could overturn any decisions of which he did not approve. The public was banned from attending municipal council meetings, and councils from different communes were strictly prohibited from meeting together or being in any sort of communication with each other (Thivot 1971: 54–5). The aim seems to have been to discourage alliances among villages or any competing power bases that could possibly challenge the authority of the centre.

High wealth qualifications were instituted for municipal electors. In the 1830s the Hautes-Alpes had 189 communes with a total population of approximately 130,000 people. Only 12,450 men were eligible to vote in communal elections, and the absentee rate was so high (35 per cent) that only about 8000 voted on average (ibid. 52–3).

From 1789 to 1848 (when universal male suffrage became law), property qualifications also restricted political participation beyond the village level. The department as a whole averaged only 400 eligible voters between 1830 and 1848 (ibid. 24). In the 1834 national elections for the Chamber of Deputies, for example, only one Abrièsois, the tax collector, possessed enough wealth to vote, and he was one of only 410 men eligible in the whole department (ADHA 38M 3). This large-scale disenfranchisement meant that Abrièsois, like most villagers, now had no institutional channels for influencing the central government. Gone was the escarton alliance, gone were the records of village politics locked away from the state, gone were the interminable suits against power-holders of the state and church, and gone were the internal taxes levied to maintain lobbyists in Paris.

The villagers of the Briançonnais did not like the Revolution, but they were at heart anti-aristocratic. They could see nothing in the counter-Revolutionary movements in Lyons and Toulon that suited them. They did, however, offer many small-scale local acts of non-compliance and some overt resistance to the new regime. In 1790, for example as the new municipal system came to Abriès, the incoming municipal council refused to receive the village books with the pre-scribed oath that spoke of the 'despotism' of the pre-existing village sec-retary. Instead, 'Master Berthelot' was congratulated for doing his duties 'always without reproach' (ADHA E545). In 1792, Arvieux, a Queyrassin village, refused to show tax agents its cadastre; the protest was led by the mayor. Similar non-cooperation with tax officials occurred in Aiguilles in 1793 and in Abriès in 1794 (ADHA L163–76). Paris viewed this local resistance to tax reform as an 'epidemic sickness' (ADHA L163) and considered sending in troops, but it did not follow through.

In 1793 and 1794 Abriès had some violence, which coincided with the billeting of troops there. One soldier was accused of striking a village woman and others of theft. Conversely, villagers were accused of stealing from the army. Sometimes individual grievances took on a more collective nature; for example, the National Guard, fearing Piedmontese infiltration of the valley, restricted movement between villages, an order that gave rise to a hair-pulling, rock-throwing fight between the guard and peasants of the Upper Queyras in 1793 (ADHA 2L202).

Abriès had long been known for producing a large number of Capucin monks (ADHA ms. 399); of 166 Capucins from the Hautes-Alpes in 1790, twenty came from Abriès. Some became famous (or notorious, depending on one's perspective) during the Revolution. After their expulsion from the monasteries in 1790, many returned to Abriès. The best-known Abrièsois cleric was Joseph Bourcier (Père Jean-Louis), born in 1766 and in orders in Vienne on the eve of the

Revolution. He refused to swear loyalty to the Constitution, persisted in wearing his clerical robes despite the law of 1792, and appeared constantly on lists of suspicious persons. Considered the leader of the Capucins hidden in Abriès, he walked armed with a cudgel and escaped arrest several times. After many exploits he left Abriès in 1795, but he was never captured and died a 'hero' in the Capucin monastery in Crest in 1834 (ADHA ms. 399, 22).

On Bourcier's account alone, the village was suspect. The fact of a mobile and literate population raised more suspicions. One Abrièsois trader was charged with distributing anti-Revolutionary pamphlets with his merchandise. The police were adamant that he was guilty, but all the witnesses gave testimony in his defence. The pamphlets, they claimed, were quite unrelated to the Revolution. The trader was acquitted (ADHA 2L202).

Similarly, state customs officials found it very hard to win local cases against smugglers, who were usually fined and their merchandise confiscated. Apparently, they were arrested only if they actually struck customs officials (ADHA 2L195). Local attitudes towards the 'foreign' authority of customs officials are epitomized by an incident in 1797. Ristolas men, dressed as women, attacked a customs outpost (ADHA 2L193). There is no evidence that any of them were caught.

BLAISE RICHARD-CALVE: USURER AND REVOLUTIONARY ADMINISTRATOR

Throughout the Revolutionary era the Abrièsois were suspicious of the new government, and the new government was suspicious of the village. The situation was ripe for the emergence of a new power-holder to mediate between the two levels. One political entrepreneur was to seize the opportunity, Blaise Richard-Calve. A local nineteenth-century biographer tells us that Richard-Calve came from a well-to-do Abriès family, able to provide him with a good education so that he acquired 'fame and influence' in his region (Albert 1889b: 41). His parents were merchant shopkeepers; the father, Daniel (in some documents, François or François-Daniel), died in 1781, and the widowed mother, Catherine Veritier, continued to run the family business. Daniel had occasionally made loans or advances on tax payments, but it was his son Blaise who made a career out of money-lending.

Most of the information we have about Blaise Richard-Calve comes to us from his account book, an extraordinary document that is also a diary, letter file, and history (ADHA F2293). It is a large, leather-bound book, almost a foot and a half high and close to seven inches wide, crammed with letters, scraps of notes, receipts, fragments from accounts, copies of court cases, proclamations, and extracts from various civil records. Two hundred pages are numbered and stamped, indicating that debts were registered in Grenoble. The left-hand leaves are marked 'debit'; the right-hand leaves are marked 'credit,' and each is initialled by Richard-Calve. The earliest reference is from 1756, to a debt owed to his father, Daniel, which years later Blaise tried to collect. The last reference is to a debt pursued in 1820 by Blaise's widow. (After Richard-Calve's death in 1818, his heirs scoured the book, working out remaining debts and methods of collection.) Thus we have sixty-four years of money-lending history.

Combining information from this diary and from the civil registry of Abriès, we find that Blaise was one of six children. He may have been the eldest, but it is possible that his brother Barthelemy was older.[1] We have no other information about Barthelemy. The three other brothers, Chaffré, Claude, and Pierre, became, respectively, a registry official and tax collector in the canton, a cheese merchant near Arles, and a priest. All of these careers were launched and supported by Blaise. His sister married a notary in the neighbouring village of Ristolas.

In 1795, at the age of thirty-four, Blaise married into the most prominant family of Abriès, taking Magdelaine Berthelot, age thirty-one, daughter of the notary François, as his wife. Magdelaine died fourteen years later, leaving no children. In less than a year Blaise took a second wife: Euphrosine Gonssolin, from an even more powerful legal family in Grenoble. That the twenty-two-year-old Euphrosine accepted the hand of the forty-eight-year-old usurer-politician was a tribute to the success he had found under the Revolutionary regime.

The Gonssolins settled a large dowry of 15,000 francs on their daughter, 13,600 francs from her father and 1400 francs from her mother. The marriage contract specified that 6000 francs were to be paid over six years from the date of the marriage, with 5 per cent interest, and that an additional 9000 francs were to be paid after the parents' death but with no interest on the mother's portion. Euphrosine herself provided a trousseau valued at 1500 francs. In the same

---

1 There is some confusion over Blaise's birthdate. The civil registry lists 1 January 1761, but the biographer Albert (1889b) gives 20 December 1756.

contract Blaise promised 6000 francs to his wife if they had children, and the usufruct of one-third of his possessions at his death. When Blaise died in 1818, he left two young daughters.

Money-Lending

The groundwork to Blaise's political career in the Revolution was laid in the village of Abriès. The business he inherited from his parents was a general store specializing in leather goods. It was centrally placed in the main business quarter and serviced all parts of the town, the other eleven hamlets of the community of Abriès, two nearby French villages and their hamlets, and several Italian villages. In addition to being a storekeeper, Richard-Calve was also a cheese merchant and a merchant-industrialist in Abriès's tiny woollen industry. His earnings and his access to large liquid assets through these enterprises launched him on his career as a money-lender.

By local standards Richard-Calve's interest rates were very high. A prefectoral inquiry in 1823 estimated that the average interest rate in the Queyras was between 2 and 3 per cent (ADHA 10M 1, 1823); thirty years earlier Blaise was charging 5 per cent. Nevertheless people borrowed from 3 to 2000 livres from him because he was the only source available to them. Many of the borrowers were local traders and merchants who needed the money to expand their operations. They borrowed large amounts, usually more than 100 livres. Presumably they were willing to go into debt in the expectation of high profits at a later date, but for some the profit would have had to have been very high indeed in order to repay the amounts eventually owed Richard-Calve. For example, in 1790 the money-lender claimed that a mule trader who had once been in business with Daniel, Richard-Calve's father, owed more than 2500 livres (ADHA F2293: 81).

Richard-Calve did not restrict his lending activity to the merchants and manufacturers of Abriès. He also made loans to merchants in the Queyras, in Briançon, and in Piedmont and served as a banker to similar entrepreneurs within the region. In 1812 Richard-Calve calculated that he was owed more than 39,000 francs by debtors outside his immediate family.

Although much of this money went to expanding business and industrial enterprises within the region, about half of Richard-Calve's debtors were peasants who bought food or small items on credit. These people were frequently unable to repay their debts, and the amounts they owed grew and grew with the high interest rates. Very often their

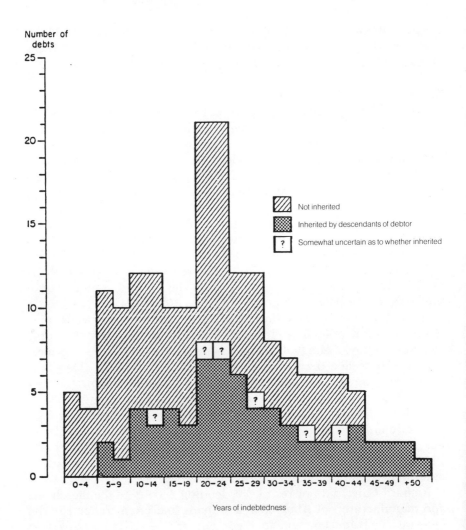

FIGURE 3 Duration and inheritance of debts owed Richard-Calve

children or grandchildren found themselves having to pay large amounts. An analysis of 185 debts owed Richard-Calve for which complete information exists shows that about 60 per cent of the cases dragged on for more than twenty years. Of these, almost half the original debts were passed on to heirs. (See Figure 3.) In other words, once a family began borrowing from Richard-Calve, chances were that they would be involved with him for the rest of their lives. For example, an original debt of only 7 livres involved one family with the money-lender for thirty-six years (ibid. 113). In another case, a person had borrowed from Blaise's father to pay a pre-Revolution tax, and forty years later Blaise took the heirs to court (ibid. 198).

Blaise Richard-Calve wrote that he did not like to loan small sums, but he was persistent in trying to collect them. His own heirs went the same route; in 1818 they felt it a victory to collect 5 francs on a 1788 debt of 41 livres (ibid. 164). Sums as small as 23 livres could be reason for taking legal action (ibid. 179). Large debts were generally paid off in shorter periods of time (ibid. 114, 141, 180, 182, 214), but poor people, with fewer resources, took longer to pay.

Blaise acted as intermediary for his mother and brothers in their financial dealings, and in turn Blaise's mother looked out for his interests in the village when he was working in the departmental capital of Gap. His Berthelot father-in-law often provided his legal services, notarizing promissory notes, and pressing recalcitrant debtors (see especially ibid. 59, 76, 196).

The history of Richard-Calve's interaction with his godson Claude Estachon is quite revealing in terms of defining the basis of Blaise's power; ties of family had no hold on him when it came to collecting a debt. The Estachons began borrowing from the Richard-Calves in 1769. The first loan was for 200 livres at 4.5 per cent; the interest due had grown to 123 livres by 1793, when the total owed, including some accumulated smaller debts was 473 livres. In that year Claude Estachon went before justice of the peace Berthelot (his father-in-law's brother) and offered to pay the money-lender that sum in the Revolutionary currency of assignats. But Richard-Calve figured that 100 livres in assignats was really worth only 34 livres, and he noted in his account book that he would lose 322 livres on the transaction (ibid. 18). In presenting the case before Berthelot, Estachon claimed that Richard-Calve refused to accept payment in assignats – a somewhat embarrassing stance for the money-lender, who was an administrator in the Revolutionary government (ADHA 2L202).

Richard-Calve's version was different. He claimed that his godson had come to him before witnesses asking for a loan of 100 livres in assignats; just as he was about to oblige, Estachon suddenly berated him for asking interest on the 100 livres, hurled insults, and finally threatened his life. Richard-Calve, acting as a 'True Republican' and 'public official called to the administration of the Hautes-Alpes,' saw no choice but to bring the case before the justice of the peace (ibid.). He called his father-in-law Berthelot and his wife as witnesses on his behalf in the matter, and, needless to say, Estachon was fined and charged to pay all his debts.

In general, however, the people who took a stand against Richard-Calve were outside the village and kinship networks. A striking example of solidarity in opposition occurred in the case of Jean Ferrus of Ville Vielle (ADHA F2293: 193). In 1789 Ferrus took a business loan of 570 livres at 5 per cent; by 1800 the interest alone on this and other debts was more than 650 livres. A third party paid off a small part of the amount owing at this time, but by 1813 Richard-Calve had the bailiff after Ferrus. The community of Ville Vieille responded to the arrest and imprisonment of the 'poor miserable' Ferrus by assembling five property owners who agreed to pay part of the debt; the rest was paid by the mayor of nearby Château Queyras, where Ferrus was imprisoned. The letter these men sent to Richard-Calve included a long description of the ills that had befallen Ferrus, including the death of his wife and many kinfolk and the fact that he was left without any property of value. They pointedly commented that Richard-Calve knew the latter fact as well as they, implicitly censuring his actions.

Richard-Calve was not hasty in employing legal action, but neither was it a tool he hesitated to use. His account book reveals some detailed information about thirty of his legal involvements. Until 1790, when he began his political career in Gap, only five of the cases involved co-villagers, but after that date approximately 60 per cent were directed against people from Abriès. From 1799, when a mortgage registry bureau was set up in Briançon, he began holding mortgages, seizing property, and forcing foreclosures (ibid., 35, 36, 63, 7, 60, 195).

Political Career
Richard-Calve's behaviour in ignoring kinship constraints and disregarding local public opinion defines him as an upwardly mobile power-holder. His actions were based on his entry into the political arena beyond the village, an opportunity which appeared in the local

system with the intersection of two large-scale events: the spread of merchant wealth into the region, and the political revolution which created new power-holding opportunities.

Richard-Calve described himself as a Revolutionary and a Republican. In 1790 he was elected to the administration of the department of the Hautes-Alpes at a salary of 1000 livres a year. Of the thirty-six men elected to administer the department, most were mayors or lawyers; three, including Richard-Calve, were merchants; only one was a peasant. These men constituted a council from which eight members were named as an executive, called the Directory. They functioned as a deliberative body and oversaw administration, public works, and budgets.

Richard-Calve's financial experience, wide networks, and acquaintance with legal affairs suited him well to his new job. By 1792 he had combined his home-learned skills with his political career – he became mayor of Abriès and a member of the Directory (ADHA introduction series L 1911). From that time on, he was able to enlarge his networks to make a place in the vertical chain of patronage politics and to include power-holders from other villages who occupied positions comparable to his own. He began making large loans to power-holders in the key centres around the department. An exchange of favours and services, usually financial, marked these horizontal relationships, which continued even after Richard-Calve left departmental politics (ADHA F2293).

Richard-Calve could not afford to cut his ties with Abriès completely since his control over that large and prosperous village was a key element in the package of attributes that made him attractive to his superiors in the new regime. But his power in the departmental administration permitted him to take a tough line in the village. In 1795 its municipal council wrote to him asking a favour: to cancel, as representative of the government, what the council members said was a communal debt for the purchase of 3500 livres worth of grain. In a sharply worded note Richard-Calve replied that they were making a grave error. He had been mayor in those days, but the loan had been a private one to the individual members of the council. He wanted to be repaid. He waxed the high-minded revolutionary as he accused the council of being 'rotten, reprehensible crooks' who were insulting him with this scheme. Launching into a long statement in praise of himself as an honest politician voted into the public administration to make sacrifices and serve his fellow citizens, he offered a definition of the

Revolution: 'Citizens, the Foundations of Our government which we have desired for such a long time, which has cost so much Blood and ... so many victims Are Love of Homeland, Justice, Truth, probity, And respect for persons and property' (ibid. 196). (Given what we know about Richard-Calve's career, one suspects that the sentiment to which he was most attached was respect for property.) He concluded his letter by warning the council to be vigilant in really important matters and guard against 'anarchists, Royalists, thieves' (ibid.).

In a later letter the municipal council quietly dropped its request for debt cancellation as it countered the serious matter of the accusations of disloyalty made against Abriès. The council assured Richard-Calve that the village had no religious problems that need disturb the government: 'We see with Sorrow that you have communicated to us that the National Agent for the district of Briançon has denounced our Commune with respect to religion. Our Duty to execute Laws includes that of Surveillance of ministers of Religion. We assure you that the most complete peace reigns over our commune in this Respect' (ibid.). (In fact, there were a great many religious/political problems in the village. Abriès was thought to have been one of the chief centres in the region for smuggling refractory priests into Italy.)

The exchanges of goods and services between patron and client – and their limits – are very clear here. Richard-Calve would not use the Revolution to do a favour for villagers if doing so would affront his sense of property; he had lent money and he wanted it back. However, he needed the village's support to remain in office and to control the religious issue, which was a threat to his political position. In return, he was willing to aid the village in matters in which he had no personal stake.

This kind of patronage system differed from the Berthelot pattern. Given the new municipal organization, which disenfranchised and disarticulated villagers, more and more power flowed directly through Richard-Calve's hands as he became the main mediator between the people and the new regime. The peasants had no systems of checks and balances to circumvent this burgeoning despot. Under the old regime, they had had access to many channels of articulation and had been able to circumvent the Berthelot power-holders and seriously challenge them in the courts. The new system reduced peasant access to alternative channels of power and set the pattern for increasing dependence on mediators for linkage to mainstream politics. In brief, organization and integration at the supralocal level entailed *dis*organization and *dis*integration at the local level.

In 1793–4 and again in 1794–5 following the lead of Paris, the administration of the department was purged. Only Richard-Calve and one other official survived the purge of 1795. The Constitution of the Year III did away with directories at the department and district level, leaving the administration in the hands of five men and one executive commissioner named in Paris. Richard-Calve became one of these five administrators and president of the executive.

In this position, Richard-Calve completed the division of property of the Archbishop of Embrun and promoted new curricula in the school system (ADHA L48). He also occupied himself with roads and bridges and the encouragement of trade with Piedmont – a position which caused difficulties for him later. In 1796 Richard-Calve became the provisional attorney-general of the departmental Committee of Public Safety. His avowed aim was to provide the Revolutionary government with a good accounting system.

For the next few years he was also in charge of public works, and he named an Abriès friend and debtor to take charge of affairs in the canton (which now comprised Abriès, Aiguilles, and Ristolas). He also appointed his brother to the job of chief tax collector in Briançon. At the same time, he made frequent appeals to higher levels of government to reduce the tax burden within the department. Thus until 1797 he was able to serve his own interests, the village's, and the Revolution's simultaneously and comfortably.

In September 1797, however, the situation blew up, and Richard-Calve lost control of his power base and his village clients. By that time the role of Abriès in pro-clerical activities had become obvious. There was a confrontation between villagers and gendarmes over the clandestine re-entry of two deported priests; two gendarmes were killed, and the justice of the peace and local cantonal officials were charged with not taking adequate measures to punish the criminals. Furthermore, assemblies of Piedmontese on Abriès territory were being reported.

Officials were ordered to Gap to explain their conduct (ADHA L51). Richard-Calve attempted to mobilize support for the actions of the municipal council of Abriès. He failed. Two months later he was dismissed from the departmental directory and charged with not giving any proof of his attachment to the republican regime or inspiring any confidence in the administration (ibid.). His political career in Gap was over.

Richard-Calve had been caught between trying to keep the support of his pro-clerical clients and remaining in an anti-clerical revolutionary government. It would probably have been impossible for him to be repressive on the issue – his own brother was a priest, and part of his reputation came from being a great benefactor of the church. An outsider was brought in to be the village's justice of the peace; he seized the property of two local emigré priests, an action which would obviously have destroyed Richard-Calve's position had he attempted it (ibid.).

Richard-Calve was not forgotten in the department, however. Mail to him was often addressed to 'Richard Président' or 'Richard ex-Administrateur' long after he was deposed. He was even nominated for another position later on, though his name was crossed out (ADHA L48). He retired to Abriès to become tax collector and eventually justice of the peace.

Richard-Calve, 'Ex-Administrateur' and Patron

Richard-Calve's downfall from the departmental directory by no means deprived him of all power or administrative responsibilities; he was entrenched in the local system and not sufficiently threatening to the Revolution to be eliminated. Within a small arena where his debtor/client relations were still intact, he continued to operate as a power-holder.

Bundles of letters inside Richard-Calve's account book give us insights into his behaviour in patron-client relationships. Most of the letters are dated after the time that he left the Revolutionary administration, but many refer to relationships built up over those earlier years. For instance there is an 1806 communication from an old friend and ex-villager living in Paris, requesting that Richard-Calve look into some business for him in Pignerol (Piedmont). One chore concerned a friend's sister-in-law who was rumoured to have died leaving some land in the Abriès hamlet of Le Roux. Another task was looking into some land in Abriès on which the friend held mortgages. In return, the friend mentioned that he might still owe Richard-Calve money. The letter makes constant references to kinship and friendship relations, including some through Richard-Calve's powerful Berthelot brother-in-law. The whole tone is one of formal etiquette, acknowledging the client/debtor status, but at the same time a conscious playing on all possible social ties to obtain a favour.

Other letters from clients have a more pleading tone. The mother of a former Abriès priest wrote, without the elegance or subtlety of the Paris friend, begging Richard-Calve to accept a third-party's promissory note in payment for her own and her son's debts. The nature of these debts is interesting; they were mostly foodstuffs – meat, lard, spices, oil – as well as some small cash loans. From this we can infer that the priest was not rich. We know too, from the debt records in the account book, that one of Richard-Calve's specialties was advancing credit to the professional men of the village and valley – priests, doctors, and customs inspectors who moved around and were often on small salaries and without sufficient land to provide for their needs.

Other members of the Richard-Calve family also acted as patrons, for they too were involved in money-lending and creating a kind of family banking system. Blaise's brother Chaffré, who was a tax collector in Guillestre, received a letter from a teacher who had once lived in Ristolas and was in debt to both Chaffré and Blaise for, among other things, services rendered in settling his father's estates. The teacher hoped that Chaffré, with his wide contacts, would help him find another teaching post for, at his present one, he had few students and they attended school only in the summer. (Presumably this situation prevented him from paying his debts.) Like correspondence of other clients, this letter is extremely polite and full of flattery: 'If you could discover anything I would be greatly obliged, there is hardly a family in the Queyras (notably our own) that has not received great benefits from the ex-president of the Department of the Hautes-Alpes, since you are as generous as he, would you in the near Future find me ... something better?' (ADHA F2293, letters, 1810).

Blaise's younger brother Claude and his mother were also involved in money-lending. The account book holds a short New Year's greeting from Claude and long letters concerning various debts owed him. The mother's letters reveal that debtors frequently paid to her amounts owed to her sons and that the sons exchanged such services among themselves. She was very active on Blaise's behalf in Abriès when he was in Gap, collecting debts and selling land.

But Blaise did not rely solely on the kinship network. He also developed a friendship network which he was able to mobilize on his behalf in various towns in the region. His lawyer, Faure, in Briançon, pursued many important cases for Richard-Calve. There is also clear evidence of exchange of services: Richard-Calve looked out for Faure's children, and Faure lodged Blaise's brother in Briançon. Contacts with other members of the legal profession were, of course, cemented after Richard-Calve's second marriage and appointment as a justice of the peace. But even when his career was just beginning, Richard-Calve created and kept up strong contacts with various lawyers, for whom he performed favours such as obtaining pensions for their clients, collecting debts, finding conscription replacements, or intervening with local mayors for them (ibid., letters).

A letter from a judge in Briançon sums up the quality of Richard-Calve's relationships (ibid., letters, 1818). Sent to Richard-Calve's brother just after the money-lender's death, it briefly expresses formal condolences and refers to the long reciprocity of services that tied the writer and Richard-Calve together. Then, having taken care of the 'dette de l'amité' (the debt of friendship), the judge swiftly turns to financial matters – various outstanding debts which are now the brother's responsibility. The concept of 'debt' of friendship was the hallmark of Richard-Calve's social relations (ibid., letter 1818).

Power-Holding in the Revolution: A Summary
In colonizing village government, the Revolutionary government created a system of local despots within the Hautes-Alpes.[2] Richard-Calve was one of the many men who rose to prominence as bureaucratic reform penetrated and controlled the countryside. Ceillac, a village near the Queyras, provides another example of this process. Ceillac was well known for its autocratic mayor, Fournier, who held office for close to fifty years. Not only did he perform all the usual executive functions, but he also set codes of manners, dress, and decorum. He chastised young ladies who wore unsuitable ribbons in their bonnets, he exiled people from the village for weeks or months for legal infractions, he forced minor delinquents to spend Sundays on their knees on the 'stone of penitence' outside the church, and he imprisoned people for as long as he saw fit. He did not like trials and adjudicated all village disputes himself. He also checked the books of all the village cafés – and thus knew who drank and what they paid – and acted as marriage broker and deathbed scribe to will makers. As Delafont, a contemporary observer who whole-heartedly approved of Fournier's tactics, put it: 'This remarkable man who has ascended because of ... moral strength and rare energy, has appeared, in the midst of unfolding democratic principles and has created the phenomenon of a paternal and despotic government' (1838: 313–14). The

2 For interesting parallels, see Lucas's remarkable study of the power-holding career of Claude Javogues, of the department of the Loire, in the same time period. Javogues was a 'violent, choleric, excessive man' who abused his power with a viciousness unknown in the Briançonnais (Lucas 1973: 77).

prefect also supported Fournier's method of power-holding, and ultimately he was rewarded by a Legion of Honour decoration from the government of Louis-Philippe (Thivot 1971: 56).

Power-holders such as Richard-Calve and Fournier operated as supralocal agents in villages. They were like the chiefs created and controlled by colonial regimes to keep natives quiet and obedient. The Berthelots, by contrast, usually acted as community advocates. They were so identified with village interests and so independently powerful that the successive regimes of the Revolution and the Restoration were not interested in nominating them to office.

Furthermore, the increased mercantile-industrial activity at the time of the Revolution opened economic opportunities to the wealthy Berthelots and involved them in international commerce at a level beyond the reaches of a petty merchant-usurer such as Richard-Calve. One branch of the Berthelot family, for example, developed a large operation for manufacturing woollen cloth in the Piedmont community of Torre Pellice, across the border from Abriès, which allowed them to get around the problems of tariff and smuggling (ADHA 2 Guillemin, ms. 5051). The Berthelots held onto their Piedmontese factory all through the Revolution and when, in 1793–4, the property of thirty-six Briançonnais merchants who traded out of the country was seized, theirs was not. The Berthelots were still powerful and still well-connected (ADHA Q100–4). The revolution allowed them to move out of the village into a wider political and economic arena. Villagers were left to contend with political entrepreneurs like Richard-Calve as best they could.

DEMOGRAPHIC AND ECONOMIC CHANGES IN THE VILLAGE

At the same time, villagers were confronted with changes in their economic system. Despite the turmoil of the Revolution, Abriès's population remained high. In 1790 it was estimated at 1812 (ADHA L350); between 1796 and 1797 it was about 2005 (ADHA 2L203); in 1806, 1820, 1831, 1836, and 1841 the figure hovered around the 1800 mark (ADHA 6M11, 6M33, 6M6 stat 66).

During this period village birth rates declined, but death rates declined even faster. A five-year running average based on the Abriès parish register shows that in the periods 1781–90, 1791–1800, 1801–10, 1811–20, 1821–5, and 1826–30, the crude birth rate averaged thirty per thousand population; after 1831–5 it declined to about twenty per thousand. From 1781-90 to 1826-30 the crude death rate was approximately twenty-five per thousand; in 1831-5 it fell to nineteen per thousand, where it remained until 1846-50. The reasons for the decline in mortality included the introduction of the potato as a staple crop and the disappearance of plague and smallpox. The municipal council of Abriès recorded the last subsistence crisis in the village in the year 1789. The threat of plague had also gone (ADHA C14), and by 1823 the use of the smallpox vaccination was widespread in the Hautes-Alpes (ADHA 10M 1).

   This demographic upturn was coupled with new economic opportunities for the villagers. During the ancien régime the most common non-agricultural employment had been hemp-combing in Italy. By the end of the eighteenth century this option had almost disappeared as both the French government and the Piedmontese discouraged French migrant workers (Albert 1889a: 313-31), and montagnard seasonal employment became increasingly oriented to southern France. The nature of winter work changed in a fundamental way: proletarian labour (hemp-combing and farm work) declined, and individual entrepreneurial activities increased. In addition, merchant activity in the village increased. Thus, although population grew in the 1780-1840 period, there was no crisis of overpopulation in the village. New forms of employment added to the existing subsistence base were adequate to support the population.

   In the beginning of the nineteenth century the Prefect of the Hautes-Alpes, Ladoucette, collected data on seasonal migration occupations. We can use his data (in Van Gennep 1946: 270) to uncover the pattern shown in Table 4. Even if we remove the somewhat ambiguous category of 'Other professions,' we find that entrepreneurial activities accounted for more than twice as many jobs as did those involving more proletarian kinds of labour.

Mule Traders and Peddlers
In Abriès, peddling ewe's milk products was the chief winter occupation. Cheeses were collected by village entrepreneurs during the summer months. In the late fall and winter they dispatched young men to Marseilles, Toulon, and other southern cities to handle the retail trade. Muleteers supplied the peddlers during the winter season and profited not only from the distribution of cheeses but also from the import of wine, sugar, coffee, oil, and soap (ADHA L401, Abel mémoire: 40).

TABLE 4
Seasonal migrants, Department of
Hautes-Alpes, ca 1820

Proletarian occupations	
Hemp combers	501
Shepherds	245
Harvesters	469
Total proletarians	1,215
Entrepreneurial occupations	
Peddlers	1,128
Teachers	705
Knife sharpeners	404
Cheese merchants	250
Butchers	83
Haulers (muleteers)	25
Other professions (weavers, shoemakers, umbrella sellers, dyers)	469
Total entrepreneurs	3,064
Unclassified	34
Total migrants	4,313

Source: Ladoucette, 1820, in Van Gennep
1946: 270

Some Abrièsois sold butter, directly or through muleteers, in the lowland Embrunnais region. The sellers returned with wheat flour from the valley towns (ibid.). The job of beurrier or burriaire was quite dangerous. A letter dated 1788 from muleteers of Abriès, written on behalf of Pierre Bec, tells us much about the conditions under which the muleteers operated. Bec had delivered his weekly load of butter to Embrun and was returning with a shipment of white flour and fine cloth when treacherous snow conditions overtook him. His mules toppled into the Guil River, and he lost goods valued at 316 livres – a substantial amount in an era when a cow cost 60 livres (ADHA C23, 1787). Twelve muleteers who witnessed this accident appealed to state officials in Grenoble for compensation for Bec. Assuming that the government had procedures for compensating merchants in distress, they explained that this 'petit commerce' was the way many people in the village earned their living (ADHA C13).

Another indicator of the importance of trade in the village economy was that traders used even the highest mountain passes throughout the winter. In one year alone, thirty men lost their lives in the Col de la Croix. The municipal council of Abriès repreatedly petitioned the government for assistance in building a refuge at this important pass (ADHA E405).[3]

Some muleteers conducted a long-distance trade with Marseilles. One set of records (ADHA 2L202) describes six men who set out for Marseilles in September 1792 carrying ewe's-milk cheese valued at 18 livres per quintal. Two were considered leaders of the mule train. The group, which was to join two other men already stationed in the city, sold their wares not only at the final destination but also along the way. They expected to be gone until March.

Because of the increase in peddling in the south, the mule trade (often called 'le commerce de Poitou') became increasingly important. It was not seasonal; it often involved expeditions that lasted a year or more. Contemporaries considered the mule trade the most essential commerce of the Briançonnais, and especially in the Queyras, where 'l'ornement des foires' brought high profits (ADHA L401). Mules would eat almost anything and required no special care. According to figures for 1787 (ADHA C23), mules sold at two hundred livres each at a profit of thirty-six livres per animal at fairs in the Queyras. Profits from sheep and cows ranged from only two to nine livres. The mule trade continued to be an important feature of the Queyras economy into the early nineteenth century (Crubellier 1948).

We do not have descriptions specific to Abrièsois trading activities in the south. However, Van Gennep has collected general material about alpine peddlers who descended from the mountains to work in the Mediterranean basin. These rough montagnards, with their strange speech, long flowing hair, and loose-cut clothing, were the butt of many jokes. Observers in Marseilles and Toulon at the end of the eighteenth century give us the following picture:

Cheese was formerly (toward the end of the eighteenth century) sold mostly by men who came down from the mountains, the *gavouas* [gavots[4]] who went down the streets of Toulon shouting: Oou goood cheese!

3 Another important pass in the region was the Col de la Traversette. Sir Gaven de Beer argues that Hannibal's elephants marched up the Queyras and through this pass to Italy (1967: 96-113).
4 Seasonal migrants from the Alps were called les gavots, a term of scorn signifying a rude, stingy country person (Van Gennep 1946: 270-1).

Those people had titled clients to whom they sold an excellent blue cheese. Their clients were *bourgeois* and shopkeepers who would buy whole cheeses for the winter season. In turn, the gavots always found their old clients when they returned, even if they had moved.

After their walk through the town ... the gavots installed themselves all along the gutter running down the Rue des Orfèvres; they would stand there, with their baskets in front of them on the ground, and lit by a piece of tallow candle, there they would await business ...

The gavots sold excellent cheese, and they showed themselves very honest on the question of weight. (Letuaire, 'Vie toulonnaise,' in Van Gennep 1946: 274).

When a gavot, wearing a coat made of square pieces of green cloth, circulated through the city [Marseilles] shouting 'Goood cheese,' young rascals would reply in the same tone, 'Shiiit on you.' The gavot would reply, 'Keep your peace, rascal', or 'you little rogue' (Régis de la Colombière, *Cris de Marseilles*, in Van Gennep 1946: 32)

To the urbanites, the montagnards appeared as simpletons – poor, backward, honest, and religious countryfolk. Some modern scholars agree with this vision. Terrisse (1971), for example, argues that the distress caused by the Revolution forced marginal people from the mountain villages into the 'floating population' of Marseilles, where they earned their living as best they could.

Yet, a different interpretation is possible. Viewed from the city, the montagnards may have looked like the lumpenproletariat, but within the framework of the countryside, they were hard-working entrepreneurs who economized during their periods of winter migration by skimping on food and housing so that they could return home with maximum profits.

Furthermore, people from the same villages were perceived as shrewd and tough when they operated as mule traders. It is paradoxical that the same population projected such an opposite image in the role of seasonal migrants. Why did the sophisticated, literate mule trader transform himself into a backward country person in the Mediterranean cities? Van Gennep argues that the gavot represented the fusing of cultural and economic role-playing aimed at maintaining and expanding trade networks. An apparently pliant personality made customers feel that they were not being taken advantage of. The gavot worked in the interstices of the southern economy and retained a polite distance from the culture around him. Van Gennep records virtually no instance of cultural borrowing in vocabulary or in customs (1946: 275).

Rural Manufacture
In addition to the expansion of entrepreneurial seasonal peddling during the Revolutionary era, small-scale industries began to develop in Abriès. These rural industries were organized on a putting-out system by contractor-merchants who supplied the raw materials and sold the finished products. In Abriès, woollen cloth and belts were manufactured and animal hides were tanned. In 1787, Briançon, Château Queyras, and Abriès produced more than 5000 livres worth of woollen cloth. The same year the Queyras sold more than 15,000 livres worth of hides, and Abriès was the leading producer of the valley (ADHA C26).

The hides and cloth were sold, in the main, to Piedmont. Because of the tariff agreement related to the Treaty of Utrecht, these items could not legally be sold directly across the border at the point of production but were supposed to be exported further north, through the Savoyard pass of Mont Cenis (ADHA C23). Local producers and government officials tried unsuccessfully for years to have this requirement changed, arguing that it impeded the expansion of local industry because of the added cost of routing merchandise through Mont Cenis (de Germane, in ADHA z Guillemin ms. 5041; ADHA C23; Crubellier 1948). Meanwhile Abrièsois merchant-industrialists coped with the situation by smuggling. In order to keep up with the demand for woollen belts, contractors smuggled in some of the raw materials from Italy and then smuggled the finished product back across the border. One merchant operated this way quite openly and with impunity (ADHA C26; L401).

There were three major merchant-contractors in Abriès (ADHA C26), as well as small-scale operations in which two families associated to set up their children as carders and weavers (ADHA E545, 1781).[5] During the Revolutionary era such commercial-industrial activities expanded in Abriès: in 1792 there were forty-six villagers who paid a patente (commercial tax) on stores or workshops; by 1798 the number had risen to seventy (ADHA L622; L630). But by 1820 the number who paid the tax dropped to thirty (ADHA uninventoried P2, no. 243). It is likely

5 In a contract of association registered with an Abriès notary, two fathers of the hamlet of La Monteite agreed to set their sons up in business to card and weave wool. They provided rooms, tools, and food (ADHA E545).

that when the Napoleonic conquests in Italy opened the border, manufacturing expanded in the Queyras, but when the border and tariffs
were reinstated with the Restoration, the wool industry contracted.
However, the cheese industry and trade, which was directed towards
southern France rather than across the frontier, continued to expand
through the first half of the nineteenth century.

Cheese Making

In the post-Revolutionary period, the chief industry of Abriès and the
Queyras came to be cheese production. An 1823 departmental inquiry
described Abriès production and sale of cheese as 'very considerable'
(ADHA 10M 1), and another in 1848 called cheese production the principal industry of the entire Queyras valley (AN C944).

Cheese making grew for two reasons. First, the small-scale textile
and tanning industries of the region declined during the course of the
Revolution (Crubellier 1948: 294–341); to compensate for the resulting
loss of revenue, many peasants increased their emphasis on cheese production, which could be done at home without hiring labour (AN
C944). Second, by the 1840s Queyrassins had added the production of
a blue cheese (similar to Roquefort) to their already highly prized
tommes, a white cheese made from fermented buttermilk (Froud and
Turgeon 1976: 342). Intensive production of the bleu de Queyras,
made from ewe's milk, continued until 1884 (Guicherd 1933: 248). According to the Abbé Gondret in 1856, making the new blue cheese required less labour and wasted less time and material and thus offered
higher profits than did the production of tommes (in Devos 1973: 61).

Industry was still ancillary to the peasant economy but crucial in
determining the shape of things to come. The opportunity for expansion and increased profit came from Abriès's connection with markets
in southeast France. The general trend in the Haute-Alpes was away
from proletarian seasonal occupations to entrepreneurial pursuits.
This trend continued and expanded in the 1830s and 1840s as part of
the economic boom of the southeast. (For discussion of the expansion
of the silk, hat-making, and gloving industries in southeast France in
the first half of the nineteenth century, see Léon 1958, and Vigier
1963.) Montagnard cheese production soon became geared to and
dependent on that expanding market. Cheese producers in the Hautes-
Alpes as a whole made annual profits of about 200,000 francs in the
early 1840s (Thivot 1971: 428). Abriès and the Queyras, as leading
cheese-producing areas, certainly had a large share of this profit.

The Politics of Roadbuilding
There was also interest in Queyrassin villages in developing other industries to take advantage of the labour force available during the winter. An 1848 departmental inquiry indicated that Queyrassins wanted to participate in the industries that were creating wealth in the lowlands – silk-reeling and hat-making as well as the more traditional industries of producing woollen cloth, knitting socks, tanning, and nail-making (AN C944).

Establishing such industries proved to be difficult. It was not peasant unwillingness to take risks but a series of supralocal bureaucratic policies that kept the Queyrassins out of the cottage industries of silk-reeling and hat-making. One crucial policy concerned road construction. The Abrièsois were eager to expand their trade networks to Provence and to Italy, and they wanted roads that could take wheeled vehicles so they could export their own products and import the products of the plains. But the 'politique routière' (the politics of roads) favoured the plains (Vigier 1963: I, 70–86). Although it is more difficult to construct roads in the mountains than in flatlands, the main obstacle to expanded construction in the Alps was not the terrain. During the July Monarchy, the army controlled development in frontier regions, and it pursued a systematic policy of protecting frontier forts such as Briançon and Embrun in the Hautes-Alpes and Sisteron in the Basses-Alpes. In practice, this policy worked to stop construction of roads within the regions. The rationale was to prevent the enemy (Italy) from easily penetrating France's border regions. In 1846, Chaix, a Haut-Alpin, spoke with the anger of many montagnards when he said that it was intolerable that 'large interests remain dependent solely on the whims of the leader of the army engineer corps, who in this way puts a region outside the law during peacetime ... under the pretext that the enemy ... should not ... find anything but the greatest poverty at the frontier' (in Vigier 1963: I 86).

Despite such clear contemporary statements of a desire for expansion, some later observers argue that the Briançonnais peasants did not develop local industries because of the 'law of isolation, of separation ... the traditionalism of rural peoples ... a kind of natural awkwardness or slowness seems to have handicapped, up to the present time, the peasant from the Briançonnais or from the Queyras' (Crubellier 1948: 341, 369). In fact, the Briançonnais peasants, handicapped by the decline in their political leverage, were thwarted not by a predilection for isolation or the psychological problems of adjusting to change but by a defence policy which they could not influence. This was a political issue, a conflict of interest between peasant and state, acted out in economic terms. (See also Wood 1981, for changes in the meaning of economic and political as capitalism evolved). The outcome for the department was to keep commerce quite local and secondary to the plains' expansion.

Agriculture
The most striking feature of Abriès's agriculture in the first half of the nineteenth century was its large herds of sheep and cows. In 1823 this village of 1800 people had more than 4300 sheep and 1300 cows (ADHA 10M 1), so many animals that it had to rent pastureland from the neighbouring village of Ristolas (ADHA 13 O 1), uninventoried). By 1836 herd size, although still very large, was beginning to decline, in large part because of harassment by the national Forest Administration, which began limiting access to pasture as part of new control policies over communal forests in France.

Animals and their sale continued to play an important part in the Abriès economy, as in the region as a whole. In 1836, the animal population of Abriès – 754 bovines, 3200 sheep, and 242 mules, donkeys, and horses – was valued at 108,610 francs (ADHA 6M stat 66). An 1840 Ministry of Agriculture inquiry into the Arrondissement of Briançon (that is, the Briançonnais region) noted that one-tenth of the cows in the region were bought elsewhere, fattened in the summer pastures, and sold at the fall fairs, as were one-third to one-half of the sheep (ADHA 6M stat 4). The mule trade, which had considerably expanded after the Revolution, was also significant in the region. Thus we see that stock-raising continued to integrate villages into the market-place. But the economic system was still not predominantly capitalistic. Money was sought to pay taxes and to provide necessities such as salt, as it always had been. But the family was still the basic unit of production and decision-making and the basic source of labour.

Within that system of production, technical changes had been made. The expansion of canal irrigation made possible the support of larger herds, especially of cows. So did the introduction of new fodder crops, such as sainfoin and clover (ADHA 10M 1). These crops provided more food for animals, which in turn provided more fertilizer to sustain food production for both people and animals. The food supply for the human population was also enhanced by the increased cultivation of the potato. In 1836 Abriès had twenty hectares in potatoes, producing about 6400 hectolitres (ADHA 6M stat 66). Yet, unlike other rural societies of that time, Abriès did not become dependent on the potato. Its main crops continued to be rye, oats, and barley. Abriès's peasant economy remained as non-specialized as it had been during the ancien régime. The aim was still to provide for as many subsistence needs as possible within the village.

Social Concerns
The stereotyped idea that present-day underdevelopment is caused by ancient, unrelenting poverty finds little substantiation in the history of Abriès. The first half of the nineteenth century was a time of prosperity for the village. Walking its now-abandoned hamlets, one can still see signs of that prosperity: chapels and church towers built in the 1830s and early 1840s. Those were the years when the village bought new bells (ADHA 13 O 10), repaired the church and presbytery (1836–46) at a cost of 7500 francs, and started the construction of a very elaborate new school building (1843) to serve more than a hundred students. The building was to cost approximately 7000 francs, to be paid for out of municipal funds (ADHA 18 O 1).

The school project was the natural outgrowth of the concern with education which had always been the hallmark of the region. Figures for 1823 indicate that the village of Abriès was paying six teachers to instruct more than a hundred students (ADHA 10M 1). An 1848 national-level inquiry which included the Queyras found that 90 per cent of the valley population could read, and its report urged that the young people of the region be admitted free to more advanced schools. 'The means to encourage ... professional training ... would be to offer the young people of the region, who are used to work and are full of good will, to attend the applied arts schools free of charge' (AN C944). The concern with education and with the need for more specialized technical training is an important indicator that the peasantry of the village were eager to participate in the changing conditions of nineteenth-century France.

The Abrièsois also continued to assume collective responsibility for the poor in their village. Table 5 gives the results of an 1841 departmental questionnaire. Abriès cared for close to thirty indigents and beggars a year, a service valued at almost 8000 francs a year. No support was available from the department or state for the village poor, sick, orphaned, or unemployed. Meagre private charity (1350 francs) cared for 101 children in two departmental asylums (ADHA 216M 13).

Village relief was distributed in the form of food, clothing, and firewood, as well as some cash. The commune also provided for some
medical care. (Exactly how much is not known, for these figures were
kept separately and have not been found.)

This secours à domicile (household aid) by the Office of Village Welfare came entirely from municipal sources. Since the population of
Abriès was about 1800 during the first half of the century, the number
of beggars and indigents represented quite a small percentage of the
population. Until mid-century, these people were quite adequately
cared for.[6]

Abriès did not consider itself a poor or backward place. It is true
that the montagnards probably had a lower standard of living than
many cultivators of the plain, especially those involved in the cultivation of new industrial crops such as silk or the root dye madder. The
key point, however, as one anonymous nineteenth-century montagnard of the Haut Dios observed, was that in the mountains there was
no widespread poverty: 'The poor regions do not have poor people,
and the rich regions have a great many' (in Vigier 1963: I, 55). The
mountains had a much more homogeneous social structure than the
plains. There were neither large absentee landlords nor sharecroppers,
and there was a sense of collective responsibility for maintaining a standard of living below which no one could fall.

CONCLUSION

The economic changes that were occurring in Abriès at the end of the
eighteenth century and in the first half of the nineteenth century were
part of a nationwide process involving the spread of mercantile operations and rural industry (Cameron 1966: 51–3). Agriculture still dominated the economic life of the village, but many peasants supple-
mented their incomes with work as seasonal peddlers or mule traders.
The village was charged with an atmosphere of commercial activity
that went far beyond its role as a market centre during the ancien
régime.

6 After the economic crisis of 1846–52 the village was never able to provide such
  services again. Even then it was not assisted by the department or the state
  (ADHA 6M stat 24, 1853). In 1852 the village attempted to care for sixty-eight
  indigents out of receipts for this purpose of only 193 francs (ADHA 216M 13).
  From 1852 to the First World War the average amount spent on aiding the poor
  in their homes was about 300 francs a year (ADHA 6M stat 25–55).

TABLE 5
Indigents and beggars of Abriès, 1841

Case	Duration of aid	Annual aid (francs)	Sex	Age	Marital status[a]	Cause of poverty	Previous profession	Family assistance
Indigents								
1	15 years	400	M	66	M	wife's debts	cultivator	some from 2 children
2	10 years	110	F	37	U	infirm	cultivator	none
3	15 years	200	F	50	M	husband blind, son crippled	cultivator son	some from
4	since birth	300	M	45	M	born indigent[b]	cultivator	none
5	since birth	800	M	45	M	born indigent[b]	cultivator	2 of 6 daughters give some
6	since birth	120	F	47	W	born indigent	cultivator	none
7	15 years	300	M	60	M	plague	cultivator	1 child provides some
8	20 years	500	M	71	M	illnesses	cultivator	2 grand-children provide some
9	since birth	110	M	23	U	born indigent	cultivator	none
10	since birth	380	M	50	M	born indigent	carpenter	1 child provides some
11	20 years	370	M	52	M	debts	cultivator	none
12	since birth	180	F	53	W	born indigent	cultivator	none
13	20 years	480	F	46	W	large family	cultivator	none
14	since birth	420	M	60	M	large family	cultivator	none

No.	Aid	Duration	Sex	Age	Status[a]	Cause	Occupation	Infirmity
15	620	9 years	M	45	M	large family[b]	cultivator	none
16	170	18 years	F	55	U	infirmities	cultivator	none
17	720	12 years	M	44	?	large family[b]	cultivator	none (8 young children)
18	500	13 years	M	50	M	large family[b]	cultivator	none
19	110	since birth	M	35	U	born indigent	cultivator	none
20	190	10 years	M	39	U	father's debts	cultivator	none
Beggars								
5 from Italy	560 (for all 5)	?	1F 4M	12–60	?	?	?	?
3 habitually resident in Abriès	120	?	F	70	U	?	?	?
	120	?	F	65	M	?	?	?
	120	?	F	60	U	?	?	?
Total aid to beggars and indigents	7900							

[a] U = unmarried; M = married; w = widowed.
[b] Self-help through some seasonal migration.
Source: ADHA 216M 13

This commercial/manufacturing expansion required capital. Would-be entrepreneurs needed access to more than just the money that had circulated through the pre-existing marketing networks. That had been sufficient for paying taxes and purchasing staples. But at the turn of the nineteenth century, capital to invest in new enterprises was required. In that situation, mortgaging land, which became possible with the creation of mortgage bureaus, and borrowing became essential, and the creditor/debtor tie emerged as an extremely important economic, social, and political relationship.

An analysis of cases brought before the village justice of the peace in 1791 and 1798 demonstrates just how important borrowing had become in village life (see Table 6). About half of the 160 disputes for which complete records exist were debt cases. The reason underlying this situation was the changing economic environment. Through the previous centuries Abrièsois had worked out and refined mechanisms for the efficient transfer of property through marriage and inheritance and for the protection of forest and water rights. Disputes in these categories were rare because people were very experienced in such matters. Borrowing and mortgaging, however, were new. There was no centuries-tested machinery which met community standards for fairness for transferring money from creditor to debtor and back again.

In these new circumstances, pre-existing community-levelling mechanisms were no longer effective. Property and money were beginning to circulate outside village reproductive circuits through the expanding network of capitalism. Blaise Richard-Calve was an extractor of these resources. Through high interest rates, mortgages, foreclosures, and small-scale industrial enterprises, he 'liberated' capital from community regulation. Richard-Calve's power was further enhanced by the fortuitous arrival of the Revolution, which broke the Berthelot grip on the local power arena and created new political opportunities.

Thus, Blaise Richard-Calve became a power-holder by means of economic control. He was very different from the Berthelots, who owed their power to legal expertise. Richard-Calve's domination was more direct and more penetrating. He operated in the region much more in terms of supralocal needs and much less as an advocate of community interests. In this he foreshadowed the power-holders of the nineteenth century. But he could not dominate the village completely. Not everyone was in debt to him. Neither could he control all behaviour. In other words, Richard-Calve did not rise to power simply by means of coercion. Many of his debtors were willing supporters because they had similar interests in commerce, industry, and profit, and Richard-Calve

TABLE 6
Cases brought before Justice of the Peace, Abriès, 1791 and 1798

	1791		1798	
	N	%	N	%
Debts	83	52	35	47
Tax, cadastre	14	9	1	1
Property sales	6	4	4	5
Business contracts	7	4	3	4
Marriage contract / dowry	10	6	2	3
Inheritance	13	8	10	14
Pensions	1	1	0	–
Resources (land, boundaries, trespass, water rights, theft)	24	15	14	19
Physical violence	1	1	0	–
Smuggling	0		5	7
Other	1	1	0	
Total	160	101	74	100

Note: The records have incomplete information for six cases in 1791 and thirty in 1798; these cases are not included in the totals.
Source: ADHA 2L202

became their banker and their friend in government. He made large loans to such people throughout the region. Apparently these people prospered, because we have evidence that they were able to repay their loans and borrowed from him repeatedly.

Within the village some people were also prospering. Throughout the Revolutionary era the wealth differences within Abriès increased. During the ancien régime, the rich had been only four or five times wealthier than the poor, with wealth measured by dowry size. But as we shall see, this difference grew enormously between 1780 and 1820.

What was happening in Abriès and the region during this era was the penetration of capitalist forms that were gathering momentum throughout France. Within the village the new social relations of capitalism were not yet consolidated, but they were expressed in terms of increased social differentiation by wealth and occupation. This differentiation was the antecedent to full-fledged class stratification, which clearly emerged in the region in the second half of the nineteenth century.

5

Village, State, and Capitalism

During the first half of the nineteenth century, the Abrièsois experienced contradictory forces. The new top-down administrative system pushed villagers out of politics and into a world of bureaucratic mystification where important resources, such as roads and forests, were annexed by supralocal administration and taken out of the realm of political discourse. In place of the old regime's institutional/legal channels of articulation, there arose village chiefs, monopolistic power-holders, who transmitted Paris orders and profited from their positions. Peasants were thus administratively integrated with but politically isolated from the centre.

At the same time, mountain villages were caught up in expanding commercial and industrial operations. Perhaps this boom period distracted them from their political woes. By 1846, however, economic expansion began a devastating decline, and the Abrièsois found, as the rest of the century unfolded, that they were losing control of economic autonomy as well as political autonomy.

Having been inserted into a capitalist economy, Abriès was transformed from a system based on labour-intensive polyculture in which production decisions were made by the domestic unit embedded in kin and community relationships to one based on capital-intensive monoculture in which the crucial decisions of production were outside the control of the family and the community.

What happened to Abriès during this period is better understood as underdevelopment rather than modernization. The key change, which affected almost all aspects of everyday life, was that loss of control over decision-making in crucial economic and political areas. At the end of the eighteenth century the population of Abriès was approximately

1800. By the beginning of the twentieth century, the population had dropped to one-third that figure. The decrease reflected massive out-migration. The Alps saw no single change, such as an enclosure movement, that threw peasants off the land and created an urban proletariat, although there were signal events, such as the economic crisis of 1846–51, that marked peaks in the process. Rather, the economic system in southeast France was transformed in a series of steps that both pushed and pulled people out of villages. In valleys north of the Queyras, some of the individuals who left the land ended up in urban industry. Queyrassin men who migrated followed different networks into urban society and often became integrated as capitalist wage-workers in the tertiary sector, as shopkeepers or clerks or functionaries.

As urban capitalism evolved, peasant villages did not disappear, but they were greatly transformed. In Abriès, villagers turned to capital-intensive dairy farming. Here the lines of dependence stretched to the central government and the Forest Administration, which promoted large-scale installations using a carrot-and-stick approach that virtually outlawed sheep-rearing and made financial assistance available only to cow-keeping dairies. This dependence on the state for capital accumulation meant village-state relations that differed greatly from Abriès's old regime strategy of keeping the crown at arm's length. Power-holding within the village arena became increasingly less meaningful. More important were connections to patrons within the supra-local administration who could secure capital and markets for peasants.

FORESTS AND TAXES

In 1827 the French central authorities implemented a complex forest code that defined all forests as a national resource over which the state could exercise strict control. Commercial and industrial interests were granted major concessions, but peasant access to forests and pastures was sharply limited. This legislation transformed a local resource into a national one, and from the point of view of mountain communes, which were especially dependent on the forest for heating, building materials, and pasturage, the annexation was devastating. There was peasant resistance all through France, and virtual guerrilla war broke out in areas of the Pyrenees (see Merriman 1975, for an account of this struggle in the Ariège).

We have seen how crucial collective ownership and management of forest and pastureland were to the economy of the Briançonnais. This local control had been briefly challenged by the crown in 1735 and again in 1769, but Briançonnais villages were successful in resisting the central authority's attempts at regulation and retained local autonomy in forest management until the nineteenth century. Then state policy once again focused on village forests as a national resource that was potentially very attractive, especially for use in naval shipbuilding. The military's desire for lumber coincided with a civil service campaign to implement 'scientific' management techniques to enhance forest productivity. In 1827 and again in 1841 the Department of Water and Forest Administration began to act in the Hautes-Alpes. In 1841, A. Surell, a forest administrator, published *Etude sur les torrents des Hautes-Alpes* ([1841] 1870), which became the bible for the departmental Forest Administration. The work provided justification for taking forest management away from peasants by apparently demonstrating that communal practices of pasturing sheep in forests, as well as extravagant woodcutting and clearing, had drastically increased river flooding, thereby denuding large areas of the Hautes-Alpes forests during the previous two hundred years.

Surell's statistics and categories have since been refuted by a number of authorities, who have disproved his claim that there was a golden age of forests destroyed by reckless peasant practices (Lenoble 1923; Blanche 1923; Fourchy 1944; Vigier 1963). We know now that the deforested regions Surell pointed to were, in fact, above the tree-line and had never been forest covered. We also know that the lack of undergrowth in Hautes-Alpes forests, which supposedly increased the flooding, was not caused by sheep and goats' eating the ground cover. Mixed pine and larch forests simply do not have the thick undergrowth of deciduous forests; build-up is prevented by the high acid content of larch needles, which fall in the autumn. Furthermore, sheep do not eat pine needles and are never pastured in such forests (Lenoble 1923).

In the 1840s, however, Surell's theories held sway. Given the state's interest in controlling forests, it was very convenient to view peasant land management as incompetent. Pasturelands, wastelands, heaths, and whole categories of terrain which peasants regarded as pastures could be classified as areas to be reforested and protected from the 'devastation' of sheep herds. Armies of forest agents invaded villages for anti-sheep campaigns. Peasants were prevented from grazing sheep and sometimes cows in their traditional pastures. Thus the flocks of the high alpine villages declined in the 1840s, and the peasants were deprived of one of their major sources of money-making and market participation.

The 1841 report of a Briançonnais subprefect noted that the forest regulations were creating a subsistence crisis for the population because herd size was going down so rapidly. 'If the greater part of the communal forests continue to be interdicted as was done in 1841, there will always be a shortage of animals relative both to the needs of both agriculture and local consumption' (ADHA 6M stat 4). He argued that the reduced sheep population was driving meat prices beyond the means of most villagers. In 1830 an average Briançonnais sheep had cost 12 francs; a decade later it cost 16.5 francs. Such great fluctuations were bound to create difficulties for peasants, the subprefect pointed out, even though widespread poaching provided some meat. Official forest policy did, in fact, combine with a larger economic crisis in 1846, and the results caused great hardship for montagnards.

The forest legislation not only restricted peasants in their production and marketing operations; it also threatened their finances. Forest agents could levy extremely steep fines and often did so. In some alpine communes the sum of fines levied was higher than the villages' annual tax payments (Vigier 1963: I, 50). Abrièsois incurred fines as high as 85 francs for the felling of one tree (ADHA 3UP129). By 1848 the situation in the Queyras as a whole was grim; one official wrote: 'The extent of the pastures being severely limited by the consequences of the region's forestry policies, the production of cheese and the raising of animals, main causes of prosperity in this canton, have suffered a great deal for several years' (AN C944).

Taxation
Abriès, like other alpine villages, was caught in the 1840s in a series of structural contradictions. On the one hand, government policies, which hampered road construction in border areas and restricted forest usage, were pushing the montagnards away from commercial expansion. On the other hand, the need for cash kept villagers trying to connect with commercial markets.

One of the most important uses of money at this time was to pay taxes. The impact of taxation on village life had been totally transformed by the abolition of the pre-Revolution tribute-paying system and the streamlining of the tax-collecting bureaucracy. To put the matter simply, peasants could no longer negotiate whether they were going to pay taxes or how much. In 1791 the Revolutionary government created four direct taxes: the foncière, a land tax; a tax on property, personnelle et mobilière (personal and real), that combined the value of three days' labour within a commune with the rental value of the furnished house of the taxpayer; a tax on doors and windows; and finally the patente, a commercial licensing tax that varied by size of commune and the nature of the business enterprise in question (Thivot 1971: 122–30; Van de Walle, 1974: 21–5). (These taxes came to be called les quatres vieilles (the four old ones) because they were the basis of direct taxation until 1925, when the window and door tax was suppressed.)

Initially these taxes were met with overt opposition in the Queyras; later, deprived of any substantial political leverage, the peasants paid regularly but complained bitterly. Montagnards objected that the land tax did not take account of differential productivity; mountain fields were in the same category as the much more fertile fields of the northern French plains. Complaints about the personal and real property tax concerned the manner of administration and how the basis for the tax was calculated. In principle, it was supposed to be assessed by a council of repartiteurs (dividers) within the commune, a system that would have given local people some say in the matter. In practice, however, everything was done by the departmental administration 'without any guarantees for the interested parties' (Thivot 1971: 128). The situation was another example of the transformation of politics into administration.

Disputes about the rental value of furnished houses were among the most bitter. At mid-century, when this value was being assessed, the objections led to riots in many parts of France, including the Hautes-Alpes (but not the Queyras), and the violence became aimed partly at the 1841 population census, which happened to be going on at the same time (Van de Walle 1974: 21). Many people considered the window and door tax to be the most unfair of all; as Le Dauphinois, a regional newspaper, put the matter on 15 January 1832, the authorities made no distinction between a giant glass window in a country estate and a small piece of oiled paper 'in a miserable proletarian hovel' (in Thivot 1971: 128).

With the exception of the disturbances in 1841, however, the montagnards did pay their taxes regularly throughout the nineteenth century. Records for Abriès show that the personal and real property tax rose steeply in the 1840s. The village as a whole paid about 800 francs a year in the 1820s. By the 1840s the amount had increased more than 80 per cent to the 1500-franc range; in 1838–43 it peaked at more than 1900 francs. The total then declined to about 1300 francs, as depopulation lowered real estate values, and remained at that level until the 1870s, when it began to rise again. The foncière also rose sharply, from 3209 francs in 1824 to 4655 francs in 1849 (ADHA P2 uninventoried, no. 244–5).

The tax that rose most steeply was the commercial tax. In the 1840s it was applied to peddlers on foot and at a higher rate to peddlers with pack animals. In 1840 Abriès paid a total patente of 447 francs. By 1848 it was 1779 francs (ibid.). Vigier argues that the 1844 change in regulations caused a crisis among peddlers, and many were forced to abandon their seasonal métier (1963: I, 86).

ECONOMIC CRISIS AND OUT-MIGRATION

Until the mid-nineteenth century the village managed to contain the contradictory pressures on its economic system and maintain an average population of about 1800 people. But, as reflected in Figures 4 and 5, the economic crisis of 1846–51 began a pattern of out-migration that sent population statistics on a permanent and rapid slide downward. By 1961, the count was 205 – fewer than the 245 of the Black Death years in the fourteenth century (Guillaume 1968: 185).

Because of the speed and magnitude of the demographic decline, we know that the main cause of the change was permanent out-migration, the result of a major transformation in the village.

To see what happened to Abriès, we must step back for a broad perspective. The underdevelopment that began in the mid-nineteenth century must be traced to what Hobsbawm has called 'the most important event in world history ... since the invention of agriculture and cities' (1962: 46), the Industrial Revolution and the global spread of capitalism that touched Abriès in the 1840s.

When the Industrial Revolution began in England in the 1780s, it was based on an agricultural transformation very different from France's. In England the peasantry disappeared; in France it did not. The Enclosure Acts of England (1760–1830) swept away the remaining structures of an ancient, collective economy and created a profit-oriented commercial agriculture of landlords, landless rural proletarians, and some smallholders (see Brenner 1964: 82). But when industrialization began to develop in France, villages such as Abriès adapted

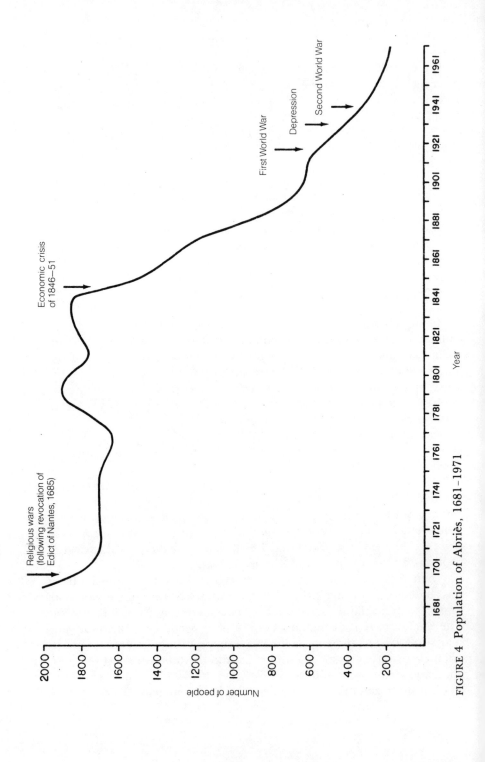

FIGURE 4 Population of Abriès, 1681–1971

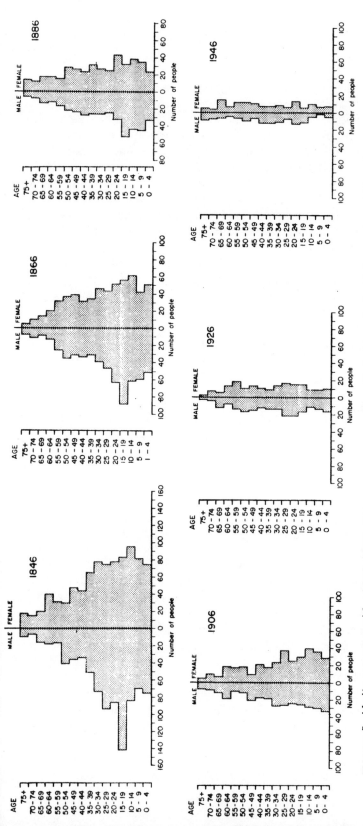

FIGURE 5 Abriès age pyramids, 1846–1946. The bulges on the male side of the pyramids for 1846, 1866, and, to a far less extent, 1886, represent a temporary population of doméstiques (immigrant farm workers considered household members). The 1846 nominative census lists give only their first names, usually in French, but later censuses showed Italian names. Nationality was not listed until 1886, when most doméstiques were shown as Italian.

Source: Constructed from the nominative censuses available in the departmental archives (ADHA 192 M66, 70, 74, 78, 81, 85).

to the process by virtue of remaining oriented to a peasant economy – that is, by not being geared to profit.

Thus, the fact that the Queyras and Abriès were not heavily involved in capitalist agriculture or major textile manufacture, as so many areas of southeast France were, is no indication that the village was protected from the boom and bust cycles of capitalist development. In fact, we have seen the important connection of market involvement through animal sales and cheese production. When crisis struck the evolving capitalist economy of France, it had direct ramifications for seemingly isolated villages and set in motion a pattern of underdevelopment which continues to this day.

Such capitalist crises differed in basic ways from old-regime crises. As Fourastié says: 'Whereas the crises of the Ancien Regime were phenomena of shortage suddenly experienced and for thousands of years the very idea of crisis was linked with underproduction and famine ... crises since the Revolution are always, except during wars, phenomena of overabundance of an explosive nature, which also lead to deepgoing social changes' (1949: 141). Subsistence crises of underproduction gave way in the nineteenth century to capitalist crises of overproduction, falling rates of profit, widespread unemployment, and financial collapse.

In such circumstances only those sectors of the economy with wide profit margins were able to survive. Peasants, who generally participate in capitalism by discounting their own labour investment and accepting very slim profits, suffer heavily during economic crises. They do not have the capital margin to ride out the storm. Guitton (1951: 94) provides some very interesting information which suggests how poorly those who have not accumulated super-profits during boom times can expect to fare during depressions. In nineteenth-century France, he estimates that in boom periods prices rose by 17 per cent and in depressions fell by 16 per cent. Wages rose by 12 per cent in booms and fell by 3 per cent in depressions. Profits rose 40 to 200 per cent in good times and fell 14 to 38 per cent in economic slumps. Thus, only those enterprises with high profit margins could weather depressions. As part-time entrepreneurs working at low productivity levels, the Abrièsois were hit very hard. They could not hope to accumulate sufficient profits in good times to survive bad times. (See also Mandel 1971: 342–73.)

Crises in capitalism recurred throughout the nineteenth and the twentieth centuries. Cameron (1966: 52–60) provides a thumb-nail sketch of France's boom and bust economy in the nineteenth century.

A mild post-war depression, from 1815 to 1820, was followed by a period of steady growth in production and national income; the largest part of the income increases gravitated to wealthy landlords, industrialists, and financiers. In 1846/7 a severe depression began with a financial crisis in Britain which affected railway investment in France. As well, France experienced its own agricultural and industrial crisis. Railway construction and public works were paralysed, coal and iron production went down, and harvests were poor. A potato blight spread throughout the countryside.

Another period of growth followed in 1852 to 1857. These years saw the highest capital accumulation of the nineteenth century, and national income grew by 5 per cent per year. But again only a small fraction of this wealth accrued to the general population. In fact, real wages declined slightly because of the rapid rise in prices. This boom was followed by another depression, from 1857 to 1859, and another period of recovery, from 1859 to 1863, the latter aided by free trade treaties and liberalized incorporation laws. Both 1863/4 and 1873 were times of depression. From 1874 to 1881 France experienced a boom similar to that of the 1852-7 period but following came the worst depression in the nineteenth century.

The prolonged depression of 1882 to 1896 combined financial panic, losses in foreign investment from defaulting governments and bankrupt railways, a world-wide return to high protective tariffs, stagnation in domestic industry, and blights that devastated the wine and silk industries. The years 1897-8 brought a modest recovery connected to the new industries of electricity, aluminum, nickel, and automobiles; the growth rate returned to about 2 per cent per year.[1]

THE DEPRESSION OF 1846-51

With this background, let us look at Abriès as it confronted France's first major capitalist crisis.

1 Cameron's sketch of economic crisis is helpful for its chronology, but it does not tie depression and recovery to world-wide trends such as expansion into colonial markets; neither does it provide any theoretical explanation for recurring crises. Marxists such as Mandel (1971), Hobsbawm (1962), and Wolf (1982), inter alia, argue that crises in capitalism are inherent within the system itself, are produced by its internal contradictions. Others, like Cameron, argue for more proximate causes, such as South American governments' defaulting on loans. Whatever causes analysts name, all agree that capitalism operates in boom and bust cycles with far-reaching repercussions.

The agricultural crisis of 1846-7 in the mountain regions of southeast France brought to a head the contradictions we have been discussing. For montagnards the crisis began not with poor cereal harvests and high grain prices, as in the rest of France, but with the potato blight. Some alpine communes were reduced to an eighth of their regular crop; in others the whole crop was wiped out (Vigier 1963: I, 76). We do not have 1846 agricultural data for Abriès, but we can compare 1836 statistics with 1853 figures (ADHA 6M stat 66-7). In 1836 the village had 20 hectares in potatoes and produced 320 hectolitres per hectare. By 1853 only 7 hectares were given over to potatoes, and the yield was 140 hectolitres per hectare. The market price per kilogram had gone up from 5 centimes in 1836 to 3 francs in 1853.

The region was not as dependent on potatoes as some areas in the Drôme and the Isère, which were particularly hard-hit (Vigier 1963: I, 76). Although elements of an old regime subsistence crisis of underproduction resulted from the potato blight, regions with mixed crops managed to survive shortages by compensating with other crops. By 1847, however, the situation worsened in the high mountain animal-raising areas. Hay production was down, so many peasants were forced to sell their animals at low prices or to pay high prices for sufficient feed to winter the stock at home and hope for higher spring prices. Here the peasants were very much tied to market conditions, and their plight was seriously aggravated by Forest Administration policy, which restricted the much-needed pasturing areas. (We can compare this situation to that in Ireland, where a much worse subsistence crisis was also compounded by state policy.) Peasants began going into debt to make ends meet (Vigier 1963: I, 78).

Later the same year, following the agricultural crisis, an industrial and financial crisis paralysed railway construction and lowered coal and iron production. The results affected those industries - silk, gloves, straw hats - which had expanded during the July Monarchy and were dispersed through the countryside. The silk industry managed to survive the crisis and even to expand, but others, including the older industries of hemp production and leather-working, which were still important in some high mountain areas, were hard hit, cutting off an additional source of income for peasants. Profits declined in all areas, and there were many bankruptcies and expropriations for debts. Peasant indebtedness began to take a tragic turn.

Usury was rampant in the Hautes-Alpes, and local notables, usually notaries or justices of the peace, forced many expropriations. In the

Gap region, for example, 1849 expropriations for debts were up 260 per cent from 1840-5 (Vigier 1963: II, 34). It was almost impossible for mountain peasants to get access to cash during these crisis years. Even when harvests improved in 1848, animal prices continued to decline (ibid. 26). The crisis was now clearly one of capitalism, in which over-abundance and low prices were part of economic collapse.

The Abriès documents for the 1844-56 period (ADHA 3UP20-3) are incomplete, so it is not possible to calculate trends. It is clear, however, that during those years some Abrièsois were mortgaging their property and losing their lands and houses and that notaries were heavily involved as creditors and as debtors. Statistics from nearby animal markets reflect Abriès conditions. In October 1849 sheep prices in Briançon were 90 centimes a kilogram – artificially high in comparison to Gap prices, which were already down to 48 centimes. By 1850 Briançon prices had fallen to 50 centimes a kilogram; in 1851 they reached a low of 33 centimes. Prices began to rise slowly in 1853 but stayed at about the 50-centimes level until the 1870s, when they rose by 20 centimes. Beef and pork prices showed similar trends (ADHA 162M6 1-9, 1848-74). No money could be made from the sale of animals in the crisis years. Market figures for 1849 show that of 180 sheep brought for sale in Briançon in October only 30 were sold (ADHA 162M6 1).

It seems likely that the cheese industry was also in great difficulty in this period. The 1844 change in commercial licensing legislation caused a crisis for many seasonal peddlers, who became subject to commercial taxes and had to pay high licence fees (Vigier 1963: I, 86). Since the rest of the region was undergoing financial problems, people were not in a position to buy as many dairy products as they had before. The departments surrounding the Hautes-Alpes were also suffering from a great shortage of money, high debts, and many foreclosures (ibid. II, 30-8).

Many mountain regions were affected by the 1846-51 crisis, some of them more than the Queyras, but not all of them responded with the large-scale out-migration that the Queyras sustained. The difference there was the pre-existing pattern of seasonal migration and high literacy. Peasants from these valleys had experience in a wider world and perhaps enough money to make leaving their villages feasible. They knew where to go and had more understanding of what was possible in terms of work than other, more isolated peasants had. Some Queyrassins went to the big cities of southern France, such as Marseilles, but others went to Algeria, to California to search for gold, and to South America and Mexico (ibid. 126–33). Eventually Abrièsois turned up in Bogota, Colombia, and a whole colony from nearby Aiguilles established themselves in Mexico. There are villas throughout the Queyras built by 'Americains' – migrants who left the region in the 1850s for South America and later returned home to retire. Most who left, of course, did not return.

Thus, in the crisis of 1846–51 pre-existing patterns afforded the montagnards an exit. This explanation of the outward movement – crisis combined with the possibility of exploiting pre-existing networks – varies from arguments that Queyrassins began migrating in the nineteenth century because they suddenly realized they were poor and backward (Blanchard 1950: 762–7; Veyret 1952; Weber 1976). Such psychological theories are both hard to test and ineffective in explaining differential patterns of migration from the Alps. Furthermore, the evidence that the standard of living was improving in alpine villages in the first half of the nineteenth century suggests that it was a crisis in new sources of wealth, not ancient poverty, that produced permanent out-migration.

Experiments in Directed Development
Between 1851 and 1875 the government became an even more influential actor in the montagnard economy. The changes begun at mid-century through the activities of the Forest Administration were substantially expanded. The simple limitation of access to pastureland was followed by systematic intervention in an attempt to create capitalist agriculture in the Hautes-Alpes. The new policy was aimed at creating fruitières (creameries – the French word is the alpine term for dairies specializing in cow's-milk products) that would serve southern French cities on a large scale and reorienting local agriculture to their support. Forest agents undertook to modernize agriculture by suppressing sheep-raising and promoting the break-up of communal land, the expansion of cow herds, the building of large dairy installations, the purchase of new equipment, and the turning to fodder production of land being used to grow subsistence staples. This capital-intensive plan was to be supported by large transfusions of loans from the government. However, the idealized picture drawn by Forest Administration officials and agriculture professors did not work out in quite the way the experts had planned.

There seems to have been no discussion of why such a massive reorganization of agriculture should have been the task of a government agency whose official charge was to conserve and protect forests. Since the 1840s, however, official discourse had made it clear that the government controlled not only the forests but the pastures of the Hautes-Alpes, and by the 1870s major economic decisions about these resources were firmly lodged within the Forest Administration.

In the 1850s Abriès became the first commune in the department to create a creamery devoted primarily to the production of gruyère cheese. It was run on co-operative lines: members pooled their resources to buy the equipment, hire expert cow's-milk cheese-makers (women from the Jura and Switzerland), and build the dairy facilities. The members of the dairy were paid pro rata to the amount of milk they brought in. Eventually the creameries also became credit agencies, extending loans to members (Briot 1881: 42–71). By 1872 Abriès had eight creameries with 140 members, producing cheese valued at 56,000 francs – the highest revenue from cheese production of the sixty cheese-making communes in the department (ADHA 270M 1). The Forest Administration often pointed to the Queyras co-operative dairies as models for emulation by the rest of the department.

In 1878, the Forest Administration went further than promoting the spread of creameries: it became involved in marketing and capital-raising. In that year it sent Elie Bellon, a member of a dairy association from a high Alpine village, to tour southern French cities and scout markets for Hautes-Alpes products. The official responsible for this mission was a forest inspector named Briot. (His area of expertise was reforestation – a fact that points up the Forest Administration's tendency to expand its mandate.) His report and Bellon's (ADHA 270M 1) are significant partly because they show the close interlocking of dairy development and the Forest Administration. A fundamental principle of both reports is that this relationship should continue and expand. The real aim of the Bellon's mission was to convince the government to provide large loans to the Hautes-Alpes to expand dairy production. The argument Briot and Bellon made was that southern markets were enormous and large profits could be had if only the capital to improve and expand alpine installations was forthcoming.

This early example of market analysis is fascinating in its optimism about rural development and the potential for huge profits. It is also important for the contradictions it reveals.

Bellon toured Marseilles, Toulon, Aix, Avignon, Nîmes, and Cavaillon, trying to convince cheese merchants of those cities to buy from the Hautes-Alpes instead of Switzerland or the Jura. He argued that Hautes-Alpin cheeses were equal in quality to the foreign products which filled the cellars of the southern merchants and would be cheaper because of the shorter distances between Midi cities and the Hautes-Alpes. He succeeded in placing a number of orders immediately but soon ran into a series of problems. It was winter, the weather was bad, the unimproved roads were in poor condition, and the montagnards were unable to fill the orders in time. The cheese wholesalers turned back to their previous suppliers. Bellon was not discouraged by this episode, even though it revealed the problem of the inadequate transportation infrastructure, which was to handicap distribution of Hautes-Alpes products in southeast France and which gave a great competitive advantage to Swiss and Jura villages with access to better and more direct railway facilities.

Bellon also appealed to the cheese merchants' regional or village chauvinism. Most of them were of Hautes-Alpin origin, and many, especially in Marseilles and Toulon, were Abrièsois. Bellon argued that they should stock products from 'home.' This appeal to homeland solidarity in a competitive situation is intriguing because it became the idiom for much future masking of southern wholesalers' exploitation of village producers. By 1878 some ex-Queyrassin wholesalers had begun to realize the advantages of vertical integration. One had bought the rights to all the dairy production of Ristolas, a Queyras village. Bellon encouraged other wholesalers to do the same. From his perspective it meant a steady market for products; for the wholesalers it came to mean a cheap supply of cheeses and eventually control of production within alpine villages.

Both Bellon's and Briot's reports were extremely optimistic about the large profits to be made in the southern market. They quoted cheese consumption figures for Midi cities and argued that gruyère production in the Hautes-Alpes could increase up to fiftyfold and still find a market. On this basis, Briot urged his superiors in the Forest Administration to provide subsidies to the Hautes-Alpes to increase its gruyère production and break into the southern market bonanza.

Bellon and Briot touched, in passing, on a problem which was in the end to sink their optimistic expectations. They noted that market conditions in Nîmes, Cavaillon, and Avignon were not very good because of the 'mortalité des vignes' (the phylloxera epidemic) that was devastating the vineyards of the region. Bellon remarked: 'Today, the disease is found among many of these properties. Two or three cheese merchants have declared bankruptcy' (ADHA 270M 1, 1878).

Despite these bankruptcies, Bellon was positive about marketing outlets in the Midi and the goodwill of ex-Queyrassin merchants. He concluded his report; 'After this trip is finished I can say in all certainty that the doors are open to great market opportunities; all that has to be done is to produce great quantities of cheese because the more there are the more merchants will come forth from the Midi' (ibid.).

Unfortunately, Briot and Bellon's predictions were wrong. They wrote in a period of economic boom. But in a few short years, France was to enter its worst depression of the nineteenth century. In 1881 Briot, by this time head of the Forest Administration's newly created Dairy Service, was beginning to detect some problems, though his mood was still positive. He believed that any problems could be solved by technological solutions, such as the extension of canal irrigation, the building of permanent shelters in the high pastures to protect cows from the elements, the use of finer instruments for measuring temperature and fat content, the hiring of better-trained cheese-makers, and, of course, the purchase of more cows of improved breeds (Briot 1881). Neither he nor Allier (1882), an agriculture professor in the department, nor Faure (ca 1881), a Gapençais pharmacist and member of the department's agriculture society, could explain why profits were not as high as had been expected. In 1877 when dairy expansion was at its peak, milk prices were 15 to 17 centimes a litre (DCG 1889: 316). Prices fell all through the 1880s, and by 1889 had dropped to 8.5 to 10 centimes (ibid. 315; Guicherd 1933: 250).

Briot had no comprehensive analysis of the instabilities inherent in the larger economic system. He looked for simple answers, and he found them. To him, the decline of alpine dairying was the fault of the peasants, especially of their placing continued importance on the commons in their villages. He argued that the cheese industry worked most efficiently when the commons were alienated and individual entrepreneurs could erect shelters in the high pastures for their cows. 'Since we have thought of increasing production within an industry that requires buildings and intelligent management, the commons necessarily tend to disappear. We can thus foresee for the Hautes-Alpes, as a consequence of the development of the cheese industry, this happy result: the decrease in communal pastures, *which all economists agree are always exposed to bad management* (1881: 60-1, emphasis added). Other experts agreed that communal holdings were impeding progress and that division was advisable, even though the poor might suffer. What they wanted were factories in the fields (see Servolin 1972).

The experts also thought profits could be improved if only peasants were more willing to expand operations, turn grain fields to fodder production, buy their grains on the market, and build larger stables for wintering more cows in the villages. Briot asked the state for a 20,000-franc subsidy for this purpose (1881: 58–9). Allier (1882) was particularly adamant that only complete concentration in fodder production and dairy cows – that is, complete acceptance of capitalist specialization and the abandonment of grain production – could solve the Hautes-Alpes problems. He viewed the department as extremely poor and felt that the Briançonnais peasants were the poorest of all. According to him they had only the sad alternatives of migrating or dying of hunger (ibid. 116).

Asking why such an educated people should be reduced to such a state, Allier argued that 'an era of true prosperity' was just around the corner for montagnards who made a full commitment to capitalist dairying. The profit from cheese sales, he claimed, would enable peasants to expand production even further, turn more fields into irrigated pastures, and buy their grains on the market (ibid. 117).

In another section of the article Allier did admit that the poor road and rail network in the department were making trade almost impossible (ibid. 118). He offered no reason why peasants should rely on this inadequate transportation infrastructure to meet subsistence needs when they were already having a great deal of trouble getting their products out for sale. Rather, he said that, seeing the large profits to be made, he hoped they would stop holding back milk for home consumption; this, too, would increase the profit margin. Another way to increase profit, according to Allier, was to discourage small-scale dairies, which were inefficient, and to replace them with larger installations. All this needed capital – 'enormous capital' – which the peasants themselves could not accumulate. Thus, like Faure and Briot, Allier argued that it was the duty of the state to provide the necessary capital: 'state intervention will in this case be … indispensable' (ibid. 130).

Faure (ca 1881) essentially agreed with Allier but did not feel the region to be quite so poor. Faure too believed that the dairy industry was the future for the department and that the Queyras, with the most beautiful pastureland in the department, could benefit greatly because its excellent pastures produced an excellent product. He felt that the Queyras was especially open to ideas of progress; all that was needed were more state subsidies, more dairies, more perfected technology (ibid. 30).

Only Briot associated continued low profits with difficulties in marketing and distribution. Yet he was still optimistic about the cities of the Midi and felt that Algeria would also provide a major market (1881: 55). He too fought for more loans.

Thus, on the eve of the 1882–96 depression, the economy of the Hautes-Alpes, especially Queyras, was geared to expanding dairy production on the advice of the experts and with the aid of state loans. During the next twenty years the creameries were wiped out. In 1882 Abriès had nine creameries; two years later it had only six (ADHA 6M stat 12).

PRIVATIZATION

A 1903 Ministry of Agriculture inquiry on the state of France's dairy industry noted: 'In the past few years, the [cooperative dairies in the Queyras] have almost totally disappeared; they have been replaced by private establishments, whose owners buy milk for the whole year at a set price. This transformation ... decreases the profits of the producers' (Ministère de l'Agriculture 1903: 16). The report explained the move from co-operative dairies to individual producers (who sold their products to wholesalers at lower prices) by blaming first peasant suspicions and disagreements in managing the dairies and then the difficulty in finding markets. No mention was made of the 1882–96 depression or of the fact that state subsidies to the dairies were sharply curtailed during that depression.

In the late 1880s and early 1890s the Queyras villagers wrote desperately to Briot trying to get subsidies from the Forest Administration. In the 1870s, almost anyone who asked had received a loan. In 1873 sixteen Abrièsois received 100 francs each to create a new dairy. In 1875 the village got another 2000 francs, but by 1877 the subsidies were getting smaller (ADHA 270M 1, 1873, 1875, 1877; see also DCG 1889: 311–19).

In 1889 a Queyras dairy asked for a loan of 3500 francs to cover expenses but received only 100 francs. In 1890 fifteen Abrièsois petitioned Briot for 13,000 francs but received only 500. Two other Queyras dairies asked for a total of 9000 francs but received only 700 (ADHA 270M 1, 1889, 1890, 1892). Villagers were astonished to find their co-operatives in terrible debt and failing.

With the Forest Administration unable to help them, the villagers turned to private sources of capital. In 1890 an association of fifteen Abriès and Queyras dairies signed a historic agreement with a large

Marseilles dairy wholesaling company owned by Marius Toye-Riont, an ex-Abrièsois. Toye-Riont agreed to buy all the products of all fifteen dairies. Profits were divided so that the first 9 centimes on each litre would be invested in the new association while any amount above 9 centimes would be divided equally between all the associated dairies on the one hand and Toye-Riont on the other. Toye-Riont reserved all rights 'with respect to the nature of the products manufactured' (ADHA 270M 1, 1890; DCG 1890: 318). He also obtained complete control over all decision-making in matters of production.

In effect the transition from a peasant economy to a capitalist economy was complete. Abrièsois cultivators now worked for Toye-Riont.

Briot and the department's Conseil Général hailed the contract as an enormous step forward. Since they could not come up with loans to bail out the villages, they were only too happy to applaud the efforts of private enterprise. Speaking to the council, Briot welcomed the Toye-Riont contract as an important precedent: 'This type of combination clearly deserves to be encouraged because it is founded on the fruitful mixture of [local co-operative] association and private enterprise, which cannot but encourage progress' (DCG 1890, 318).

By 1891 the department had stopped giving out any subsidies to dairies, because of arrangements like the one between Abriès and Toye-Riont. 'Ever since the dairy owners and others have been selling their products, they enjoy the most perfect comfort and can easily do without departmental subsidies' (ibid. 1891: 275).

By the beginning of the twentieth century, the direction of dairying within the department was set. In terms of production and ecology, the trend was devolutionary – towards greater simplification and de-differentiation of the productive process. Co-operative production of cheeses (and butter) in locally owned installations gave way to simple production of raw milk for major industrialists.

The first phase of the transition to simple raw-milk production began when individual entrepreneurs took over the co-operative creameries. By 1903 the buildings which had been used for 'the collective production of milk' were for the most part rented to individual entrepreneurs who purchased raw milk (Ministère de l'Agriculture 1903: 17). Of the forty-six such establishments in the department, only three remained co-operative (two of them in the Queyras and one in an Abriès hamlet). At this time, raw milk could not yet be transported efficiently, so it was transformed into butter and cheese in the village dairy buildings as before. But it was the milk – the raw product – not the cheese or butter which was sold to the individual entrepreneurs.

Who were these individuals – these owners of the milk product? (Notice that one cannot call them dairy owners because the buildings still belonged to the villagers.) Were they the wholesalers who eventually marketed the product in Midi cities and North Africa? This was the case with Toye-Riont, but the record is unclear as to whether his was the general pattern. The Ministère de l'Agriculture's 1903 report on dairying refers simply to individuals who operated the industrial establishments, bought the milk, and hired workers to make dairy products. Whether these individuals were local people, villagers, or distant wholesalers we do not know. The Abriès records suggest that it was not individual villagers who took over the former co-operatives because no villager had sufficient capital to do so. It seems likely that milk-buyers/cheese-makers also ran the wholesale and retail aspects of the industry. But it is also likely that at this stage there were slots for a number of middlemen who may have produced the cheese and sold to wholesalers.[2] Whatever the case, we do know that these middlemen did not remain in the picture for long because the trend was towards vertical control by the milk purchaser.

By the period after the First World War, the picture had become simplified. Industrial dairyists purchased and transported raw milk, first in horse-drawn carts and then in trucks. Their employees supplied containers, weighed and measured the milk, loaded it into wagons, returned the empty containers to the villagers, and drove off to the factories. They organized the routes of collection and the centres for pickup (which required cold-storage areas).

The Nestlé Corporation pioneered this method of organization. Already one of the world's largest multinational food businesses when it moved into the Hautes-Alpes in the 1930s, it quickly became the most important industrial dairy in the department.[3] Although infor-

2 Some middlemen may have transported the cheese. The records do not say who was responsible for cheese cartage. We do know that butter, produced mostly in the winter, was sent from the Hautes-Alpes to the south by mail in three-kilogram packages wrapped in parchment paper (Ministère de l'Agriculture 1903: 18).

3 Historically, Nestlé's investments have always been in processing, not in agriculture, which has a much lower rate of profit.

Nestlé traces its origins to two sources. In 1866 two American brothers, George and Charles Page, founded the Anglo-Swiss Condensed Milk Corporation

mation on Nestlé is difficult to obtain,[4] I did find local sources in the Hautes-Alpes showing that in 1932 it received almost 8 million of the 13 million litres of milk produced in the region (Guicherd 1933: 246).

Before the First World War two Briançon dairies, Montana and Gravier, had been the major purchasers of Queyrassin milk, but after the war Nestlé dominated there as well. In dealing with Montana and Gravier, villagers had formed sellers' co-operatives to negotiate prices with the dairies. Nestlé, however, would not negotiate; it insisted on using a scale based on milk prices in the Savoyard city of Annecy. Nestlé also made its purchase of Queyrassin milk conditional on culti-vators' calving their stock in the fall so that the company would have a winter milk supply. This schedule meant added expense for the vil-lagers, who had to provide winter fodder and care to cows and calves. Despite the bad weather and poor road conditions, Nestlé found winter pick-ups in the Queyras profitable because it paid producers there 40 per cent less than the Annecy price.

In the rest of the department, especially the regions of Champsaur, the Gapençais, and the Dévoluy, Nestlé came to dominate the market by joining forces with agricultural officials in encouraging dairy cow-raising to replace sheep. The company advanced capital and assured purchase of milk. It also opened a major factory in Gap for the produc-

in Cham, Switzerland; their method of production was based on a process developed in the United States by Gail Borden in 1856. In 1867, in Vevey, 200 kilometres from Cham, Henri Nestlé developed an infant food of cereal mixed with milk; he also set up shop in the milk business. The two companies soon began competing with each other for markets, especially after 1875 when Nestlé sold his company to three Swiss industrialists. Finally, after years of intense competition, Anglo-Swiss and Nestlé merged under the name Nestlé. At that time the corporation owned seven factories in Switzerland and eleven more in five other countries. By 1918, it had eighty factories, forty of them in the United States. By 1930, it had factories in Australia, Norway, Spain, Italy, Germany, Holland, and Belgium, as well as the United States and France. Although the early 1930s were somewhat rocky for Nestlé, by 1938 it had more than 500 plants operating from Europe to South Africa to Panama to Japan.

4 Because Nestlé maintains headquarters in two Swiss cantons, it is permitted by law to keep its financial records closed to the public. Thus, information about its financial history and its operations in France between the wars is scarce. Sources include Moskowitz, Katz, and Levering (1980), Harrisson (1982), Gar-reau (1977), Wolfisberg (1966), International Union of Food and Allied Workers' Associations (1977), and George (1985).

tion of condensed milk. This plant connected Haut-Alpin producers with a world-wide system. Railway cars from many parts of Europe pulled in and out of Gap, and its condensed milk was sold throughout the world (Guicherd 1933: 241-52).

CONCLUSION

In eighty years the village economy was transformed from independent production to monopoly capitalism. Rosa Luxemburg, a contemporary observer, described this process and theorized about it:

> Capital must get the peasants to buy its commodities and will therefore begin by restricting the peasant economy to a single sphere – that of agriculture – which will not immediately and, under European conditions of ownership, only with great difficulty submit to capitalist domination. To all outward appearance this process is peaceful. It is scarcely noticeable and seemingly caused by purely economic factors ...
>
> In reality, however, the process of separating agriculture and industry, is determined by factors such as oppressive taxation, war, or squandering and monopolization of the nation's land, and thus belongs to the spheres of political power and criminal law no less than with economics ...
>
> Only the continuous and progressive disintegration of non-capitalist organizations makes the accumulation of capital possible. ([1913] 1968, 395-6)

Luxemburg, drawing examples from Europe, North America, and South Africa, outlined a general devolutionary and dependency-creating process which places villages such as Abriès in the context of global trends. A key aspect of the transition to a capitalist economy is the role of the state in capturing the power to define and monopolize resources. A crucial step in the decline of peasant communities and peasant communalism in villages such as Abriès was the forest legislation of 1827 and 1841, which moved control of forests and pastures outside peasant hands. In this transfer of resources, politics may have been disguised as administration (Balandier 1970), cloaked in an aura of bureaucratic language; but the move created an irreversible rupture in the political economy of the region.

At the individual level local administrators of the Forest Administration, such as Briot, probably had the well-being of peasants at heart. But such a man implicitly represented a bureaucracy whose agents were stationed in the village, a bureaucracy with which peasants could not openly disagree. Villagers who disliked the direction of change could express opposition only by nuancing their co-operation with external change agents or by migrating out of the village. Under such circumstances, preserving pre-capitalist institutions became an expression of resistance.

The experiences of Abriès in the second half of the nineteenth century suggest the vigour with which the French state was prepared to act when it wished to regulate local economies directly, moulding them to capitalist development. The interplay between village and state also reveals the greater flexibility of the supralocal system, which had the option of reorienting or curtailing its inputs into the local system as conditions changed. Those peasants who did not benefit from being drawn into an increasingly monocrop version of capitalist agriculture were not nearly so flexible; it is difficult to reproduce a peasant society in a world of capitalists.

6

Resistance and Compliance

Like people all over the world, Abriès peasants participated in the new economic system in a variety of ways. Their strategies included resistance, co-operation, and migration, depending on time period and circumstances.

COPING STRATEGIES

During the 1870s, Abrièsois were in the forefront of co-operative dairy development. Pre-existing patterns of collective responsibility and pasture management undoubtedly facilitated this type of expansion. Abriès had one of the first creameries in the department, and by the end of the 1870s it had eight, one of them, in the hamlet of Valpreveyre, a model dairy almost completely subsidized by the department. These co-operative creameries received many subsidies and much official support; furthermore, before the crash of 1882–96, they made profits. Meanwhile, the Forest Administration ran an active and continuing campaign against sheep-raising. All of these forces combined to make a transition to cow-keeping attractive to many Abrièsois.

Nevertheless, the transition from sheep to cows and hence to an increasingly capitalized economy also had its detractors and opponents. In the pre-creamery era, cheese and butter were made by individual households with local women in charge of production in the chalets of the high alpages (Guillaume 1901: 251–2). Women received significant revenue from the cheese and butter production, and they were opposed to the creameries, which hired specialists, depriving village women of an important source of income (Briot 1907: 184–5).

Women were also opposed to the increased labour that cow-raising meant for them. Producing chalet cheese from ewe's milk in the summer months was hard work, but it had compensations. It was done in groups, and its rhythm was integrated into a rich ceremonial life of gift and meal exchanges between chalet groups and shepherds who accompanied transhumant flocks. Teasing, joking, and flirting were part of summer chalet experiences, and the skills of women in producing high-quality cheeses were extolled in winter story-telling gatherings (Guillaume 1901).

Agricultural experts in the 1930s argued that women were in favour of the new system of production because it meant less work for them. For example, Guicherd claimed: 'At first skeptical, producers quickly saw the benefits of selling la vente en nature [unprocessed milk]: fewer manipulations, less waste and *simplification of women's work on the farm* ... all this was sufficient compensation for the loss of profit from bi-products especially since the price of milk in the last ten years has been satisfactory' (Guicherd 1933: 250, emphasis added). Yet village women who were active cultivators in that time period told me that the work was boring and isolating. The transition to cow milking and privatized labour tied women to a monotonous responsibility that was daily rather than seasonal. Cows must be milked twice a day every day. There is no break from that kind of work. This change in the working life of women undoubtedly influenced some of them in the decision to migrate from the village.

Other evidence that dairy development did not benefit all interests can be seen in the rapid abandonment of the hamlets. By the 1880s almost all the hamlets except Valpreyvere, which had the model dairy, were rapidly depopulating. One reason was that the installations were centralized in the agglomerations of Abriès and Le Roux. Another was the official policy of turning fields into meadowland. (A member of the Council Général admitted in 1891 that this policy probably contributed to out-migration from the villages of the Hautes-Alpes [DCG 1891: 318].) As the population of the hamlets began to fall it became increasingly difficult to obtain the labour necessary to terrace fields and maintain canal irrigation. It was easier to convert fields around the hamlets to hay production, which required less labour; cultivators could live in the central agglomerations and go out to the hamlets for haying in August. This strategy, in turn, encouraged further depopulation of the hamlets with the inevitable cut-off of road maintenance, schools, and religious services, and finally complete abandonment.[1] Service workers from the hamlets – masons, shoemakers, blacksmiths – were also under pressure to leave since they were now in competition with people in the central village.

Another group that was pushed out by dairy production consisted of the people too poor to raise the capital to buy cows. Most of them probably had a few goats and sheep, but cows were eight or nine times more expensive than sheep. Since the official campaign of the Forest Administration was aimed at eliminating sheep and goats, these people were under considerable pressure. In 1836 Abriès had 3200 sheep; in 1904 there were 550 (ADHA 6M stat 4-102).

Even those Abrièsois who could and did convert to raising dairy cows were selective in the co-operation they gave the new system. On the one hand they were highly mobilized around the construction of creameries and the procuring of loans; on the other hand, they were unwilling to alienate the commons, to eliminate collective practices such as vaîne pâture, or to reduce the production of grain for household consumption. These areas of resistance may have saved the village from even worse depopulation when the subsidies ended and milk prices began to tumble in the 1880s.

From the cadastre (land survey register) of 1827 to the present, one constant has been the total amount of land held in common by the village: approximately 6200 of the commune's 7500 hectares or about 83 per cent of its area (AMA, cadastre 1827; 1913; 1943; 1957; 1960; 1964; 1966; 1967; 1972). Most of the commons is pastureland which was (and is) rented by the commune to transhumant sheep herds from the Midi, ensuring a steady flow of money into the village. The retention of these practices suggests a continued cultural commitment to collective responsibility, especially for the poor, in the face of very strong countervailing pressure.

The Forest Administration opposed common holdings as it opposed vaîne pâture, considering both inefficient practices and impediments to individualization in agriculture. In 1889 the prefect announced the abolition of vaîne pâture, which the Abrièsois strongly supported because it was an important source of fertilizer for the fields. The

1 One villager told me that one of the hamlets had had a hermit living nearby, but he too migrated in the 1880s, perhaps because he was getting lonely!

municipal council responded with a strong letter of protest calling for 'the preservation of the right of vaîne pâture ... an immemorial custom ... [which] has always existed as a communal right ... its prohibition would harm the majority of inhabitants' (AMA, *Délibérations du Conseil Municipal* 1889). Thus began a letter campaign reminiscent of the tactics the village had used with the 'Administration supérieure' of the old regime. The resistance lasted until the 1950s, when the department's administration finally gave up. Vaîne pâture still continues in Abriès.

The village also continued to produce as much grain as possible and to resist, for the most part, the government's urging to specialize in fodder production. Cultivated fodder crops, such as clover, lucerne, and sainfoin were added to production – eighteen hectares of them by the turn of the century – but not at the expense of cereals (ADHA 6M stat 73). By 1892 two cultivators did specialize in fodder production for the market, but this pattern was not general (ibid., stat 75). Most people were concerned with meeting as much of their subsistence needs as possible within the village.

The continuance of labour-intensive grain production struck agricultural observers as a prime indicator of the backwardness of the region (see Blanchard 1950: 912–14), but from the villagers' perspective that subsistence cushion was crucial. They had no guarantee that they would have enough money to buy what they needed and since road conditions were still extremely poor, no guarantee that imported grains would actually reach the village.

SCRAMBLING TO MAKE ENDS MEET

By the end of the nineteenth century, Abriès, the Queyras, and most of the high alpine regions of the department gave evidence of seemingly contradictory traits of development, underdevelopment, and modernization. In fact, these processes were connected. Abriès had a few people who were profiting from the capitalizing economy. The 1892 agricultural statistics show that one cultivator owned more than 200 of the village's 571 cows in the village; another had more than 500 of a total of 1617 sheep; a third specialized in pig production, a forth in potatoes, and two others in fodder (ADHA 6M stat 75). The other animals and resources were distributed among the rest of the population, which stood at 748 in the 1891 census.

For most people it was a time of shortage and scrambling to make ends meet. A series of desperation industries were considered or tried in Abriès as in many parts of the Hautes-Alpes.[2]

One scheme to provide work and money for the inhabitants was an 1881 plan by the department's Conseil Général to promote basket weaving; this project did not find much favour in Abriès. Another plan was to create an atelier lapidaire (workshop for gem-cutting). Some 2600 francs of municipal funds were devoted to the scheme and petitions for subsidies were sent to the prefect in 1887, but the plan died after three years. Another project was an attempt by two ex-villagers to open a marble quarry. The commune granted these entrepreneurs a thirty-year concession and extracted a payment of 2 to 3 francs per square metre of marble, but this scheme also foundered. Yet another project which failed was an attempt to create wood-working shops to specialize in toy-making.

To make ends meet, some of the villagers turned to smuggling. The customs officers and village gendarmes tried to stop it, but the Abrièsois still tell tales of everything from tobacco to whole herds of sheep being smuggled across the border. These stories may be exaggerated, but the villagers undoubtedly had a better command of the terrain than did the forces of authority and were probably successful smugglers at least some of the time.

Some women took up wet-nursing as a paid employment, an occupation usually associated with the poverty of old regime economic conditions. A village register kept between 1881 and 1909 shows that twenty-nine women were officially engaged in this occupation and that the village itself was running an office to recruit infants to be nursed. The register notes whether the connection between parents and wet nurse was made under the office's auspices or through personal networks. For the most part, the parents of the infants were ex-villagers living in Marseilles or Toulon who had become cheese merchants or hotel keepers. About half the women who took up this profession were married; they usually breast-fed the children in their care. The other half were widowed or unmarried, and bottle-fed the infants. Wages varied from 23 to 35 francs a month, and the duration of employment was usually one year.

2 Müller and Peguy (1944) describe much the same process in the Briançonnais: the destruction of village industries, such as tanning and nail-making, in the first half of the nineteenth century, the later decline in seasonal migration, and unsuccessful attempts to find replacement industries.

An industry which did take root in the village was tourism. In 1896 the ex-villager and cheese merchant Toye-Riont put forward a massive plan for the construction of the Grand Hotel des Touristes. The commune absorbed the cost of providing the land and bringing water to the building, but the hotel was in private hands. This early experiment in tourism set the pattern for future tourist ventures. The commune would create a favourable environment and financial concessions in return for the promise of jobs. Profits went to the entrepreneurs.

Meanwhile, Abriès was showing various signs of underdevelopment. It fought a losing battle over improvement of road and transportation facilities. It could not raise sufficient revenue for fountain repair and depended on private donations from wealthy ex-villagers for repairs to church buildings. Its welfare services to poor villagers were severely curtailed in comparison to those of the first half of the century (ADHA 6M stat 25–55). Attempts to raise money for improved medical services were ignored by the department (ADHA 216M 13). Villagers offered to pay a doctor 1600 francs a year, but could get no one to come. Once again they had to turn to wealthy ex-villagers such as Toye-Riont, who promised assistance in hospital construction. An architect was actually employed in 1912, but the project was abandoned after the First World War.

One of the persistent problems facing Abriès was constant attempts by the authorities to reduce the number of teachers and eventually the number of schools in the area. The Abrièsois were particularly bitter about these curtailments and attempted to raise private money to keep teachers on. The closing of schools in the hamlets hastened out-migration.

At the same time that Abriès was showing these signs of underdevelopment, many other signs of modernization appeared. In the 1880s a specialist baker who imported wheat flour and baked white bread moved to the village. In 1899 a gas-lighting project was undertaken under the entrepreneurship of an ex-villager; only the central village was equipped. In 1905 construction of a small electric generating station also began in the village, and before the First World War some Abrièsois had electricity. In 1907 telephone lines were installed in the village, and in 1910 residents were given access to military phones in Le Roux. These services undoubtedly made life more comfortable for some, but they did not forestall the deterioration of the economic base of the community or out-migration.

TABLE 7
Seasonal distribution of births, Abriès, 1806-1902

	% of births in				Total births (N)
	1st quarter	2nd quarter	3rd quarter	4th quarter	
1806-12ᵃ	45	25	15	15	361
1813-22	45	27	12	15	557
1823-32	40	26	14	19	526
1833-42	39	29	14	18	245
1843-52	44	25	15	16	340
1853-62	37	24	21	18	345
1863-72	33	22	25	20	282
1873-82	31	24	26	20	219
1883-92ᵇ	25	30	26	19	212
1893-1902	27	24	28	21	199

ᵃ The 1803-5 records are missing.
ᵇ Figures do not include one illegible entry.
Source: ADHA 204M 1-10, Etat Civil, Table Decennale des Actes de Naissances, Mariages, Commune d'Abriès 1803-1902

MIGRATION

Seasonal migration had long played an important role in the economy of the village. In the first half of the nineteenth century many turned to profitable entrepreneurial jobs as peddlers of local products, especially cheeses, in the Midi. All through the 1850s, 1860s, and 1870s, the transportation networks of the south had enough interstitial slots to allow for individual petty traders. But when the southern cities, developed large retail stores and expanded railway and tramway lines into suburban areas people no longer had to wait for pack-carrying peddlers to come to them. The markets for peddlers began to shrink. At the same time, the village creameries became more and more oriented to selling their products to large wholesalers in Midi cities, bypassing individual retail sales. The era of small traders marketing home-produced products was drawing to a close.

We can date this change in seasonal migration patterns by looking at the birth months of the Abrièsois over time (Table 7). Random distribution of births would put about 25 per cent in each quarter. Instead, we find that in the first half of the nineteenth century, an average of 43 per cent of all births occurred in the winter quarter. Because so many village men would leave in the fall and return in the spring, children were conceived in the spring and summer, so January, February, and March were the common birth months. This pattern broke down in a very striking way in the second half of the century. By the 1880s births were spaced relatively evenly throughout the year. Seasonal migration was no longer dominant in the village.

A parallel way of confirming this hypothesis is to look at the months of marriage (Table 8). In the first half of the century about 90 per cent of all marriages took place in the spring and summer, after the men had returned from their seasonal expeditions. With the decline of seasonal migration, more people married in the fall and winter (although the spring and summer were still preferred seasons). By 1883-1902, some 35 per cent of marriages in Abriès were in fall and winter, as the ancient pattern of seasonal migration disappeared.

One area of seasonal employment that did open up for some Abrièsois after the First World War was selling roasted chestnuts on the street corners of Marseilles. This occupation lasted only from the end of October to January, a much shorter season than previous employments. Many villagers still recall their stints as chestnut sellers between the wars. Some women participated, but usually more men worked at this job, which the peasants themselves defined as low-status work.

Permanent Migrants

Pushed by the growing difficulty of making their livelihood in Abriès or even in seasonal migration elsewhere and pulled by the knowledge that a wider world with available work existed, the peasants adopted migration as their dominant strategy for dealing with change in the village.

Where did the migrants go? What did they do? Occasionally one reads in the 1870-1930 death records about men who became merchants and died in South America, Algeria, or even Russia. One young soldier had died in Senegal. But those scattered data do not give a complete picture. Villagers today say that relatives who migrated at the end of the nineteenth century went to the cities of Marseilles, Toulon, and Aix to become cheese merchants.

This perception is verified in data about registrants for the army. Every year twenty-year-old men were registered for national service. Registers kept about young men indicate professions and places of

TABLE 8
Seasonal distribution of marriages, Abriès, 1806-1902

	% of marriages in				Total marriages (N)
	1st quarter	2nd quarter	3rd quarter	4th quarter	
1806-12ᵃ	5	52	38	5	114
1813-22	6	37	52	4	143
1823-32	3	63	29	4	108
1833-42	3	60	29	9	104
1843-52	5	47	42	6	102
1853-62	2	77	15	6	53
1863-72	0	49	39	12	59
1873-82	5	63	20	12	76
1883-92	11	49	11	28	53
1893-1902	9	43	26	21	53

ᵃ The 1803-5 records are missing.
Source: ADHA 204M 1-10, Etat Civil, Table Decennale des Actes de Naissances, Mariages, Commune d'Abriès 1803-1902

residence, in addition to whether each was conscripted immediately, exempted, or placed in reserve. We thus have data about occupation and residence for twenty-year-old Abrièsois men from 1856 to 1899 (see Tables 9 to 11).

Between 1856 and 1874, about one-third of these young men were listed as residing outside the village. Soon the proportion reached one-half and even two-thirds. It was not that these young men were simply off on seasonal jobs; registry entries were all made in the summer – usually in June – when any seasonal migrant who also engaged in local farm work would have been back in Abriès. Rather, these men were living and working outside the village, many of them in the process of becoming permanent out-migrants.

Most of these non-residents were in Marseilles, Toulon, and Aix (Marseilles was the most common destination). Very few migrated within the Briançonnais or the department, where there were few work opportunities. Despite their farm backgrounds, few actually worked in a farm environment. Most worked as clerks, often involved with selling cheeses. None were working in the industrial sector. (In fact, although there were a few factories in the region – one in Argentière and another in Briançon – there is no evidence of any Abrièsois residing in these

TABLE 9
Registrants for military service (age 20), Abriès, 1856–99

	Total	Residing in village	Residing outside village[a]	
			N	%
1856–60	52	36	16	30.76
1861–5	44	30	14	31.81
1866–9[b]				
1870–4	41	27	14	34.14
1875–9	49	27	22	44.89
1880–4	37	12	25	67.56
1885–9	27	11	16	59.25
1890–4	42	14	28	66.66
1895–9	29	14	15	51.72

[a] Registry entries were made in the summer (May and June). Thus the men listed as residing outside the village were not on seasonal migrations but were actually working outside the village.
[b] The records for 1866–9 are missing.
Source: ADHA, series R, uninventoried

TABLE 10
Abriès military registrants, place of residence outside the village, 1856–99

	Marseilles, Toulon, and Aix	Hautes-Alpes	Paris and Lyon	Other, France	Other	Total
1856–60	12	2	1	1	0	16
1861–5	10	1	2	0	1[b]	14
1866–74						
1875–9	15	1	6			22
1880–4	21	0	2	1	1[c]	25
1885–9	12	1		2	1[d]	16
1890–4	20	1	6	0	1[d]	28
1895–9	12	0	2	1	0	15

[a] The records for 1866–9 are missing. The records for 1870–4 have no specific data on place of residence.
[b] Tunis
[c] Algeria
[d] Italy
Source: ADHA, series R, uninventoried

TABLE 11
Occupations of non-resident military registrants, Abriès, 1856–99

	Farm worker[a]	Merchant/ clerk[b]	Student[c]	Soldier	Customs	Chestnut peddler	?	Total
1856–60	0	14	2	0	0	0	0	16
1861–5	4	9	1	0	0	0	0	14
1866–9[d]								
1870–4	2	8	1	0	1	0	2	14
1875–9	7	4	0	0	1	0	10	22
1880–4	11	9	0	1	2	1	1	25
1885–9	3	6	1	1	1	0	4	16
1890–4	21[e]	5	1	1	0	0	0	28
1895–9	8[e]	6	0	0	1	0	0	15
Total	56	61	6	3	6	1	17	150

[a] Included here are men listed as domestiques and garçons de peine but not those listed as cultivateur except as explained in note d (see below).
[b] Included here are marchand de fromage, negociant, and employé de commerce.
[c] All students listed were ecclesiastical students at the Embrun Seminary.
[d] The records for 1866–9 are missing.
[e] Occupation listed as cultivateur, but urban residences, including street addresses, are given. Some of the individuals may have been recent migrants to the city. Or perhaps the language of record-keeping was changed.

towns.) The preferred choice was definitely the tertiary sector. Thus Abrièsois who were leaving the village were rapidly making the transition from peasants to clerks. They used the pre-existing networks of seasonal migration, which had set out the main directions, and followed their co-villagers to jobs in the cities of the Midi. While those who remained in the village were being integrated into a capitalist economy through industrial dairying, those obliged to leave often found their niches in another phase of that same industry.

It seems likely that the men who left the village in the second half of the nineteenth century had hopes of returning. After all, the data discussed so far were for military registrants listed as residing outside the village, not as permanently domiciled elsewhere. Data are also available on the migration of men in the army reserve from 1878 to 1894 (ADHA series R, uninventoried). The patterns here show that many men moved several times before taking up permanent residence outside Abriès. For example, one young man, a commercial clerk, was listed as residing in Marseilles in 1882 and 1883, moving to Paris in 1885, returning to Marseilles later that year, and then going back to Paris. In 1889 he was listed as domiciled in Marseilles and in 1892 in Toulon where he died in 1898. Thus between 1882 and 1889 this person considered himself domiciled in Abriès but residing elsewhere. It took seven years for him and the authorities to acknowledge that he was no longer an Abrièsois.

Of eighty-eight Abriès men who were in the reserve between 1878 and 1894, twenty-nine were eventually domiciled outside the village; it took them an average of almost nine years to make this transition.[3] These figures suggest that the decision to leave Abriès was a difficult one and that they long held out hope of returning to the village.

Throughout this book I argue that it was primarily economic factors that pushed people out of Abriès and economic factors that pulled them to places where they knew they could find work. In this I disagree with some alpine demographers who attribute emigration primarily to psychological factors, the 'psychose du départ' (emigration psychosis) (see, for example, Veyret 1952: 153). That approach is a mystification of the very real consequences of capitalist economic transformation. Veyret argues that people simply followed one another like sheep – an 'esprit moutonnier' – out of alpine villages which they left because everyone was doing it. Yet for many of the reservists at least, the decision to migrate permanently was not quick, and one cannot help but suspect material causes.

Women
There are other categories of people who left the village about whom we know very little. For example, we do not know very much about the women who left Abriès – who they were or where or why they went. Women who migrated between the wars but returned to the village say they went to keep house for their brothers and other male family members who went to the Midi and that they helped out (that is, were probably not paid) with work in the establishments which employed their kinsmen. Some sold roasted chestnuts on the street corners of Marseilles. Many women also worked as domestic servants.

3 The median was eight years. The shortest period of time to become domiciled outside Abriès was three years; the longest was twenty.

'Americains'

Not all the migration was within France. Some people went overseas. All through the Queyras are villas, large summer or retirement homes owned by Americains, Queyrassins who were successful migrants to South America and whose descendants have returned home to retire. Abriès has its Villa Bogota owned by the daughter of a man who made his fortune in Colombia. He is buried in the village, where his tombstone tells us that Guillaume Alphonse Richard, born in 1887, was a vice-president of the Chamber of Commerce of Bogota; he died in Panama in 1918. Richard left Abriès as a young man to join his uncles who had already established a department store – a general store which carried everything from guns to perfume – in Bogota. According to his daughter, Richard left home, seeking adventure, and as an act of rebellion; he wanted to study art, but his father wanted him to maintain the farm or go into commerce. He ended by becoming a successful businessman.

Richard returned to France to marry a Frenchwoman, and their children were born in Bogota. The sons who took over the business became Colombian citizens, but the daughter retained French citizenship. She too married a Frenchman and continued to keep contact with Abriès. During the political unrest in Colombia between 1945 and 1955, she and her husband and one daughter decided to return 'home' to France. Another daughter remained in Bogota, married to an Italian who owned a factory and a casino. But this daughter too retained her French citizenship, kept ties with Abriès, and returned to baptize her child in the village.

The Americains are mythologized in the Queyras. They are thought to have numbered in the hundreds and to have made great fortunes. Yet department data on the 559 passports issued between 1877 and 1909 shows that only thirty-two people were destined for Latin America or Mexico (ADHA 107M 2-3). In contrast, 326 went to Algeria. Yet villagers do not talk about those who went to North Africa. It is the Americains who returned home rich that people choose to remember.

In other words, those colonists who did not prosper have been dropped from popular consideration. The giant economic forces at play at the end of the nineteenth century have been reduced by many to a social-Darwinist equation of individual responsibility. As one Americain said to me, 'those who were clever went far ... those who were not sold chestnuts in Marseilles.' Similarly, Blanchard, who interviewed people in Aiguilles, a village four kilometres from Abriès, about

Latin American migration, argues that two-thirds to three-quarters of the migrants were unsuccessful. 'People talk about those who succeeded, always forgetting the unfortunate ones who sank into oblivion in the faraway continent of America without leaving a trace' (1922: 147).

CONTRASTS OF WEALTH AND CLASS

Italian Immigrants
One result of the massive out-migration in the second half of the nineteenth century was a severe summer labour shortage in Abriès. Historically, labour shortages in the village had been household-specific. Families that could not recruit labour from within, because children were too young or because only old people were left, hired workers. This hiring was as an adjunct to the domestic mode of production, compensating at a particular phase in the family life cycle for a lack of workers. Households aimed at generating labour from within by reproducing, not at hiring workers. For example, even at mid-century, most families that had domestiques had only one (Abriès 1846 census, nominative list).

By the 1880s, however, the labour shortage was a structural fact pervading the whole village economy. Almost all families had to hire labour. This widespread introduction of wage-labour into the village – a significant link in the transition to a capitalist economy – was done on a seasonal basis to cope with the demands of summer farm work.

The labourers who came to the village were Italian peasants working out a seasonal migration system which permitted them to take care of their own fields earlier in the summer and then come to the Queyras. (Given the ancient and persistent links between the Queyras and nearby Italian valleys, it is not surprising that Italians were aware of the French labour shortage.)

Older Abrièsois still remember the process of hiring Italians in annual spring labour markets held in the central square of Abriès, during which contracts for the coming season were struck and sealed with a handshake. The villagers today agree that hundreds of Italians came to the Queyras and that each Abriès family employed at least three people. Specialists at haying, the highest-paid workers, made about 90 francs for the season. Women and children were also hired to harvest and look after animals; women were paid less than men, and children received the lowest salaries – about 50 francs. Some day-labourers were hired for shorter periods at 3 to 10 francs a day. The seasonal workers received room and board, but the day-labourers did not.

Many of these workers eventually settled in Abriès, for if the Abrièsois were poor, the Italians were even poorer. For example, one Italian woman who married an Abrièsois man was happy to meet someone who owned a 'domaine,' even if it was only three hectares. Other Italians came to work as masons, shoemakers, and dressmakers. Still others rented land in Abriès, becoming fermiers who paid just enough to cover the property tax. By 1911, some 12 per cent of the 668 people resident in Abriès were Italian citizens.

Merchant Emigrants
One of the fundamental characteristics of the transition to a capitalist economy in France was the movement outside the village of control of decision-making in production. It was no longer Abrièsois peasants within the household or even the co-operative creameries who decided what to make and how to make it. Starting in 1890, when Toye-Riont signed his contract with Abriès and other Queyras dairies, decisions of production were made by the milk purchasers who lived outside the village. This pattern was reinforced after the First World War, when the Nestlé Company came to dominate the scene. The Abrièsois, although still living on the land, meeting some of their subsistence needs within the village, and technically owning the means of production, had become part of a wage system which proletarianized their labour in so far as it related to dairying. This is the difference between peasant production in a peasant society and peasant production under capitalism.

Before the Nestlé Corporation took over, it was wholesalers such as the ex-villager Toye-Riont who determined what kinds of cheeses would be made and controlled major production decisions. Other prosperous ex-villagers living in Marseilles, Toulon, and Aix also played important roles as potential employers for migrants and as people who involved themselves directly in village affairs. They acted as patrons and benefactors, often providing the capital for village projects which the state would not provide. The *Délibérations du Conseil Municipal* from 1887 to 1913 (AMA) show that ex-villagers left money in their wills for hospital construction, for school construction, for church and cemetery improvements, and for charity to the poor. They also intervened directly in the village economy with various projects.

Wealth and Class

Thus the ties between the ex-villagers and Abrièsois were very strong. Many of the former returned to marry within the village or the valley. Some had their children wet-nursed by village women, and most retained land and houses in Abriès, renting out the land and maintaining the houses as summer residences. To this day some retired merchants return to Abriès in the spring to participate in the annual path-clearing corvées which prepare the transhumant routes. In the late nineteenth century many Marseilles, Toulon, and Aix merchant families considered themselves part of the village, and the villagers agreed with this definition. Given these families' economic relation to the village, they actually formed its upper class.

At the same time that the Abriès elite was consolidating outside the village, the residents began to hire labour systematically for the agricultural season. These Italian workers were also part of the wage system and the proletarianization of labour. They were the lower class of the village. Like the upper class, they lived outside its geographical confines for much of the year. When they worked in Abriès they were called 'les troussiers' after a word describing the burden a mule carries. The term was used not with scorn but as descriptive of their hard work – and in a real sense they did bear the burden of production. (The importance of the wage to the Italian seasonal migrants can be seen in the fact that they continued to come to the Queyras all through the 1920s and 1930s, even after the border had been closed by the Italian Fascist regime.)

In the middle, between the elite and the lower class, were the Abrièsois cultivators. They hired labour, yet they worked for others. There were, of course, wealth distinctions within this group. The man who owned 200 of the 571 cows in the village in 1892 was obviously wealthier than the villagers who owned fewer animals, but in terms of the relations of production and the control of decision-making in production he too worked for the Midi merchant families and later the Nestlé Corporation. The Abriès cultivators *sur place* formed the middle class of a class system whose boundaries must be traced to networks beyond the village.

The old regime had also seen power and wealth distinctions among the Abrièsois. But the eighteenth-century elite of the village did not control decisions of production. The Berthelots had wealth and power, but they did not have people working for them. Their power came from their legal expertise. They were local functionaries who were gradually differentiating themselves out of village life. The Midi merchants of the late nineteenth century, such as Toye-Riont, were capitalists who intervened directly in the village economy and, as we shall see, used it as their basis for political power-holding.

This class system of Abriès was also ranked by wealth. The Italians were the poorest; village testimony, to their situation is confirmed by a study of Italians who married into Abriès. Unlike most villagers, they tended not to make marriage contracts because they did not have enough wealth. Those who did make contracts were usually Italian men who had a trade such as shoemaker. Three marriage contracts described in the registry of civil acts (ADHA series Q, uninventoried, Bureau d' Aiguilles) in 1885, have the phrase 'ne possède rien' (possesses nothing) in relation to the men while the Abriès women involved did bring a few hundred francs to their marriages.

At the other end of the spectrum were the extremely wealthy Midi merchant families, usually officially domiciled in southern cities but coming to Abriès for rites of passage such as marriage ceremonies. We can get a sense of their wealth from their marriage contracts, many of which were drawn by local notaries and registered in the village. An example is the 1864 contract between Pierre Audier-Merle and Benoîte Adrienne Audier-Merle recorded by the notary Laurens of Abriès (ADHA 1E7374). Pierre is described as a businessman domiciled in Marseilles but born in Abriès of Abrièsois parents. Benoîte, also born in the village, was still domiciled there. Pierre brought into the marriage the considerable fortune of 100,000 francs 'en numéraire' (in cash). Benoîte brought a dowry of 100,000 francs, money compiled from the estates of her father and her aunt, and 'the profits she has realized in commerce together with her brother ... Cheese Merchant in Marseilles (ADHA 1E7374). Obviously, large sums of money could be made in the cheese trade. The dowry money was to be invested at 3 per cent interest for the benefit of both spouses acting jointly.

This contract was not an isolated case. Several out-migrant merchant families were enormously wealthy. In 1878, Hyacinthe Martin, born in Abriès and domiciled in Toulon, signed a marriage contract in Abriès with nineteen-year-old Marguerite Martin, who was born in Toulon. Hyacinthe, a property owner of means brought 100,000 francs into the marriage; Marguerite, whose father was a cheese merchant in Toulon, brought railway stocks to the value of 49,482 francs. Hyacinthe's brother, Pierre Ernest Martin, a Marseilles cheese merchant, signed a marriage contract at age thirty-two with Abriès-born

Marguerite Audier; she brought 51,000 francs into the agreement, and he brought 110,000 francs. Other merchant out-migrants brought lesser but substantial wealth into their marriages.

In marriages between Abrièsois cultivators we find much lower dowries. For forty-eight marriages between cultivators in the twenty years 1871–85 and 1895–9, the three highest dowries were 5500, 6000, and 7500 francs. The remaining forty-five dowries were between 200 and 2300 francs – a far cry from the huge sums the Midi merchant families brought to their marriages.

Villagers who were not cultivators tended to have higher dowries. Several women with high dowries married men whose occupations were listed as 'rentier' or 'propriétaire' – that is, they made their living through investments and the renting of land and property. To be able to marry such men, these women had to bring relatively large dowries into the marriage; thus their cultivator families must have had more wealth than other cultivators in Abriès. During the 1895–9 period, the records show eleven marriages between cultivators; the average dowry was 690 francs and the median 600 francs. But in 1897 one woman whose occupation was listed as cultivator married a 'propriétaire' and she brought more than 16,000 francs into the marriage. During the same five-year period a village businesswoman brought the enormous dowry of 66,805 francs into a marriage with a 'propriétaire.'

Thus, it is clear that there was some wealth in the village and that it was unevenly distributed. That five-year period was a time when most Abrièsois were desperately scrambling from one project to the next in an attempt to make money. The merchant woman likely obtained her wealth from her position as village banker/creditor (much as Richard-Calve had during the Revolutionary period); her family also had alliances with Midi merchant families. The registry entry noted that she had numerous debtors in Abriès and Embrun and many investments in French, Italian, Austrian, and the trans-Siberian railways (ADHA series Q, uninventoried, Bureau d' Aiguilles).

If we compare the range of women's dowries through the end of the eighteenth century with those of the nineteenth, an interesting pattern of increasing inequality of wealth emerges (see Figure 6[4]). In Chapter

4 The data used for Figure 6 were assembled and calculated in the following manner.

Between 1780 and 1865, all marriage contracts that were registered were also recorded by the authorities in tables which indicate the cash value of dowries,

2, we calculated the difference between the 20 per cent of Abriès women with the highest dowries and the 20 per cent with the lowest dowries in the 1744-8 period and concluded that in the mid-eighteenth century the rich were only about four or five times richer than the poor, using dowry amounts as the criterion. If we construct a similar index of wealth distribution through the end of the nineteenth century, we see that the differences grow sharply and then decrease. I attribute the increase in the first part of the nineteenth century to an early period of capital accumulation, when many people were profiting from cheese sales and the general economic boom. After the crash in mid-century, wealth differences within the village were markedly reduced as migrants from both ends of the scale left the village, though the relative homogeneity of the mid-eighteenth century never returned.

In ideological terms, however, these differences were not recognized within the village which placed more emphasis than ever before on

including trousseaus (ADHA, series Q, uninventoried, 'Table des contrats de mariages, Aiguilles,' vol. 1-6, 1780-1865). The marriage data for 1807 and 1808 are missing; so are some tables from 1821 and 1830. Excluding the two years for which there are no data, Abriès had 692 marriages between 1780 and 1865; of these, 631 (91.8 per cent) had contracts.

Sometimes the tables also show the amounts men brought into marriage, but these records were not kept systematically. Therefore the data base used here is female dowries only.

Some contracts specified not a particular amount but a promise of future rights on maternal or paternal succession. In these cases, I considered the dowry amount to be zero, taking the arrangement as an indication that the bride's family could not mobilize any wealth at the time of the marriage.

I chose not to try to retrieve dowry figures directly from individual contracts to offset the missing tables for 1821 and 1830. I did, however, take that route in compiling figures for 1871 to 1890, for which there are no separate listings of dowry amounts. I retrieved the data directly from the civil acts (ADHA, series Q, uninventoried, Bureau d'Aiguilles). During those nineteen years, 101 marriages were registered in Abriès and 90 marriage contracts were signed. Of these, usable data were ultimately available for 59 marriages.

Where possible, I grouped all these data into ten-year periods. An index of wealth difference was calculated by comparing the highest 20 per cent of the dowries to the lowest 20 per cent. The scale on the y axis of Figure 6 is thus an indicator of how many times richer the top 20 per cent of brides' families were in comparison to the bottom 20 per cent.

To compare these data with data from the mid-eighteenth century, see Chapter 2, Table 1.

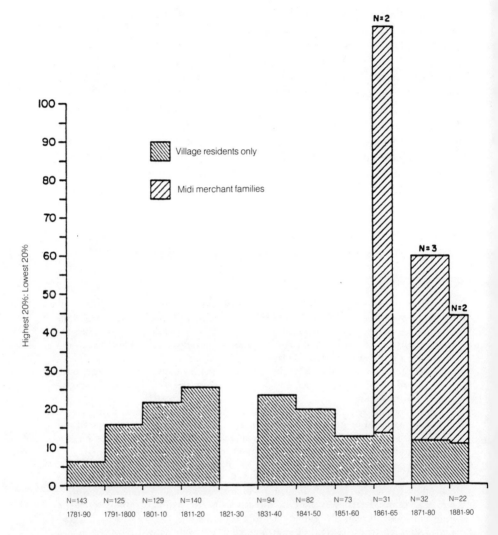

FIGURE 6 Wealth inequality of Abriésois, 1780–1890 (see footnote 4 for method of calculation)

egalitarianism. 'We are all the same here' is the phrase used in a manuscript of village and valley history undertaken by the Abbé Berge, writing in Abriès circa 1920. He could write, with some justification, that
most villagers were poor but equal because he did not consider the
Italian labourers or the Midi merchant families in his equation. Conspicuous displays of wealth within the village were still frowned upon,
and there were many outward signs of shared poverty. Berge argued
that the village had always been poor, but the egalitarianism of villagers had made the burden easier to bear. The poverty of Abriès he
explained as stemming from ancient, unchanging circumstances – an
act of God and therefore beyond human control. This opinion coincided with official explanations of poverty in the region and influenced
the views of later observers who saw the region's failure to modernize as
the typical lot of peasant societies.

'POLITICAL LIFE REDUCED TO A MINIMUM'

As we saw in Chapter 4, the property qualifications for voting in
national elections were so high during the nineteenth century that the
Abrièsois, like most Hautes-Alpins, were effectively disenfranchised
and thus had no institutional channels for influencing the central government. The qualifications for village electors were only somewhat
less stringent. Moreover, voting in local contests was an act of futility
since the system of governance imposed by the central state gave little
authority to the elected council. The real power lay with the mayor,
who was chosen by the departmental prefect. Thus the Queyras, once
the region of the egalitarian escarton system, became infamous for the
dictatorial powers of its mayors, who operated as police, tax collectors,
justices of the peace, and bailiffs. Thivot has argued that Queyrassins
accepted and even appreciated this system because it saved them legal
expenses – mayors did not accept fees as justices of the peace (1971:
56). Yet, since Queyrassins had no alternatives, one may well ask what
choice they had but to accept the imposed system.

By the Revolution of 1848, when universal male suffrage was introduced,[5] the dominant political system of the Hautes-Alpes was
patronage. Throughout the Second Republic (1848–51), when other

5 Silver (1980) argues that even after universal male suffrage was introduced, the
   domination of local notables continued until the legislative elections of 1876 and
   1877 throughout France.

departments were turning to the left, the Hautes-Alpes remained in the grip of patronage politics. Vigier (1963: I, 128–33) has described the situation as entirely corrupt – so 'pourri' (rotten) and pervasive that the revolutionaries of the Second Republic felt they could make no serious effort to change the system but worked through it.[6] For the Queyras, the shock of depoliticization introduced by the post-Revolutionary regimes, in contrast to the political system of the Escartons, had been paralysing. Queyrassins had been used to working with and through a system that exerted some leverage on the centre. Suddenly they had been thrust into a situation in which most decision-making came from the centre. Furthermore, state surveillance and repression had become a feature of daily life.

Power-Holders

In addition, debtor relationships now tied many Queyrassins to a particular patron. In the mid-nineteenth century, Puy, a former justice of the peace for the valley of the Queyras, for example, controlled an enormous number of debtors there, much as Richard-Calve had done before him. With this power at a time when foreclosures for debt were increasing, Puy was able to control and direct votes right through the Second Republic (ibid. II 413–29). The prefect of the department, while deploring Puy's power, did not take the step of cancelling debts. And if the Queyrassins had attempted to cancel debts on their own initiative, the government would likely have come to Puy's aid, opposing any peasant resistance as a threat to the established legal/property system, as it did when it suppressed peasant uprisings over forest occupation in 1848. (This contradiction within the Second Republic suggests the key to its willingness to accept support from, and perpetuate patronage politics in the Hautes-Alpes.)

Queyrassins made the transition from the Second Republic to the dictatorship of Louis-Napoleon without violence. Other parts of France had peasant uprisings and mass arrests, but the Queyras was quiet.[7] In Abriès the same individual who had been named mayor by

---

6 See Vigier (1963: II, 413–29) for a comparison between the Hautes-Alpes and the Basses-Alpes in this regard. See Judt (1979) for a discussion of socialist mobilization in Provence.

7 Margadant (1980) recounts the uprising of 100,000 peasants in 900 communes protesting the coup of Louis Napoleon in 1851. He shows that in many communes resistance to government repression was mobilized through secret

the revolutionary commission of 1848 was named mayor again by the subprefect under Louis-Napoleon in 1852 (ADHA 70M, 1848; 71M, 1852).

Throughout the Second Empire the prefect continued to name village mayors and assistants. In 1860, Claude Richard-Calve, a merchant, was named mayor of Abriès; he continued to hold that office until 1878 – through the Second Empire and into the Third Republic. What is fascinating is that the prefect during the Second Empire and the prefect under the Third Republic approved the appointment with the same observation: Richard-Calve was 'loyal to the government' (ADHA 72M4, 1860; 75M21, 1874). Similarly, Jean Bourcier, another merchant and an assistant mayor under both regimes, was described as devoted to the government under both.

The clue to the survival of these municipal officers can be found in a subprefect's 1874 reports on them. The most telling comment concerns Bourcier; the subprefect noted that he had held office since 1861, that he was wealthy with an annual revenue of 4500 francs, and, most important, that he was 'sans opinions politiques, probe, estimé, et convenant parfaitement' (without political opinions, upright, well thought of, and perfectly acceptable). The second assistant mayor from the hamlet of Le Roux was praised on similar grounds; he was wealthy, kept the civil registers in a neat handwriting, and was 'without marked political opinions' (ADHA 75M2 1).

Throughout the rest of the nineteenth century and well into the twentieth, praise for being apolitical is the most common compliment paid by state administrators to local politicians. In 1935 a confidential memo from the prefect of the Hautes-Alpes to the minister of the interior assured the latter that he had no reason to fear any opposition to the government in the Hautes-Alpes, where 'political life has been reduced to its minimum.' The prefect attributed this lack of political interest to the fact that the Hautes-Alpes contained an almost exclusively rural population 'where ... political questions recede into the background, only questions of personalities or of local interests matter' (ADHA 77M 3).

---

societies. Abriès was silent during these protests, perhaps because of the high levels of government surveillance within this village. Merriman (1977) offers case studies of repression under the Second Republic in Limoges and the departments of the Nord, the Creuse, Arriège, Finistère, and the Yonne.

Underlying this perception of politics with regard to the state is the equation that supporting the government is equal to being apolitical – an extremely narrow definition of politics which implies that what the government itself does is not political. This stance is closely associated with what Barrington Moore calls Catonism: a romanticization of so-called peasant virtues – simplicity, hard work, honesty – which occurs 'where commercial relationships have begun to undermine a peasant economy' (1966: 491). Romanticization of a disintegrating peasant economy was exactly what was going on under the Second Empire. Prefects and subprefects in the Hautes-Alpes eloquently extolled simple peasant virtues, one of which was not dirtying oneself with politics, at precisely the moment when the peasant economy was being commercialized. Thus in 1876 the prefect of the Hautes-Alpes could say of village political life: 'In general, the mayors and assistants elected are simple farmers – landowners who ask nothing but to peace-fully cultivate their fields, [they are] in agreement with the government and the administration' (ADHA 76M1).

Such rhetoric was quite inaccurate in the case of Abriès. Through-out the nineteenth century most of its mayors and assistant mayors were not cultivators but merchants. Of the ten men who were mayors in Abriès from 1807 to 1912, six were merchants, one was a notary, and three were described as property owners; none was a cultivator. The three 'propriétaires' may have engaged in some agriculture, but we cannot consider them full-time cultivators because we know the word 'cultivateur' was used to describe the occupation of the few con-tempory municipal council members who actually made their living from agriculture (ADHA 68M4–77M1; 80M1).

Official Surveillance
The romantic ideology of honest peasant virtue has historically been combined with a repressive social order that buttresses the position of those who hold power. 'It denies the need for further social changes, especially revolutionary ones. [It] ... may also relieve the conscience of those most responsible for the damage' (Moore 1966: 491).

In the case of Abriès and the Queyras, the political discourse which made a virtue of equating rural simplicity, local political apathy, and support for whichever government was in power was closely linked to bureaucratic surveillance within villages. Throughout the nineteenth century, the political life of Abriès was constantly watched by represen-tatives of the state – gendarmes, forest agents, customs officials, and, in the late nineteenth century, special railway police who patrolled the border.[8] In addition, soldiers constantly patrolled the border between the Briançonnais and Italy. Reports from the 'commissaires spéciaux de police aux frontières' (special border patrol) to the Ministry of the Interior from 1887 to 1893 reveal just how closely watched life was in Abriès (ADHA 92 M1 3; 2Z 122, Briançon). In those years all travellers, especially Italians, to the village's Wednesday market were stopped and questioned by the border police or the army. The mule trade and all animal fairs were watched, and reports written on the trade. The presence of any notable in Abriès was the occasion for a descriptive report. Anyone visiting Italy, trading with Italians, hiring an Italian, or marrying an Italian was the subject of memoranda to the army, the minister of the interior, or the prefect.

The implication of all this activity was that war between France and Italy was imminent and that the central government was, as always, suspicious of Abrièsois (and Queyrassins) for having such close ties with Italy. Many reports described the movements of suspected spies in the border region, and most complained of the lack of co-operation that Abrièsois exhibited in spy-catching activities.

One 1882 report provides a good example of this intense scrutiny. The report, written by a 'commissionaire spécial de police aux frontières' and destined for the minister of the interior, described the celebration of 14 July in the Queyras. The commissaire found that only functionaries and state employees celebrated the holiday with any zeal. The people of the Queyras were cold and indifferent to the 'national celebration' and thus without patriotic feeling – 'No French fibre causes their hearts to beat.' He concluded by saying that he thought the Queyrasins would welcome the Italians with open arms rather than fight them if war came (ADHA93 M1 3).

Such surveillance is a very concrete form of social control and certainly would have inhibited overt expression of political opposition. Not surprisingly, we have no specific documentation of collective violence in Abriès during this period – not even during the opposition to the Forest Administration in the late 1840s.[9] What we find instead of overt action is tales of opposition expressed by non-cooperation with

8 Other Hautes-Alpin villages probably did not have this full complement of surveillance officials but they would have had gendarmes and forest agents at the least.

9 Vigier (1963: I, 204–6) does note popular revolts and occupations in the Briançonnais as well as most stock-raising areas of the Alps. He also describes the fearful response of the new administration of the Second Republic to such 'disorders': it used military force to reclaim the forests for the state.

the surveillance authorities: villagers saying they knew nothing when asked questions by such officials. Smuggling in Abriès probably had political overtones of defiance and resistance. Present-day Abrièsois are certainly very proud of having outwitted customs officials during the 1930s, one elderly cultivator from a nearby Briançonnais village described to me exploits of the late nineteenth century in which whole flocks of sheep were brought in from Italy. Village solidarity rallied around smugglers if they were caught. In sheep-smuggling cases, for example, customs officials had been instructed to auction off the animals, but no villagers would bid except the smuggler himself, who would get the sheep for a trivial sum, pay the fine, and come out ahead.

Another form of depoliticization was the Forest Administration's seizure of local resources and of control of economic development in the villages of the Queyras. (Balandier [1970] describes similar situations in which important resources are taken over by a colonial regime which disguises its control as an administrative rather than a political matter.) Even in this matter, the supposedly apolitical Abrièsois managed some political resistance. Again it was in the form of non-cooperation (refusing to abolish vaîne pâture and keeping the commons undivided) rather than collective violence, which would have been very difficult considering the policing agencies within the village as well as the village's dependence on the state for financial assistance. This careful political manoeuvring between compliance and resistance was the hallmark of political life in Abriès in the nineteenth century as it is today.[10]

POWER-HOLDERS: MARIUS AND MAURICE TOYE-RIONT

Another aspect of the depoliticization of Abriès had to do with particular client-patron relations which connected the village to the supra-local political and economic system. By the end of the nineteenth cen-

---

10 'I have seen nothing to indicate that the silent masses kept silent because of repression rather than indifference' is Weber's introduction to fourteen pages of description of government manipulation of nineteenth-century local elections (1982: 372–86). It is not clear to the reader why government interference should not be considered part of a modern political system or why the state would have bothered with such concerted efforts if the peasantry had been as indifferent as Weber claims.

tury the most powerful person in Abriès was Marius Toye-Riont (1849–98). His method and arena of power-holding provide a striking contrast to those previous village notables. In comparison to his prede-cessors, the Berthelots and Richard-Calve, Toye-Riont had the most direct control over the economic life of Abriès. He combined that economic power with political office to become the most important patron in the life of the village. (The biographical data on the Toye-Riont family in this section is from Pons [n.d.].)

The Father: Marius Toye-Riont
Significantly, Marius Toye-Riont did not live in Abriès. His father, Jean, had migrated to Marseilles, where, in 1867, he founded a cheese business that was destined to become one of the most famous in the city. Marius was raised in Abriès by his aunts, his mother having died in childbirth. At age twelve he went to study in Marseilles, and, as soon as he was able, he joined his father's business. In 1875 he married a woman who was originally from Abriès but whose family had gone into business in Lyon.

Marius was one of the first Midi merchants to recognize the economic benefits to be gained from direct control of Queyras dairy products. As early as 1878, when an agent of the Forest Administration was drumming up business for these products in the Midi, Marius had already begun to make contacts with the village of Ristolas for all rights to its production. By 1890, when the co-operative dairies were going under, Toye-Riont was able to step into the situation, in the guise of a concerned fellow-countryman and benefactor, and take effective con-trol of fifteen Queyras dairies. The contract, as we have seen, was enor-mously advantageous to him and assured him a dominant role in the economy of Abriès and the Queyras.

In 1891, Marius entered politics as a candidate for member of the departmental council. The election was disputed, but he eventually took office, and held it until his death in 1898. Office-holding greatly enhanced Toye-Riont's economic power. He had the ear of the govern-ment and was in a position to get all-important subsidies to Queyras cultivators, in return for loyalty. For Marius, the exchange always returned to his entrepreneurial activities. He was a champion of improved roads for Abriès, not solely because of agricultural needs but also because he had built a large tourist hotel in Abriès and needed access to it. We find in the General Council debates (DCG 1897) that

Toye-Riont argued vigorously in the interests of agriculture for roads connecting Abriès to Aiguilles and Le Roux. He did not deny that the hotel would also benefit, but he claimed roads and the hotel would benefit the economy of such a poor region.

The records on the hotel project reveal just how Toye-Riont was able to use his political position for economic benefit. In 1897, he had worked out a deal with the mayor of Abriès in which the village was to supply the hotel with free water (that is at public expense). A member of the Arrondissement Council was aghast that the mayor of Abriès should grant such special favours, saying, 'This free appropriation for the profit of a private company is prejudicial to communal interests' (ADHA 2Z428). He, the subprefect, and the agent for the Water and Forest Administration all argued in letters to the mayor that the hotel should at least pay an annual fee for the water and should attempt to get it from a different source because the hotel would deprive agriculturalists. The mayor made occasional replies to these letters, saying that he had never received any complaint. The outraged subprefect wrote that Toye-Riont was abusing his position: 'The General Councillor for the Canton has initiated the construction of a Hotel at Abriès merely in order to further his financial and electoral interests' (ibid.).

Toye-Riont, whose politics had been described by the prefect in 1895 as 'douteux' (doubtful) (ADHA 64M 13), triumphed over all this opposition with the help of his loyal clients in Abriès and his position as president of the council.

Needless to say, this use of the public interest for private gain did not find its way into official descriptions of Toye-Riont's role in Queyrassin life. The public version of his role as patron, benefactor, and loyal native son is found in his death notice. The author of the obituary, reflecting the economic philosophy of his time, had nothing but praise for Toye-Riont's business methods – especially with regard to the Grand Hotel of Abriès, which, he said, demonstrated why individual rather than government initiative would always be successful (Roche 1898).

In a sense, Marius Toye-Riont operated as a robber baron, buying the cheap raw materials of the Queyras for his wholesale trade and using politics to further his business interests. This exploitation was somewhat disguised by a display of village patriotism – the sort of sentiment that might, in a non-European context, be called ethnic solidarity or tribal loyalty. Thus he acted as a patron to Abriès showing his concern for the village by being a church benefactor and trying to solve the winter unemployment problem by the introduction of artisanal activities. But his main benefit to the Abrièsois was buying their dairy products.

The Son: Maurice Toye-Riont

After Marius's death and especially after the First World War, Abriès and the Queyras were converted to industrial dairying and the production of raw milk. Toye-Riont economic interests changed as well. Maurice Toye-Riont (1876–1950), who had inherited his father's business, used the accumulated capital to convert to an industrial enterprise that specialized in the manufacture of lard and margarine – products which used cotton-seed oil imported from the United States (Opperman 1926: 235, 446, 488). Thus he did not pursue dairy interests in the Queyras although he did attempt to use the village and valley to further a political career.

Although Maurice was very wealthy, his resources were more limited and his support base far less secure in the villages of the Queyras than his father's had been. He did not have clear control over the villages' economy, and he could not offer the same economic rewards. Furthermore, as a famous urban industrialist it was harder for him to maintain the fiction of being a peasant at heart – a fact thrown up to him during election campaigns. Unlike his father, Maurice encountered much local opposition to his political ambitions. Yet Maurice needed village support. He was on the far right politically, and it would have been very difficult for him to enter politics in socialist Marseilles.

At first glance, Maurice's political career is very puzzling. He was a poor politician and a poor patron. In 1914, for example, he ran for re-election – and thus had a distinct advantage – in a three-way race for the office of deputy from Briançonnais. French elections are two-tiered, and after the first round he was only 251 votes behind the front-runner. The third candidate was a socialist who had received only 507 votes and should have been the one to withdraw before the second vote. Yet Toye-Riont was so anti-socialist that rather than accept socialist votes – the newspapers described him as going into a fury at the thought of doing so (Le Petit Briançonnais, 10 May 1914) – he himself withdrew. Throwing an election on ideological grounds is certainly not the mark of a dedicated politician.

Neither was Maurice Toye-Riont a dedicated patron. The favours he secured for Abriès were on a very small scale indeed and often consisted of promises of moral support rather than any actual outlay of

cash. For example, before the First World War the Abrièsois were trying to raise money to supplement funds which had been left the village
in a will to build a hospital. Maurice said that he supported the
hospital plan, but he gave no money. In his years as deputy (1910–14)
he was able to raise only one subsidy for the village of Abriès – 700
francs for canal repair (Toye-Riont 1914).

Today in the courtyard of the church of Abriès there is a plaque
dedicated to Maurice Toye-Riont as general councillor (1919–45) and
senator (1929–45) in the department. Yet when I asked the villagers
what he did to merit the plaque, some responded that he did nothing,
that some people just *think* they are important.

And that is the clue to Maurice Toye-Riont's rather odd behaviour
as a power-holder. He really had no power; he only thought he did. He
had no power in the village, because he had no economic benefits to
offer and because he would not tap his personal resources and act as a
benefactor/patron. Neither had he any power within the central government; as an office-holder in the 1930s in the underdeveloped and
historically pro-government department of the Hautes-Alpes, he was
an expendable and unimportant person.[11] From the point of view of
the government, the region he represented was entirely safe and did
not have to be bought off with loans, which were scarce during the
depression and could be better used in more politically uncertain
areas. Thus Toye-Riont had no access to resources, and he promised
none. In a 1932 speech, for example, he proposed a plan to rejuvenate
the Haute-Alpin economy by creating co-operatives. The key to the
plan was that it would cost no money (Toye-Riont 1932: 22). A politician who admits that he has no access to money is a politician without
power.

CONCLUSION

Maurice Toye-Riont was not a power-holder; he was a place-holder, a
person simply filling a structural slot. If we compare him to previous
Abriès notables, we see that he was the end of the line of village-
generated power-holders. The Berthelots were important power-
holders, operating in a complex system. Richard-Calve too was signifi-

---

11 In 1945 Maurice, who had been a supporter of Pétain, was declared ineligible to
run for public office again.

cant to the central government and to the village. By the time of the
Toye-Rionts, however, the village was no longer a meaningful unit
from the perspective of the central government, so it was not village
power-holders who were important. Marius Toye-Riont lived in Marseilles and representing Abriès was only a fragment from his cluster of
interests. By Maurice's time, the whole department was politically
insignificant. The fact that Maurice Toye-Riont did not wield power
was a direct reflection of the powerlessness of the village and the
region. A politician without power, he was a perfect example of the
depoliticization of politics in Abriès and the whole department.

7

Tourism and Agriculture: Village Life
in the Twentieth Century

Abriès was hit hard by the depression of the 1930s and by the Second World War. During the 1920s, when milk prices were relatively high, the population of the village stabilized at about 400 people. By 1932 milk prices began to fall, from 96 to 88 centimes a litre on average (Guicherd 1933: 252). By 1935 the Nestlé Company was buying milk in the Queyras at about 55 centimes a litre (ADHA 256 M 1). Many Abrièsois remember the 1930s as a time when it was impossible to negotiate with Nestlé and producers were forced to accept extremely low prices: 'They gave us two sous per litre. Just imagine – two sous.'

RE-PEASANTIZATION

To make ends meet, many villagers took up options from their pre-capitalist past. They began to raise sheep and goats more intensively for domestic use and barter. Some families returned to making ewe's-milk and goat's-milk cheeses for use within the household and for exchange at Abriès's Wednesday markets. They tried for self-sufficiency in grain and potato production. They hired fewer Italian labourers and paid the ones they did hire as little as possible, arguing that room and board was an important payment in itself. The Abrièsois also remember the depression as a time when the only way to survive was to intensify labour. People worked long hours and used their ingenuity to make things rather than buy them. Women, especially, recall this period as one of self-exploitation, when they economized by doing as much as they could at home. One village woman epitomizes the depression for herself in terms of endlessly ripping out outgrown sweaters and reknitting them for her children. She began to dread a certain shade of blue yarn because she had reworked it so frequently.

It was a period when the village economy looked very much like a peasant society that had not changed for centuries. A little later, when agricultural experts surveyed the Queyras in the 1950s, that vision was what they thought they saw. Yet the economy of the 1930s was not a continuation of ancient tradition and ancient poverty but an adaptation to a world-wide economic crisis. Abriès was retrenching – re-peasantizing itself – to cope with a major crisis in capitalism.

There were other adaptations. Smuggling became increasingly important even as patrols and surveillance along the Italian border intensified. Some Abrièsois, despairing of the low prices paid by Nestlé, took to peddling their products directly in the lowlands. One montagnard told me that the milk they sold was sometimes watered, although others denied it. Almost every Abriès family sent a member to sell roasted chestnuts on the street corners of Marseilles between late October and January. Abrièsois had a virtual monopoly on chestnut kiosks there for which they paid the city a small fee. The money earned went towards paying taxes. The chestnuts sellers economized in every possible way while living in the city. They spent no money on amusements and as little as possible on food and lodging. They thought of themselves as very thrifty in comparison to the Marseillais, whom they perceived to be throwing money away on expensive meals.

In addition to these individual and household strategies, the villagers employed important collective strategies. Peasants organized informal insurance associations, specific to quarters and hamlets, as a form of protection against the loss or injury of draught and herd animals. If a mule went lame, the peasants of that quarter would take turns lending its owner their mules. If the animal had not recovered after ten days, the association divided the cost of purchasing a replacement. They made a group decision about the value of the loss, taking circumstances into account. If, for example, the mule owner had been careless or had neglected his animal, he was not paid the full amount. If the owner was young and inexperienced, he was awarded more money than someone who should have known better.

The same system applied if a herd animal was lost. Peasants took turns watching over their herds in the pastures in spring and fall. The work input expected depended on the number of animals placed in the herd; each member of the group put in one day of animal tending for each ten sheep or one cow. If an animal died, it was replaced by the group. Collective responsibility did not extend to the summer periods, when village herds were joined with transhumant animals; then the responsibility was that of the transhumant shepherd.

Other forms of collective labour organization persisted from earlier times. Corvées were still organized for road and canal maintenance. All villagers had access to firewood from the communal forest, and their animals could graze free in the communal pastures.

These collective forms within the economy made it possible for many Abrièsois to survive on the land. Nevertheless many people left the village in the 1930s. The out-migrants tended to come from families with five or six children. Often they were sent to work for relatives who had stores in Marseilles, Toulon, or Aix; the expectation was that they would eventually return to the village and in the meantime would send money home. But after a few years most decided to stay in the south. Of twenty-seven people I traced who migrated out permanently during the depression, most became clerks and small businessmen. One became a policeman, another worked for the French national electricity company, and two moved to a nearby village to continue working as shoemakers.

THE SECOND WORLD WAR

Permanent out-migration intensified during the Second World War. In 1940 there was heavy fighting in the region, and three Abriès men were killed. Women, children, and old people were evacuated to southwestern France for a few months as Italian troops advanced on the Queyras. Many of the older people decided to stay in the south, rather than return to Abriès. Those who returned after the 1940 cease-fire found that the boundary had placed all land east of the village under Italian jurisdiction, encapsulating the central agglomeration of Abriès. In order to move from their homes in Abriès to their fields or to the hamlet of Le Roux, the Abrièsois required passports.

Today the Abrièsois do not remember the Italian occupation as particularly severe. During the evacuation the villagers had saved some of their herd animals by driving them into the forests and high pastures; now they were able to reclaim many of them. (Most of their horses and mules had previously been requisitioned by the French army.) The change that most people remarked on to me was the teaching of Italian as well as French in school in La Roux. The Italian troups were not methodical in patrolling the border area, and smuggling continued as a source of income. The French underground blew up a few buildings in the upper Queyras but was generally regarded by villagers as ineffective.

In 1944 Italy changed sides, joining the Allies, and the village was surrounded by German troops. The German occupation is considered to have been a very bad time. There were numerous incidents between villagers and Germans, but no village casualties. One villager in Le Roux successfully hid an American pilot for ten days without being detected.

At the end of 1944, the Allies pushed through the Queyras. The Germans were driven out, but as they withdrew they shelled Abriès and Le Roux. Once again villagers were evacuated, this time to the nearby village of Aiguilles, where they stood on the roofs of houses watching Abriès burn. All of the quarter of L'Adroit and much of the Bourg were destroyed, as well as many houses in Le Roux. Again some people were able to save their animals by driving them into the woods and hiding them.

None of the agricultural land was affected by the bombardment. Some people returned to the village, dismayed by the damage but eager to rebuild their lives. Others decided that they were too old to weather the hardships of reconstruction and did not return. In 1946 the population of Abriès, which had been 414 in 1931, was down to 275.

POST-WAR RECONSTRUCTION

After the war Abriès was designated as an area of resistance, and the central government awarded large grants to help in rebuilding its houses. Much of the early work was done by German prisoners of war; later, the government hired Italian labourers. The houses they built were very large and equipped with running water, indoor toilets, and even central heating. The co-residence of people and animals was eliminated; attached to the three and four-storey structures were enormous barns.

The reconstruction took a very long time – from 1946 to 1957. At first, families whose homes had not been damaged took co-villagers in. Temporary housing was also constructed. But as the rebuilding period stretched longer and longer, some people decided that they could not remain in Abriès. By 1956 the population was down to 202.

La Zone Pilote

The new houses of Abriès had been built big in preparation for large families. Reconstruction officials expected agriculture to flourish in the area, an expectation in which they were encouraged by a variety of agricultural agencies. The Queyras had been selected as a model site for the renewal of mountain agriculture, an example for thirty-two other departments with mountainous regions.

This zone pilote (pilot-study zone) was to be a test area for demonstrating that agriculture was viable in the mountains, so the theoretical aspects of Queyrassin development were studied from 1947 to 1951. The problems were seen as almost entirely technical. Teams of experts and a few Queyrassins were sent to Austria and Italy to study the ways these countries coped with mountain terrain and insufficient labour. There they noted the use of hand tractors for haying sloping land, cables and pulleys instead of mules for moving hay and grains, and pump-driven cannons for shooting fertilizer onto the fields. The use of silos for more efficient storage was also discussed (Chauvet 1954).

Funding for the model zone began in 1952, and by 1957 agricultural renewal in the Queyras was described as a major success in an official publication of the Comité Départemental de la Vulgarisation et du Progrès Agricole (Departmental Committee for the Popularization of Agricultural Progress), which offered reports from the financial division of the Secretariat of State for Agriculture, the Agricultural Commission of the Cantonal General Council, the departmental Chamber of Agriculture, and five other local and national agencies, in addition to the Agricultural Services Division of the Shell Oil Company. In the introduction to this publication, the prefect of the department wrote: 'At this time, when the Government, with the profound support of the region, is making efforts to improve the areas suffering from insufficient economic development and to renew the regional economies, *the experiment undertaken in the Queyras constitutes a leading example full of lessons and of hope*' (Bonafous 1957, emphasis added).

The prefect, like members of the various development organizations, considered the Queyras experiment successful because the villagers eagerly adopted new technology. With the aid of state subsidies, Queyrassin peasants had bought 169 hand tractors and 39 wheeled towing vehicles, had started construction on 41 silos, and had remodelled 49 stables announced one report (Vezin 1957)

This study did not mention milk prices or the role of the Nestlé Company and industrial dairying in transforming the Queyras economy, but Chauvet, a departmental agronomist who had been with the project since 1946, did touch on the question of dairying. In 1954 he reviewed nineteenth-century developments and concluded that household cheese production and later co-operative creameries had disappeared *because* of depopulation. Confusing cause and effect, Chauvet's report offered no analysis of market or price conditions during the development of capitalism in the region. He described the hardships keeping dairy cows imposed on the family labour force but argued that they could be overcome by joining herds so that milking machines could be used. Cow's milk, he said, should continue to be the mainstay of the economy, but it should be combined with tourism on a modest scale ('bed and breakfast') and winter work, such as masonry, carpentry, and mechanics, on a Swiss model of development to supplement incomes sufficiently to prevent further depopulation. He too considered the Queyras development plan successful.

A 1959 study by the Institute of Urbanization of the University of Paris supported the position that the Queyras pilot project had worked, declaring the Queyras to be a good agricultural area with fertile soil and vast pastures. It did note the poverty in the region, which it explained by pointing to its history of dependence on milk production for the Nestlé Company: 'the only law regulating production in the Queyras is the price of milk set by Nestlé' (Aubert 1959: 247). This study advised that stock-raising, not dairying, should be the most important element in a balanced 'agro-sylvo-pastorale' economy in the Queyras.

The army of experts and the contradictory advice which invaded the Queyras in the 1950s were confusing to many cultivators. The Abrièsois say they were eager to mechanize after the war because Italian labour was so expensive and because, like all the experts, they were afraid of depopulation and were hoping to make agriculture viable. Yet at the very time the various agriculture agencies were calling the pilot project successful, many families were leaving the land because, despite mechanization, agriculture was not proving profitable in Abriès. In addition, the school and bus services in the hamlet of Le Roux closed during the 1950s, hastening the departure of several young farming families who were unwilling to board their children for schooling elsewhere.

Moreover, several problems existed in agriculture for which there were no easy or mechanical solutions. A major one was the fragmentation of holdings. The experts agreed that consolidation of holdings was necessary for efficient agriculture, but the villagers were opposed to consolidation – or at least to doing it officially.

During the ancien régime, the fragmentation of holdings had produced a levelling effect which prevented the implantation of a land-holding aristocracy or the accumulation of holdings by any one person or family. The large population of the village kept the numerous holdings circulating within and among families. With massive out-migration, much of the poorer land went out of production. But people rented or traded plots for mutual convenience. Several Abrièsois told me that when they were children their fathers would spend a few hours in a village café and then emerge having traded fields among themselves. There are many stories of Abrièsois who worked pieces of land for years only to learn, at the time of a father's death, that the land was not his but had been exchanged out of the family years earlier.

Despite such confusions, the Abrièsois were against any official con-solidation plan. Aubert argues that such opposition was rooted in ties to ancestral land (1959; 270). But the Abrièsois made it clear to me that their objections were entirely practical. They had available a kind of de facto consolidation which they considered advantageous because it was flexible and suitable to changing market and migration situa-tions. Furthermore, it avoided costly legal fees. An official, codified consolidation plan would have destroyed the flexibility and, according to many, permitted the 'gros' (bigshots) who had political influence to accumulate all the best land. Yet many gros were also opposed to offi-cial consolidation. For example, one family of shopkeepers who had accumulated some bottom land were afraid of losing it and so were vio-lently opposed to consolidation. A woman who had lost a garden plot in small-scale consolidation during the reconstruction of houses in the L'Adroit quarter was completely unwilling to let any more go. This opposition was based not on some mystical attachment to ancestral holdings but on the realization that flat land was potentially quite profitable for both agriculture and tourist development.

In 1957 the debate over consolidation in Abriès exacerbated ten-sions, which were already running high over the slowness of reconstruc-tion. During this bitter time, a flood struck the Queyras, tearing away topsoil and depositing gravel on much fertile land. Later the flood come to be regarded as the sole reason for the shift from agriculture to tourist development in the Queyras. In the late 1950s agricultural officials considered the loss of arable land a tragedy but one that could be overcome. They were convinced the zone pilote was successful, and they believed in the future of agriculture in the valley. Only in the mid-1960s, when the local economy was being groomed for tourism, was history rewritten and the Queyras suddenly found to be unsuitable for agricultural development after all.

Tourism
The Queyras, the highest inhabited valley in Europe, had always attracted some small-scale tourism. Abriès, with its Wednesday market, had inns and facilities for accommodating some tourists – usually hunters and fishermen. At the end of the nineteenth century Toye-Riont opened the Grand Hotel in Abriès. The patrons were mostly soldiers, for in 1900 the French army began to develop ski patrols in the Hautes-Alpes. (The villagers themselves rarely used skis, preferring sleds to get about in the winter.) Two older village women remember the Grand Hotel with much affection as a place of lively balls and handsome officers, but the hotel, like tourism in general, played an insignificant role in the village economy before the Second World War.

After the war, although the hotel had been destroyed during the bombardment and was not replaced in the reconstruction, the villagers and agricultural officials became interested in promoting small-scale summer tourism. Storekeepers were especially enthusiastic. The mayor at the time was a village-born shopkeeper, and he managed to promote camping facilities on the outskirts of Abriès and in the hamlet of Valpreveyre. Support for winter tourism emerged in 1958, when the Gaullist government decided to support industrial instead of agricultural development and when the price of milk fell nationally (Remy, 1972). Departmental administrators began circulating a brief which discussed the important role winter tourism could have in the Hautes-Alpes ('Programme d'expansion économique des Hautes Alpes,' May 1958). A long-time departmental agronomist told me that the two administrators who came to head the Rural Engineering Corps and the Bridges and Roads Administration in the department at that time were avid ski fans, as was the prefect. The new administrators had come from Savoy, where they had been successful in promoting large 'stations du ski' (ski centres), and they were hoping to do the same in the southern Alps. Since agriculture was now seen to be failing in the department and two urban factories had closed, throwing a thousand people out of work, it seemed an ideal time to demonstrate how tourism could revive a backward economy.

In Abriès, the 1959 conflict over land consolidation turned out the old mayor (by three votes) and brought to power for the first time a non-Abrièsois, a man who had installed in the village a small sanatorium for asthmatic children. Throughout the 1960s he and department officials searched for some way to side-step wrangles over agricultural development and to combine agriculture and tourism as equal partners in development. In 1970 the balance shifted radically towards tourism, when Nestlé stopped picking up milk in the Queyras. The next year the company pulled out of the department completely, closing down its Gap processing plant and throwing 490 Gapencais out of work.[1]

The departure of Nestlé sent shock waves through the department. There were protests in villages throughout the Hautes-Alpes and marches and demonstrations in Gap. Workers from Gap circulated pamphlets which connected the closing of Nestlé with the promotion of tourist interests: 'the department will be nothing but a reserve of labouring peons who will be subject to being moved about by the bosses' whims. And don't tell us that tourism will come to save the

---

1 Three hundred had been laid off in the previous year, and 180 were let go in 1971.

Throughout the early 1970s permanent layoffs were widespread in European food firms. Industry representatives claimed a crisis of overproduction in Europe, but the International Union of Foodworkers argued that the reason was a shift in production and pricing policies: corporations such as Nestlé were withdrawing from basic processing 'to concentrate on highly processed and sophisticated dairy products which are more profitable but do not meet the basic nutritional needs of the world population' (IUF Dairy Conference Publication no. 9-10, 1974, cited in George 1985: 157).

The IUF's claim that overproduction was not the main reason for plant closures seems to have been borne out in the case of Nestlé. Shortly after closing plants in France, it began large-scale operation in Greece aiming at the production of one million cans of condensed milk a year (see Garreau 1977, 43-7). In a secret deal, whose contents were discovered after the fall of the military dictatorship in 1975, the colonels had given the company a thirty-year production monopoly which would have killed local dairies, agreed to apply tariffs to imported dairy products, and promised to finance the export of Nestlé-Hellas products not absorbed by the Greek market although the profits from these sales would go directly to the Swiss parent company.

inhabitants ... All the ski resorts are in the hands of a few trusts[2] and there is no real creation of new jobs' (ADHA, pamphlet file on Nestlé demonstrations, 1971, uninventoried).

Other pamphlets argued that the department was deliberately being classified as an area without potential industrial development so that it could function as a 'tourist reserve for the rich' (ibid.). Peasants were reminded that if the city of Gap died, the countryside could not survive, and that many peasants had already been forced out because of Nestlé's policies. Shopkeepers and artisans were warned that a seasonal influx of tourists would not provide them with a stable clientele. And all were reminded of past, failed development schemes, such as the hydro-electric project at Serre-Ponçon, which was supposed to have benefited agriculture and commerce but did neither once construction had ended.

In the end, these protests were ineffective in preventing the Nestlé pull-out. The Abrièsois cast about for other milk buyers and became involved in a co-operative based in the village of Montdauphin. However, the pick-up was only every other day, and the prices offered were low.

VILLAGE STRATEGIES

Abriès cultivators are now in the process of relinquishing dairying and turning to stock-raising.[3] Ironically, agricultural development in the village is coming full circle as experts assure cultivators that sheep-raising is really the future of the region.

Today Abriès is a village of fragments, divided into several social groups with different histories and different economic activities. With a 1973 population of 192, the small community is over-serviced by two grocery stores, (almost side by side), a bakery, a wine wholesaler, four hotels, a trailer-camp facility that offers a restaurant, a dancehall, a laundromat, and a boules court, a ski boutique, a variety store, a small

2 This reference was to a station du ski in another valley that had started off as a communal project but been taken over by Marseilles investors. A departmental agriculture agent told me that his research showed that the station had provided no significant job opportunities for villagers.
3 The ethnographic present tense in the rest of the book refers to the period of my field-work, 1972–4, unless other dates are specified. All the names of villagers – long-time residents, immigrants, and emigrants – and of regional mayors are pseudonyms.

sanatorium which also houses Marseilles schoolchildren who come for ski lessons, and a vacation hostel for retired working-class people from a Paris suburb. The presence of all these services plus the modern appearance of many of the houses makes the village appear quite up-to-date. In July, August, and midwinter it bustles with people, but it is very quiet the rest of the year. The winter skier or summer camper, who comes to see beautiful scenery but rarely interacts with villagers, is not aware of Abriès's struggle to maintain agricultural life or its economic dependence on transfer payments – old-age pensions, retirement pensions from the post office, the army, and the police, disability allowances, and family allowances. These payments, not tourism, constitute the bulk of income in many households.

Beneath the commercial structures of modern Abriès rests the remnants of an agricultural economy which surfaces when there are no tourists in the village. In the early spring the men assemble at the sound of a small drum played through the streets by the 'garde champêtre' (field guard) for collective labour on pasture pathways in anticipation of forming collective sheep and cow herds. 'We are the bulldozers here,' announce village men who gather in mid-April to repair roads which mud slides have made unusable. During the next few weeks several paths are cleared. The men point out that in the past forty or more would show up for unpaid corvée labour. Today the crew has only ten men, who are paid from municipal funds, and they feel that they do not do as good a job as was done in the past. Nevertheless they enjoy the work – 'It's a bit of an outing.'

In the beginning of May work begins on village gardens. Women and men in heavy sweaters and leather hiking boots sift the soil through large screens, discard stones, and add animal fertilizer. All the gardeners disdain commercial fertilizers and are proud that they do not pay for 'chemicals.' Some villagers 'who own garden land but do not garden' rent it to relatives or friends. Others work out a share-crop arrangement. Some merchants, for example, say they 'give' the use of land to relatives, who in turn 'share' the produce which the shopkeepers sell in the summer. Several elderly pensioners live alone and own only garden land; they work it intensively and live off the vegetables and root crops for a good part of the year. Some combine this strategy with winter migration to Marseilles, where they go on welfare; one or two others prefer to check into a local hospital for the coldest winter months. In the spring these seasonal migrants return to their

homes and act like cultivators, taking an interest in animal prices, corvées, and religious processions to bless the fields and protect against
floods, even though they own no animals and do not work in the fields.

All 66 village-born people turn out to watch the formation of the
communal sheep herd in early May. Although only eight households
still own sheep, the occasion is joyous and lively as men, women, children, and dogs gather along the streets and in the schoolyard to watch
the animals pass. There is much shouting, whistling, joking, swearing,
and laughter as the sheep and goats trot out of the barns, where they
have been kept all winter, and head through town towards the fields.
Before the sheep ascend to their first pastures, cultivators and ex-
cultivators stand around discussing in patois the merits of the herd and
of the pastures, which used to be grain fields but are now covered with
grass and wildflowers. Although these fields are technically not communal pastureland, they will be used as if they were. Two villagers will
watch the sheep for the first week, until they are used to being out-of-
doors. Thereafter each sheep-owning family will provide one day of
labour for every ten sheep it owns. In the past at least two large herds
were pastured collectively, on the adret, (the south-facing slope) and
the other, a little later, on the ubac (the north-facing slope). Today's
small herds – 434 sheep and 50 cows – need much less space. The ubac
is a ski-run and sheep are no longer pastured there.

Above the ski slopes are rich pasturelands used to graze cattle.
Villager men put in corvée labour to clear debris from paths up to
these pastures. Men who migrated into Abriès in the 1960s and 1970s
and whose jobs are related to tourism do not participate in agricultural
corvées, though two of them watch the formation of the communal
sheep herd from a distance. By contrast, several of these men work to
clear avalanche debris from the ski slopes but no village men participate in that labour.

In June the agricultural group forms more communal work parties
to clear the high pasture pathways for transhumant sheep and cow
herds. In an average year Abriès now rents pastureland to about 5000
sheep and 165 cows. Villagers mingle their own sheep and cows with
these herds, which are looked after by shepherds hired by a consortium
of nine lowland industrial entrepreneurs. These industrialists get
access to very good pastures at very low prices, paying about 50 centimes per sheep and 4 to 6.5 francs per cow. The Abrièsois themselves
are prohibited from guarding these animals; in highly bureaucratized

France they are not considered qualified because they have not received veterinary degrees from France's national shepherding school. The Abriès flocks are guarded gratis.

In July and August, the twelve families that continue to irrigate hayfields and cultivate grains and potatoes work flat out. The old pattern of collective canal maintenance and management has virtually disappeared because of depopulation. Only three major irrigation canals remain operational, and they are cleared by individual families who have exclusive rights to the water that goes through their fields. Tiny, step like plots of terraced fields are still clearly visible on the slopes surrounding the village, but no work goes into their maintenance. The few fields that are not completely abandoned are now planted with grass or clover for animal fodder; a few small plots are used for potatoes.[4] Two households maintain hayfields in distant hamlets, and occasionally one sees an old peasant with a scythe resting on his shoulder bicycling to reach hamlet fields. Later his son will come with a wagon, load the grass, and sell the product to animal-raisers in other villages.

The French take their vacations in July and August. Abriès is packed with tourists – sightseers, hikers, 'estivants' (renters of summer apartments), campers – and ex-Abrièsois who open their village homes for the summer season. Traffic jams occur frequently in the central village square as tourist cars and hay wagons try to manoeuvre around one another. Campers complain that cultivators shoo them away from the campsite, while cultivators alternate between chuckling at the notion of 'le camping sauvage' (tent camping) and anger at working so hard while others vacation. Shopkeepers, who do half their business in these two months, keep their stores open late selling food, drink, and Korean-made alpine trinkets. The hotels, bakery, variety store, and other tourist-related structures come alive with various schemes to attract and entertain visitors. They also distance and isolate villagers. Activities such as boules play-offs and dances, which are held in the trailer park facilities, welcome tourists but tend to exclude villagers, who are either too busy or too poor to afford entrance fees, dance tickets, and bar drinks. Walking tours, wildflower 'photo safaris,' and hunting and fishing parties cater to a small clientele which rarely inter-

4 In 1913 Abriès had 209.53 hectares of arable fields; only 54.50 hectares were cultivated in 1953, and by 1971 a mere 6 hectares were in production (DDA, Etat Communal de Statistic Agricole).

acts with the villagers. However, the children from the Mont Cenis vacation colony, owned by working-class Parisian suburbanites, and the seventeen-odd summer-apartment renters who stay for extended periods of time do tend to interact with villagers.

Ex-villagers join village work parties, attend church, and help to organize religious processions to hamlet shrines. In August the ancient church of Abriès is full, the sounds of choir and congregation ring out, and animated groups stand around after services. Under the handsome bell tower, on which an inspired artist of the eighteenth century lettered 'It is later than you think,' villagers and visitors exchange pleasantries and Abrièsois and ex-Abrièsois discuss the weather, animal prices, and the marriage prospects of relatives and friends. The village's appearance of being large and thriving is in marked contrast to the emptiness of its streets in September when the tourists and ex-villagers have gone.

Villagers call September, October, and November 'sad' months. The tourists leave. So do the transhumant herds. Village animals descend from the high pastures and roam freely across the harvested hay-fields in the ancient practice of vain pâture, which was never suppressed. The larch trees turn brilliant orange, drop their needles, and stand barren against the icy blue sky. Villagers go to the forests to cut wood for the winter. They cannot afford fuel oil to heat their enormous houses and in their kitchens prefer to maintain wood-burning stoves, which often stand side-by-side with unused gas stoves. Dining-and living-rooms are rarely used and therefore rarely heated; bedrooms are never heated.

The Forest Administration no longer keeps agents stationed in the village. When asked about ownership of the forest, Forest Administration officials say that the woods belong to the communes, and the villagers say they belong to the Forest Administration. Technically the woods do belong to the communes – under the Forest Administration's supervision, which is very mild compared to that of the nineteenth century. Each household is allowed to cut some timber each year (the amount is the same for every household, no matter how large). Theoretically, forest agents patrol the valley to prevent excessive or inappropriate cutting, but the patrols are infrequent and no agents are stationed in the village. People usually carry out fallen timber and uprooted trees without bothering to ask permission. If an agent hears of timber being cut in an unauthorized spot, he often comes to some understanding with the offender and marks the logs ex post facto.

The major job of the Forest Administration now revolves around selling cutting rights to large industrial entrepreneurs. Larch wood is highly prized for furniture-making in Italy, and an Italian entrepreneur operates in Abriès, cutting before the agricultural season begins. The commune receives what many consider to be a small payment for trees cut from the communal forest; individuals who have permitted trees to grow on their fields make private deals. In essence the forests of Abriès are no longer part of the village's agricultural economy; rather they are now a resource exploited by entrepreneurs from outside. Only one young village cultivator has found any employment related to the forests. A few years ago he worked for the Italian entrepreneur hauling logs to the main road (the rest of the operation was carried out by Italian labour). Villagers do not have enough capital to buy equipment to exploit this resource for themselves.

The Forest Administration no longer concerns itself with animal husbandry and dairying and no longer considers the question of sheep-raising to be its domain. Ironically, state and departmental agricultural agencies now actively discourage cow's milk production and argue that the Queyras is best suited to the raising of stock, especially sheep.

Winter brings a second wave of tourists into the village. The pleasant small-scale, low-cost ski facilities in Abriès draw working-class families from southern cities for weekend packages. In addition, the commune has negotiated a deal with the Marseilles school-board which brings schoolchildren and teachers to Abriès for four weeks of afternoon ski lessons. It is not clear, however, in the competition among the four hotels and the trailer facility in Abriès, that any of the enterprises is prospering. Only one of these establishments, a modest hotel of eight rooms in the hamlet of Le Roux, is owned by an Abriès family, and that couple plans to retire soon. Only one hotel has had the same owner and management for more than five years. One establishment in central Abriès has changed ownership twice in the last three years and is now owned by a Paris syndicate. Another has changed management frequently in the past few years, although it is still owned by ex-villagers who live in Marseilles. Another hotel changed hands in 1968. The trailer facility profited from a period of uncertainty about land values in the 1960s, after the construction of the ski installation forestalled communal development, but then ran into financial difficulties itself. It was able to complete construction of its central building only in 1974.

Competition among these enterprises must also be seen within the context of competition among the 209 hotels of thirty-one communes in the Hautes-Alpes that now offer tourist facilities for skiers. According to an untitled pamphlet put out by the Office Départemental du Tourisme des Hautes-Alpes for 1971/2, five of these communes have 'stations nationales' – huge super-centres – with 163 trails, a variety of ski tows, chair-lifts, and gondolas, and additional dormitory facilities for 1544 people. They also have skating-rinks and swimming-pools and 225 ski instructors.

These installations draw the lion's share of the seasonal and weekend tourist trade from the Midi. By contrast, Abriès has only fifty-seven hotel rooms and dormitory facilities for eighty, four trails, three tows, and one chair-lift. Moreover, it is hard to get to Abriès; the trip from Marseilles, the major tourist pool for the Hautes-Alpes requires at least a half-day's drive. Abriès has the advantages of high altitude and assured snowfall, but fluctuating gasoline prices and reduced road speeds in France have underlined the serious contradiction of a remote mountain village's trying to draw skiers from Marseilles. Abriès was almost completely cut out of the weekend market in 1972–4 because of high gasoline prices.

In fact, Abriès hotels are completely booked for only three weeks of the ski season (two weeks at Christmas and one at Easter). For the most part, the Abriès ski facilities are used by Marseillais schoolchildren who stay not in hotels but in the sanatorium building. Neither the hotels nor the shopkeepers derive much profit from these children, although the commune does receive payment for their use of the slopes and the villagers generally say that they enjoy having the young children around.

TOURISM ON THE GROUND

Does winter tourism create jobs for villagers? It has to some extent, but there is also much dissatisfaction with ski-related employment. The major ski-rental facility is run by Pierre Toussaint, a Grenoblois who moved to the village with his family in 1970. He not only rents out most of the ski equipment, but because he has the appropriate degree from the national ski school, he also oversees the six villagers employed on the slopes as instructors and lift attendants. His salary is higher than those of the local workers, who receive the minimum wage from the commune budget. The villagers who work as lift attendants are unanimous in finding the work onerous. The job, which begins at eight in the morning and continues until five at night, requires standing outside in the snow to help people onto the tow equipment. The work is considered extremely boring, and workers say they are half-frozen when they return home in the evening.

Only three village women have found work in the hotels. They clean washrooms, make beds, and do laundry. These women get the minimum wage for their work, and it is part-time. For the most part, the hotels prefer to bring in young non-villagers for work such as dishwashing and waiting on tables because these people can be paid less and let go as soon as the season slackens. Cooking is done by the families who own or manage the hotels.

Food for these enterprises is rarely bought locally because villagers do not produce in sufficient volume. In summer and winter the hotels are provisioned by wholesalers from the lowlands, who truck frozen foods up to Abriès. Despite the fact that some Abrièsois still raise stock, they are not permitted by law to slaughter locally. In 1971 a departmental directive prohibited local butchering in all but seven approved abattoirs. The two Abriès butchers went out of the meat business, and the hotels began buying frozen meats.

Cultivators assume that the hotel owners and local shopkeepers are making a profit from tourism. The shopkeepers and hotel owners assume that tourism benefits the cultivators. In reality, the only people who may be profiting are land speculators. Two retired ex-villagers have appeared in Abriès and started to purchase land. One, who already had some holdings in the village, has been buying up plots for three years. Recently he forced a Le Roux cultivator off land that he had been working for thirty years. An agricultural agent assured the cultivator that he is entitled to bid first on the land and may be eligible for government assistance in buying it; however, he considers the price beyond his means even with assistance.

The other man is a builder who is in partnership with the mayor. They are attempting to build a chalet development of privately owned summer homes for tourists. Permits for this development have recently been blocked by a judge in Grenoble, who is considered the mayor's political enemy. There are rumours of land speculation about this development. One villager who is known to have land in the area under consideration became involved in an angry dispute with the mayor while they both examined the village cadastre. Land speculation is an issue no one wishes to discuss at length, but most people agree that it is divisive and should be stopped. At the same time they also say that it would be foolish not to profit from it if one can.

Tourism as a Development Strategy
In principle, tourism, especially winter tourism, has been developed in Abriès to prevent further out-migration and to provide Abrièsois with work in the winter now that seasonal migration is no longer an option. This is the explanation given by the present mayor and by pro-tourist villagers. Abriès tourist development, as defined by the mayor, is to be on a 'human scale'; he argues that the giant stations du ski developed elsewhere in the department would be out of place in small Queyrassin communes.

The aim of tourism, say its proponents, is to benefit the commune as a whole, not a few rich capitalists. This theme was expressed in municipal council debates as early as 1960, when the commune decided to build a ski tow and create three downhill trails. Abriès undertook to borrow 160,000 francs from the Credit Industriel et Communal of Paris at an interest rate of 6.25 per cent for fifteen years. At the same time the village also attempted to raise money for a municipal wood-working workshop to provide winter employment. This plan was rejected by the department and not funded, although only 8,000 francs was needed (AMA, *Délibérations du Conseil Municipal d'Abriès* 1960). With the refusal of the workshop plan, the village put its energy exclusively into tourist development.

Villagers were urged to fix up rooms and apartments in their houses for tourists, and the fact that the reconstruction had left many Abrièsois with white elephants was encouragement enough to do so. At the same time the two existing inns in the village and one in Le Roux were encouraged to winterize to attract tourists. The commune discussed one possibility of buying up land around the ski installation so that it could invest in any hotel development that might occur in that area. Clearly, the intention of the commune was that ski development, like the rental of land to summer campers, would be a communal project in which it would take the risks and also the profits.

In fifteen years of development, however, tourism has grown along different lines. The commune is still the risk-bearing unit, but so far it has made no profit. Abriès is now allied with the six other Queyras communes and the village of Ceillac in an intercommunal association to enable it to be more effective in raising credit for the expansion of ski installations. This organization, which used to be a relatively dormant intercommunal agricultural grouping, now has a modern-sounding name – SicaSport – and little connection with agriculture. Its president is the mayor of Ceillac, Maurice Jaubert, who is considered an important political patron in the region and its chief promoter of tourism. Jaubert's power stems from the fact that he has good political connections with the government party and is a proven money raiser. He was able to obtain millions of francs for a development scheme in Languedoc. Although he moved to Ceillac only when the Languedoc development plan went bankrupt, the fact that he was able to open the taps to government loans has defined him as a powerful person.

Abriès's present mayor, a builder from Grenoble, is a supporter of Jaubert's and explains SicaSport as a borrowing association which permits the member villages, which are legally required to balance their budgets yearly, to go into debt to develop ski facilities. Many Abrièsois are, however, appalled by SicaSport and fear the village is sinking into debt from which it will never recover. They point to the fact that in Abriès, as in most other communes they have heard about, ski-lifts never make a profit, so it is the village that absorbs the losses of ski development.

National and departmental bureaucrats now define Queyrassin agriculture as being in the service of tourism. Minister of Agriculture Jacques Chirac expressed this view perfectly in a 1973 television broadcast, declaring that peasants are important in France because they keep the landscape groomed. In fact, he said, 'Nature, without peasants – that is anarchy.' In France, according to Chirac, peasants serve an important ecological function as well as a productive function.

Departmental and local officials concur with this view and have developed practical reasons for keeping some agriculturalists on the land. One key reason in high mountain areas is the threat of avalanches. Unless people pasture animals on the slopes, the grass grows long and when snow falls it bends creating air pockets. These pockets become warm spots under the snow which may cause melting and result in snow slides and possibly avalanches. Hence tourist interests demand keeping the grass mown in the summer. The cheapest, most efficient way to do this is to use grazing animals rather than machinery. Thus, there are now subsidies for grazing animals in the Hautes-Alpes. The 'cow-that-mows' is worth a subsidy of 200 francs to its owner. (There have been disputes over the fact that only cows are eligible; cultivators are urging agricultural officials to consider seven sheep as equivalent to one cow for the subsidy.)

In the Queyras the subsidy program is part of a wider program in which the valley has just been designated a regional park. The mayors of the Queyras communes and Ceillas are enthusiastic about the park scheme, arguing that it will preserve the unique ecology of the region by, for example, making the picking of rare wildflower species illegal. The mayor of Abriès says that the designation will alert people to the fact that they are entering true 'virgin territory' where they will not encounter the crass commercialism of the superstation. Shopkeepers and hotel owners in Abriès favour the park program because they feel it will bring in more tourists, especially those interested in hiking, cross-country skiing, nature, and the architectural charms of the valley.

Many cultivators, however, are furious about the regional park designation. They were not consulted when the original proposal was made, and now that the park is a fact, they have no voting power in its management. They are designated 'friends of the park,' solely an advisory role.[5] Some feel that the park will be like the Canadian Indian reserves they have heard about and that they will be objects of curiosity on their own land. They point to an old peasant of Saint Véran who sells tours of his house for 50 centimes. 'The home of yesteryear' proclaims a sign outside his house. One Abrièsois describes this activity as prostitution.

Cultivators also point to the fact that the creation of a regional park offers them no economic advantage and several potential disadvantages. They fear that whole pastures may be set off limits for animal grazing in order to protect certain botanical species. They also fear that when the park hires rangers, villagers will be excluded because they lack the formal degrees that the government will inevitably require.

Many native Queyrassins say that they feel the park scheme will turn the valley into a museum and perpetuate the notion that they are

5 In June 1973 departmental officials called a meeting for cultivators of the Queyras to discuss the regional park and have the advisory role laid out for them. Since the meeting was held at ten in the evening during the agricultural season and at Guillestre, twenty-seven kilometres away, no Abrièsois attended. In fact only five cultivators attended the meeting, two from Arvieux and three from Guillestre. When asked why the mayors of the villages did no more about peasant representation, the cultivators present said they were lucky to have mayors who lived in their villages, let alone anyone who does anything to promote peasant interests. The mayors are officially considered peasant representatives on the committee to direct the park.

quaint and somehow different from other French people. They also object to the plan's housing code, which requires them to use authentic and now extremely expensive building materials, such as slate, in home repairs. The last point is not an issue in Abriès, however, because most of the houses in the village were built during the post-war reconstruction and thus do not have to conform to the strict code.

The park plan also calls for three garbage treatment plants (which the cultivators consider costly) and a research laboratory from the University of Marseilles. Villagers greeted the announcement of the latter with cries and hoots: what possible benefit would peasants ever get from university research?

Conclusion
Tourism in Abriès has not fulfilled its original promise. It is no longer subsidiary to agriculture; rather agriculture has become a subsidiary to tourism and is maintained to serve it. Those Abrièsois who wish to continue as agriculturalists are angry and resentful at having been cast in the role of parkkeepers to serve tourist interests (see also Franklin 1969). They point to the fact that tourism is even more unstable than agriculture. It is just as seasonal and just as dependent on weather conditions, but, unlike food, it is something people can do without during bad economic times.

Yet many agricultural officials at the department level continue to promote tourism as the only salvation for 'backward' mountain regions. One agronomist who had actively promoted the 1950s zone pilote plan in the Queyras now says that agriculture is unfeasible in the mountains (interview, 1972). The Queyras, which he once considered a model of agricultural development, must now content itself with serving the recreational needs of tired urbanites: 'The agriculturalist is the gardener of the mountain; the tourists want a change of scenery in a rural ambience.'

VILLAGERS, IMMIGRANTS, AND MIXED HOUSEHOLDS

Abriès now contains two economic systems that operate as separate networks with limited interactions. One is the system of villagers largely dependent on transfer payments and the piecing together of diverse resources. It is for the most part an economy of old people who will leave few descendants in the village. And it is an economy of people who live at a much lower standard of living than their neighbours, recent immigrant families connected with tourism. The second economy, of this latter group, provides a more stable, less piecemeal income to a group of young, city-born people with skills and capital unavailable to most native villagers.

Villagers

Most native Abrièsois today are old and have left agriculture. They live alone or in two-person households and are poor. Officially, most are retired, but almost all work to make ends meet. For no native Abrièsois household does tourism or agriculture alone provide sufficient income. The subsistence deficits are made up in a number of ways. Gathering, hunting, fishing, gardening, and the raising of small animals (chickens, pigeons, rabbits) and bees supplement the incomes of all villager households. Native Abrièsois do not have to pay rent on their houses, which is an important feature in reducing the costs of the household budget, but many complain about high home-insurance and tax payments. For many households, transfer payments – old age pensions, disability payments, and other social welfare payments – make up the dominant portion of the domestic budget.

One such household comprises the Roberts, a childless couple. M. Robert, age seventy, is a retired postman and shoemaker. He receives an old-age pension from the government and another from the postal union. Mme Robert, age sixty-three, is not yet retired; she works as a charwoman, baby-sitter, and seamstress for one of the hotel owners on a part-time, seasonal basis. M. Robert migrated to Abriès from Italy after the First World War with his brothers and father. They were shoemakers and accumulated no land in the village. Mme Robert comes from an old Abriès family, and her father's estate has given her some access to garden land. She and her husband work this land and share-crop the gardens of her brother's wife who sells the produce in her grocery store. The Roberts also keep rabbits and chickens for their own use, for barter, and for the sale to tourists. M. Robert repairs shoes in a shed in one of his gardens – usually in exchange for food but for money if tourists are involved.

Most other two-person households (husband-wife, sister-sister, brother-sister) follow similar patterns. One exception is the couple who own a grocery, the Allands. Ages sixty and sixty-one, they are considered wealthy by village standards. In addition to the grocery store Mme Alland has gardens, strategically placed throughout the village, which supply the store with some produce in the summer. The couple also have three inherited houses, as well as an apartment over the grocery store in which they live. They rent apartments in two of these houses to tourists. The Allands are eager to retire but are unable to find a buyer for their store.

The seventeen single-person households of the village-born Abrièsois include nine widows, one widower, and seven people who never married; only one is considered wealthy. Mme Belier is part of a family of prosperous merchants in Toulon and lives off investments, but she also gardens and rents apartments to supplement her income and to 'keep busy.' Born in 1900, Mme Belier is a healthy, vigorous, religious woman who was secretary to the mayor for many years. Her skills in filling out forms, aiding sick people, and organizing food and clothing collections when a tragedy occurs in a village family are important resources for many villagers. Her nursing skills, which she provides free, are crucial to several of them.

All the other retired villagers in single-person households patch together a living which depends primarily on pension cheques, free housing, and gardening. In the past some gathered mountain herbs for sale to Italian peddlers, but recently this trade has fallen off. Two widows who own some bottom land in Abriès rent it to kinfolk who still farm and receive in return money, produce, and fertilizer for their gardens. Six widows who have children, siblings, or in-laws outside the village have worked out a system of seasonal migration in which they live with their kin in southern France during the winter and return in the summer to the village, where they garden and receive reciprocal visits from their families. One of these women also supplements her income by working part-time in a hotel.

The five unmarried men who live alone are in their forties and fifties. One is a municipal employee – the garde champêtre. The ancient title used to describe the village official responsible for assembling corvées, overseeing water distribution, and levying fines. The job still requires swearing an oath of office, and the garde champêtre still wears a uniform when he circles the village with his small, flat drum to announce a corvée. However, the main part of his job now consists of sweeping animal droppings off the streets ('I sweep shit,' he says of himself). The job provides a steady income, which, in addition to previous savings from jobs as a woodcutter, has permitted this man to buy many gadgets and appliances; most other single-person households have few consumer items because the householders rarely have access to much cash.

Three of the single men are brothers, who live separately; one delivers the mail and the other two work as day-labourers. During the week, one is in Gap as a carpenter; he rushes back to the village to farm on the weekends and depends on elderly Abriès relatives to supervise his animals while he is gone. He finds the pace killing and says that unless he marries soon and settles in the village, he will give up agriculture.

Most agriculturalists in Abriès depend on additional sources of income. The Mignards, for example, call themselves 'paysans' but admit that they can survive in the village only because of pension payments from the state. These payments come to approximately 9000 francs a year (about $2000 Canadian in 1973) for a couple in their late sixties. Mme Mignard, despite being so crippled that she walks with two canes, manages two gardens which provide the bulk of the household's summer produce and winter vegetables, especially potatoes and cabbages. Although the family no longer has any dairy cows, she continues to work at the village milk weigh-scales every other day for 60 francs a month – a salary that has not changed in twenty years. The Mignards are ineligible for the subsidy for keeping grazing animals because M. Mignard, the nominal head of the farming enterprise, is of legal retirement age.

One winter evening Mme Mignard was serving coffee to visitors. She reached up to a shelf, pulled down a box of powdered milk, paused, shook her head, and sighed: 'What kind of peasant am I? I give you powdered milk – I who used to have milk everywhere. It's unbelievable.'

The Mignards feel that they have been forced out of agriculture but hope that their son, Raymond will be able to pull something together. Mme Mignard is especially interested in his scheme of expanding into sheep-herding because she prefers sheep to cows and feels that she has expertise in ovine husbandry.

Another young farmer, Noël Rollier, has just purchased an expensive tractor to use in hay production; he expects that pastoralism on a large scale will bring profits and justify the expense of the equipment. Having listened to the agricultural experts, he argues that one must spend money to make money and sees himself in the vanguard of 'revolutionary' change. Other villagers consider him foolhardy. Older villagers do not know what to make of these young farmers. The decline of agriculture in Abriès is hard for the elderly to understand, and many explain it with the stock comment 'youth doesn't know the meaning of work.' Buying machinery does not seem like work to them.

Furthermore, they no longer understand the operations of the cattle market. For centuries Abriès devoted 29 September to an animal fair in which it displayed its animals to buyers from the south. In 1973, when the day of the fair arrived, the central square held no animals and no buyers. For two nights before the fair, buyers had slipped into the village and struck private deals with individual farmers. By 29 September the buyers had left the village, and there was no point in having a fair. A few mobile merchants parked their vans in the square, hoping to sell clothing and kitchenware, but perceiving there would be no activities that day, they drifted away by noon. After this non-fair, many cultivators complained that they had been tricked by the buyers and that had all the sellers stood together publicly, they might have obtained better prices. A few families who are reported to have profited greatly are silent on the subject of animal prices. Cultivators do now agree that fairs are a thing of the past for Abriès. They reason that where animals fairs do persist in the department, they are attempts to unload stock that buyers do not want.

Villagers are also puzzled by departmental agricultural policy, and they are suspicious of agricultural agents. In January 1974 I went with about twenty Abrièsois to a meeting sponsored by departmental agriculture bureaucrats, whom the villagers privately call 'a rotten mafia.' In an atmosphere that was by turns heated and sullen, the Abrièsois demanded explanations for policies that gave subsidies to dairy-cow owners but not sheep raisers when officials publicly discourage milk production and support expanding sheep herds. An agricultural technician countered that the peasants were too individualistic and that they should consider collective ownership and management of flocks, collective purchase of machinery, and collective grouping of land to prevent speculation by tourist interests. Neither peasants nor experts realized that nineteenth-century agriculture experts had spent considerable energy supporting individual initiative, the break-up of the commons, and the dismantling of collective labour systems.

One peasant shouted from the back of the room that the really smart thing would have been to quit the village twenty years before. The mayor spoke on behalf of tourism and argued that there was no conflict between tourism and agriculture. Villagers disagreed. An older farmer said that he wished that he could return to selling chestnuts in Marseilles rather than freezing his behind on the ski slopes in the winter. He concluded by saying that if one wants to do both tourism and agriculture, one ends by doing nothing. After a short silence, the meeting ended, the cultivators drifted off, and the mayor invited the technicians – but no one else – for a drink.

Recent Immigrants
In contrast to the fragmented economies of most village households are those of Abriès's recent migrants, who depend more consistently on a single source of income. The migrants, a few of them old and many of them young, make up 45 per cent of the active population of the village.

One portion of group are transients. These are the six gendarmes and their families – twenty-three people in 1972 – stationed in Abriès, (one family was transferred out at the end of the year). The mayor of Abriès counts these people as village residents as part of a numbers game proving that the village is thriving under his administration. In general the gendarme families stay aloof from villagers and interact only with each other and the shopkeepers. They have no access to garden land, and they do not exchange goods or services with the villagers. Each of these families depends exclusively on the husband's salary, and some villagers expressed envy because the gendarmes' wives do not work for wages and are thought to have much more leisure time than village women. One seventy-five year-old woman, ankle-deep in the mud of her potato plot, said: 'Ah yes, that is truly women's liberation – to get women out of the fields and into the home!'

Other salaried officials in the village include the postal clerk and his wife, who were assigned to the village until his retirement in 1973. The priest and the schoolteacher, who came with her family, are also recent immigrants, as is the mayor of Abriès, Joseph Lebrun. The mayor is also self-employed as a building contractor and works on development projects in the Queyras and Grenoble. His wife was a schoolteacher before marriage but no longer does wage work.

The village has six self-employed households directly connected with tourism. These are the households of two hotel owners and the managers of the ski boutique, the trailer facility, and the magazine store, and the baker. All these families are young, with children age twelve and under. In all cases they expect the enterprise to provide the entire income for the household, and five of the six couples consider both spouses to be equal work partners. (The exception is the magazine store owner, who considers himself the sole support of his family, which includes three children. Although his wife appears in the store each day behind the cash register, she claims that she does not work and calls herself a housewife.)

Except for the priest, the salaried and self-employed people maintain a standard of living that is higher than that of most villagers. Appliances, cars, and colour televisions are a part of life for the migrants, though a rarity in villager homes.

The presence in the village of self-employed migrants is of course, explained by their access to capital. They came to the village with money to make money. By contrast, the presence of many of the native Abrièsois can be explained by an absence of capital. They do not have enough money to live elsewhere.

Mixed Households

Abriès has ten mixed households – that is, couples in which one spouse is a villager and the other a migrant. They divide evenly between two groups: five couples who married just after the Second Word War and five who married within the last five years. Of the three categories of households in the village, these mixed households average the youngest and they have the largest average household size – more than double that of villager households.

One mixed couple considers themselves peasants, but they acknowledge that agriculture is really secondary in a household economy which depends primarily on the salaried labour of M. Leroy, who collects garbage in the village, and of Mme Leroy, who works as a laundress. Garbage collecting has proved a valuable resource for the Leroys as it permits them to raise pigs; they are the only family in the village to do so. The Leroys are on a tight budget and value the family allowance money they receive for their two young sons.

M. Leroy is a native villager, and his mother, who lives in the same building as her son, considers her household separate. She supports herself almost exclusively on her old-age pension cheque and from the garden of her widowed daughter, who also lives in the village. She shares meals with her son's family and frequently baby-sits for them.

The Leroys have a third-floor apartment which they rent to tourists in the summer. M. Leroy, who keeps only a few sheep, says that the tourist presence does not inhibit his work. Indeed, he finds that it has increased the amount and quality of garbage in the village considerably. He claims that other cultivators used to scorn him for collecting garbage but now see that it can be valuable and envy him.

One Abriès family is adopting a deliberate strategy of moving out of agriculture into tourism. The Baptistes – the husband a villager and the wife a Queyrassin – still maintain some agricultural work, but they are concentrating their children's education on trades. The eldest (born in 1954) is already working as an electrician, and the youngest (born 1961) is expected to become a plumber. The middle daughter plans to be a secretary. The Baptistes face strong criticism from other villagers for pressuring their children into career paths, but the couple argue that they want a secure future for their children and that security cannot be found in agriculture. M. Baptiste has a long-range plan which includes building a ski boutique with the labour of his family. At present, the Baptistes rent rooms of their house and a garage which they have converted into a makeshift apartment. They work constantly, rising early to milk cows, doing agricultural work in the summer (assisted by M. Baptiste's parents), laying the foundation for the ski shop, gardening, and keeping bees, rabbits, and chickens. Mme Baptiste, like many Abriès women, economizes by doing her laundry in the icy water of the public fountain near her house. M. Baptiste works on the slopes in the winter. They sell garden produce and milk to tourists in the summer.

Another mixed family, the Romanos, are following a similar path. They have combined M. Romano's skill as mason with his wife's large inherited house and the labour of their teen-age children to open dormitory-style accommodations for young tourists. Mme Romano is hoping to work as a cook in her own establishment rather than working for others as she has in the past.

The Baptistes and the Romanos are the only families in Abriès to have accumulated sufficient capital from work within the village to launch owner-operated tourist enterprises. Moreover, they have children who are able and apparently willing to support such an undertaking. These couples are not rich enough to consider hiring labour but feel they can make it in the tourist trade by the joint efforts and skills of their families. Children are considered crucial to a successful enterprise but also unreliable. Some people think the Baptistes are pushing their youngsters too hard, and that they may eventually leave the village, scuttling their parents' investment. It remains to be seen whether tensions between children and parents will develop and how these joint ventures in tourism will be affected.

The other older mixed households depend on salaried incomes. M. Levesque, originally from Marseilles, is the mayor of a neighbouring village. He and his Abrièsois wife have three children and live with her parents in a house large enough to include summer apartments for tourists. (The income from these rentals goes to the wife's parents, who are retired.) M. Levesque also works for the Bridges and Roads Department. His two salaries as mayor and works director in the Queyras for road repair are the chief source of family income. His wife does not work for wages outside the home. The family is quite prosperous and plans to send the eldest son to the elite Ecole Polytechnique in Paris.

The younger mixed households all follow the typical villager pattern of putting together a living from various sources. Two of these families will probably stay in the village. They are a mason and a carpenter married to two sisters whose parents still live in the hamlet of Le Roux and who have access to gardens in Abriès. The other four families, each with one child, are uncertain whether they will stay in the village or not. Three of the four men come from farming backgrounds although they see no future in agriculture or in tourism, they support themselves and their families by work on their parents' farms and jobs on the ski-lifts in the winter. Two of the men married schoolteachers who still work in Briançonnais villages. Their wives board near their schools during the week, and return to Abriès on the weekends. Their children are cared for by their Abrièsois grandmothers.

Conclusion

The villager population in Abriès is being replaced by the recent migrant population, people who have brought their resources with them from the outside and who have the skills and capital to exploit the area's snow, sunshine, and landscape for tourist development. They have no inherited access to the pre-existing productive base of the village economy – its land and animals – but they require only limited access to it and to the village labour pool. All they need are enough animals to crop short the summer grass on the slopes (a service which can be supplied by transhumant herds from outside the village), a small amount of flat land for building (which can be bought from villagers) and cheap seasonal labour (which does not have to come from the village). Thus in many ways the indigenous population is irrelevant to the needs of the recent migrant population. For the latter, it is the weather and the scenery, not the productive capacity of the land, which is the chief reason for their presence in the village.

The recent migrants and their descendants will probably not replace villagers as cultivators.

The land in Abriès is still very divided; it is also expensive because of land speculation. It would be difficult for a recent migrant to buy into the farming system. Renting is theoretically possible, but most of the good flat land is now leased by village cultivators. Finally, none of the recent migrants have expressed any interest in farming, and none come from rural backgrounds. Thus, it would be extremely unlikely, as well as difficult, for recent migrants to become cultivators in Abriès. No bonds of sentiment or of land and house ownership hold this group to Abriès. If tourist development does not succeed for them, they can move on.

It is only the mixed households of Abriès that have the capacity to move back and forth from agriculture to tourism. This group is young and can accumulate capital as the older village population cannot (especially given the criteria of the Ministry of Agriculture, which sets an age limit to the active work phase and rules older people ineligible for credit or grazing subsidies). Many of the mixed families have access to arable land and farm buildings through the inheritance lines of one of the spouses, so that it is possible for them to go into agriculture. At present, the younger mixed families are undecided about what course to take; two older families have decided to go into tourist development. These households all have ties of sentiment and kin which may hold some of them in the village. The mayor has said that they are the real future of the valley, but whether the families themselves feel such a commitment is far from clear.

DEVELOPMENT OR MODERNIZATION?

Abriès is now dominated by tourist development. But tourism may not be a form of development at all. A taxi-driver/cultivator in a large tourist resort told me: 'They say that our region is developed. But that's false. We have a false development.' Many Abrièsois also argue that tourist development is a cosmetic which conceals underdevelopment in the guise of modernization. What is happening in Abriès is similar to what is going on all through the European Mediterranean. Schneider, Schneider, and Hansen make the following distinction between modernization and development: 'Modernization refers to the process by which an underdeveloped region changes in response to inputs (ideologies, behavioural codes, commodities and institutional models) from already established industrial centres; a process which is based on that region's continued dependence upon the urban-industrial metropolis. Development refers to the process by which an underdeveloped region attempts to acquire an autonomous and diversified industrial economy on its own terms' (1972: 340). I agree although I would add that the aim of modern development must go beyond an industrial economy to include the creation of a diversified productive base with some balance among the primary, secondary, and tertiary sectors (Rosenberg, Reiter, and Reiter 1973: 37).

Tourism has not developed the economy of Abriès because that industry does not have the ability to improve the village's productive capacity and because it is inherently contingent on factors such as oil prices over which villagers can exercise no control. It has offered little economic reward to villagers thus far but has diverted energy away from difficult agricultural issues, including land reform and the direction of animal husbandry. Agricultural development, in a region renowned for centuries for its animal-raising capacity, has become almost a dead issue.

Villager households in Abriès continue to display many characteristics of underdevelopment. Most of them depend on 'welfaristic capital investment' – transfer payments, via retirement pensions and grants and loans, to a dependent agricultural system subsidized to serve tourist interests (Franklin 1969: 174). Such investments are a holding operation; they maintain people on the land but offer no opportunity to improve its productive capacity. The village, in effect, has become an old folks' home in which small pension cheques are combined with remnants from the pre-existing agricultural system to maintain a population which will not reproduce itself. In the midst of this system, tourism stands like a foreign outpost, taking advantage of the recently expanded consumer market in snow and sunshine. The capital accrued in this system has little spillover into the village economy. It offers only fragments of supplementary income to some villagers. It has not significantly improved the standard of living of most villagers.

Since the Second World War, Abriès has blossomed with outward signs of modernity – especially the large houses equipped with central heating and indoor plumbing. But the people of Abriès cannot make a living in their village, and out-migration has continued at a steady pace. Villagers say that their new houses are of little value if there are no people living in them. The large, emptying houses of Abriès stand as graphic symbols of modernity without development.

8

Community Structures and Politics

Class relations in Abriès are now part of a fully developed national class structure. The village itself is not a microcosm of that structure. Rather, it is a small fragmented community of people, thrown together by circumstances, who have come from different backgrounds and have different goals. The result for Abriès social life is a marked absence of integrated activities. The social worlds of the villagers and the migrants operate independently of each other, demonstrating that even in a small, face-to-face community people can lead very segregated existences.

SOCIAL LIFE

Despite the demographic facts, the villagers tend to see themselves as the majority in Abriès. When they talk about themselves in comparison to the rest of France, villagers – shopkeepers, cultivators, and salaried or retired employees – refer to themselves as paysans (peasants). The hotel-keepers, boutique owners, and gendarmes who come from an urban background are clearly not peasants and have no interest in animal prices or the agricultural policies of the European Economic Community. Villagers, whether they are active cultivators or not, do follow such issues and think of them as being of primary importance. Furthermore, most villagers spend their days in such a fashion that they rarely encounter recent migrants, and this segregation contributes to their sense that the newcomers are a small minority in Abriès.

The difference between recent migrant and villager life is graphically expressed by the way information passes through these two groups. Notices of interest to villagers are posted on the church door by the priest or choir members. Notices which are theoretically of interest to the village as a whole are posted on the door of the variety store by the mayor or his secretary. Since recent migrants buy newpapers and villagers rarely do so, it is generally the newcomers who see such notices. And since recent migrants rarely attend church, they do not see the notices on the church door. The church itself is on a street behind the main square while the variety store is in a building at the very edge of the other side of the square. It is possible for villagers to do all their business, visit, garden, and move animals without crossing the main square at all. Even the two old people whose apartments front on the square usually locate their gossip circles on the side-streets. The bakery and two hotels are on the square; in the summer the hotels set tables outside, giving the villagers another reason to avoid the square.

Even within the village-born community, people find it difficult to maintain regular patterns of socializing. Before the Second World War social life for most Abrièsois was embedded in work life. Labour exchanges, joint work efforts, market and fair cycles, and neighbour-hood insurance associations created regular social intercourse. There were a host of work-related occasions when people saw one another informally. In other words, work used to be a crucial area of social interaction. Today it is no longer a significant forum. The three or four corvées of the year still provide the village men with occasions for socializing, but the systematic interactions characteristic of labour exchanges in the past no longer exist. The insurance associations no longer function because tractors have replaced mules and people are too competitive to be willing to compensate for someone else's lost herd animals. Households rely as much as possible on machines and family labour. There is very little need even for impromptu labour exchanges between households.

Villagers are very specific about the connection between work and socializing. They say that everyone works at home now (and those who work for wages have rigid and differing schedules). Many days may pass before next-door neighbours see each other. Occasionally people help one another out in a way that is socially identified as 'se rendre service' (being of service), but there is no regular social interaction out-side the family that allows the Abrièsois to decide spontaneously to have a dance, for example. Villagers consistently recall that in the past friends returning home together at the end of a day in the fields would decide to do something. Someone would bring out an accordion, others would find some lemonade and wine, and there would be a dance in the main square. Old people and children would attend too. 'It was very easy and inexpensive to have fun in the past,' the villagers often say.

They contrast this spontaneous fun with the present situation. Dances are now held in a large room with a juke-box in the building at the trailer camp. The entrance fee is 10 francs, and one must, of course, pay for drinks as well. Older people, who in the past would have shared in the music and liveliness of the scene, cannot afford to go; they also say they would feel out of place in that 'foreign' environment. Younger people complain about the cost, but some go because it is an opportunity to socialize with age-mates.

The Control of Institutions and Providers of Service

Privatization within the economic system has contributed to privatization within the social system. However, the church remains an important social focus for native Abrièsois. Men, women, and children attend mass on Sundays, and many women go every day of the week. In addition, the congregation holds several processions within the village and once a year organizes community pilgrimages to the Hautes-Alpes shrines of Notre Dame de Laus and Notre Dame de la Salette. Being Catholic is important to most villagers, and the fact that many of the recent migrants are either Protestants or non-practising Catholics widens the gulf between the two groups.

In 1972 I observed a vignette that exemplified village solidarity in relation to a perceived outsider. Every first of May is the procession to the high pasture oratory of Our Lady of Seven Sorrows; the purpose is to praise the Virgin at the beginning of the month dedicated to her and to ask blessings on the fields for the coming agricultural season. That year as is customary, almost all villagers attended; the only absentees were those too ill to leave their houses or to make the long climb up to the oratory. Even though most of the villagers no longer work actively in the fields, being part of this agriculturally oriented procession is an important experience in their lives.

In contrast to the turn-out of the villagers, no recent migrants of adult years participated in the procession of 1972.

The procession formed outside the church. The leaders were children, who carried crosses and banners. The priest and altar boys followed and then the choir, composed of village women. The men brought up the rear. It was the first procession of the season after a long, often house-bound winter, and there was much spirit and gaiety during the walk. People chatted and told jokes, and at many points the laughter and hubbub of the men drowned out the choir. Finally the priest, a Belgian recently appointed to the village, stopped the proceedings and severely reprimanded the men for turning the religious occasion into what he called 'a picnic.' The men were not at all chastened. They began shouting at the priest that it was their village and that they had been going on processions and talking during them long before he came on the scene. Tempers eventually cooled, and the group moved on to the oratory, where the priest blessed the fields. Afterwards the women and children followed the priest back to the church, while the men lingered outside smoking ostentatiously. Said one old man: 'They send us just anybody. That's what happens when you're a lost corner – you have to take whoever they send.'

The incident demonstrates that people are conscious of the priest as an outsider and that he cannot unconditionally impose his authority. Many villagers' sense of the occasion did not conform with the priest's definition of what the ritual required, and they felt within their rights to express objections to the priest on the basis of pre-existing solidarity.

This incident can be further interpreted within a wider social context to assess the stereotyped notion that peasants invariably resist change. In terms of their ritual life, Abrièsois villagers have declared themselves far from traditionalists, expressing approval of the reforms begun by Pope John XXIII and the Second Vatican Council. For example, many are quite enthusiastic about the mass being said in French, rather than Latin, and about other updating of Catholic ceremonies. They do not object to modernization per se. What they do express objections to is the fact that the priest sent to them is, they feel, poorly qualified ('a know-nothing'). They maintain that the religious authorities who stationed the priest in the village are like the school authorities who consistently send poorly qualified teachers to the villages. The frequent quip is that church and school authorities send their failures to Abriès for vacations.

This situation is an important feature of the social aspects of underdevelopment. In the past, the Abrièsois had some control over the quality of professional services available to them. During the ancien régime, Abriès produced many of its own priests, and the people struggled with the church hierarchy to define the economic terms of their presence in the village. The Abrièsois also once hired their own teachers and doctors. Now they have lost that control. Abriès is no longer a village of close to 2000 people that can afford to support the kind of services it wants; it is a depopulated, isolated backwater that takes what it can get.

Settings for Socialization

Older women provide the leadership for one of the most cohesive groups in the village, and they focus much of their social energy on church activities. Choir practice brings a dozen women together on a regular weekly basis; they use the occasion to exchange information, plan to visit the sick and do errands for those who cannot get out, and mobilize aid in case of an emergency in an Abrièsois family. This group exhibits much solidarity, and members have rebuked the priest on more than one occasion for meddling in affairs which they considered were not his business.

By contrast, the social situation of the village's men is very scattered. They have no regular place to meet. The hotel bars are expensive and cater to a sophisticated tourist clientele. Village men do not feel comfortable in such surroundings and usually spend their evenings standing, talking, and smoking under the old stone arches of Les Halles, which used to cover the market and have now been incorporated into the town hall. The fact that the men do not even have a café in which to socialize is considered a great tragedy by the Abrièsois.

The absence of a café setting also means that married and unmarried men rarely socialize together. This pattern is in contrast to women's social groups, which encompass married and unmarried women of varying ages and degrees of wealth. The men have no overarching structure or area of social focus which cuts across divisions of age, sex, and wealth. In the past the Wednesday market brought together men from different walks of life not only to transact business but also to drink, gamble, play boules, and talk.

Church-related functions are obviously not an appropriate setting for drinking and gambling. But the question arises: why don't Abrièsois men at least play boules together? The answer is that for most of the summer there is no place to play. The central square, the logical boules court, becomes a parking lot for tourist cars in the summer. It is almost impossible to squeeze a hay wagon through the square, let alone to set up a game. There is an open flat space outside the church, but this is not considered a place where one can freely joke and swear. A third possibility is the boules court run by the trailer camp. However, there is a small fee to use this court, and players are expected to order drinks from the bar. Only those Abrièsois with steady incomes, such as the postman and the mason, feel they can afford the cost of playing boules in this setting. Most Abriès men generally avoid the camp's boules court except to turn out once a season to watch a tournament which is dominated by tourist players.

The game of boules is not entirely dead in the village, however. One frequently finds a family – husband, wife, children, and any visiting relatives – playing on the path or road beside their house. Since no gambling occurs at such sessions, they are considered not serious games but a way of amusing the kids on a Sunday afternoon when work is not pressing.

The fact that the family rather than male solidarity groups has become a social focus for boules playing is an important clue to what is happening to social life in Abriès. Underdevelopment has stripped away most of the ties between households, and as a consequence, the family unit has become the most important social focus for many people. The nuclear family has always been important in this peasant society, but now social functions which were previously dispersed through the community are all dumped on this increasingly isolated institution. And given the present economic system, many of these families are in competition with one another.

Competition and 'Jalousie'

The outcome of this competition in social terms is 'jalousie' (jealousy). The villagers say people no longer help one another out because they have become jealous. Blaxter (1971: 121 defines jalousie within the context of a French Pyrenean village as 'the protection of one's own rights or status against a perceived challenge.' She argues quite correctly that jealousy is a statement about competition, but she misunderstands the source of that competition. For the Abrièsois, the problem is not the competition inevitable in a small-scale society but rather the competition generated by the penetration of capitalism into a community in which most economic levelling devices no longer operate and in which self-interest is no longer mediated by co-operative structures in which people can be of service to one another.

Blaxter's excessively voluntaristic explanation of jealousy versus mutual assistance makes it seem as if people can make completely independent choices about whether they will co-operate or not and can decide for completely independent reasons (attitudes and value systems) whether a particular exchange is appropriate or not. When one explores the links between value systems and the material conditions of everyday life, a different explanation emerges. Cultivators in Abriès know that they cannot all be successful. This understanding is not an 'image of limited good' said to be characteristic of backward peasant societies (Foster 1965). It is simply a fact of life, known to all Abrièsois, which finds its reality in the market-place. In Abriès, the non-fair in which animal buyers made private deals, the purchase of expensive machinery, and the rental of land by various households signal a high level of competition among remaining cultivators. Avoidance, silence, and gossip are ways in which the people deal with the tensions produced by competition. One young cultivator has expressed the contradictions of farming life in Abriès this way: 'Only the last farmer in the village will survive, only he will have enough land to use machinery and make a profit.'

POLITICS, PATRONAGE, AND PERSONNALITÉ

Patronage has been the dominant idiom of political life in the Hautes-Alpes since the mid-nineteenth century. Despite changes at the national level, (for example, the creation of a republican constitution, and the development of political parties), patronage persists at the local level because of the region's economic underdevelopment, which has unfolded in terms of increasing dependence on state subsidies. A relatively simple trade-off of interests has emerged in which national (government-forming) political parties preserve such a region as a domain for career-building. A neophyte politician is 'parachuted' into a local political arena, is elected on the promise of bringing some economic benefit to the locality, and may hope to move on to higher public office eventually. As a retired high-school teacher from Gap told me about the villages of the Hautes-Alpes in 1973: 'Here it's a "parachutist heaven" – a poor depopulated region ... it doesn't cost much to buy people.'

The Abrièsois, like other people of the Hautes-Alpes, participate in such a system because they are economically dependent on governmental subsidies and hope that the locally elected politician will indeed rise through the system of multiple office-holding and then not cut ties with the locality but distribute resource rewards for loyalty. (In France an individual may hold municipal and national office simultaneously.)

Since people can choose among potential patron/politicians and even attempt to launch patrons of their own, they do have some political choice within this system. However, to say they have a choice says nothing about the definitions of the system itself – their choice is only among patrons. Peasants expect patrons to grant them favours, to mediate for them in situations in which they have no control. Villagers are mobilized through new patrons when their older ties are weakened or their standard of living takes a downward swing. In this context, peasants are not seeking revolution or even reform but rather the protection of men more powerful than themselves. Thus they will seek out and bind themselves to new patrons as the occasion demands. In such a political context people are selectively mobilized, but they are also dependent.

Such vertical political integration has an aspect of modernity because it is phrased within the modern political party system and so outwardly stresses universalistic goals (usually French nationalism). But it is also a form of political demobilization because it inhibits the horizontal coalitions which precede the articulation of class consciousness (Huizer 1969; Berger 1972).

Peasant Diplomacy

Blok (1969) points out the important role of patronage, often disguised as friendship, within the modern political arena. The system is not one of simple domination but of selective manipulation which includes the clients' strategy for survival in a changing and complex environment as well as the career ambitions of the patron. It is a dynamic in which villagers feel they are participating rather than being the passive victims of a political system.

In Abriès, villagers call this form of participation 'peasant diplomacy,' a term which de-emphasizes the dependency aspect of the transaction and emphasizes the shrewd, realistic assessments they make within the patronage-dominated political system. Peasant diplomacy in practice means exchanging votes for subsidies and supporting someone with a long reach (and 'big sleeves') who can penetrate the system and get access to money. Therefore, the Abrièsois think it wise to support personnalités above any ideological considerations. In Abriès, people pride themselves on their flexibility, on having supported extreme conservatives and socialists at various times. Said one politically conservative villager: 'I'd vote for a communist if he had good connections.' What is important in politics is a personnalité, such as Toye-Riont in the past and Maurice Jaubert, the present-day SicaSport dynamo.

The word 'personnalité' is easier to explain than to define. A personnalité is someone who is well-known and well-placed and can bring subsidies and loans from the state. A good personnalité is someone like the famous Briançonnais member of the cantonal general council who never campaigned during an election. All he did was publish in the newspapers what the department had paid out in taxes and what he had brought in in government grants. His prowess in bringing in money was characterized as 'c'était bien arrosé' – the phrase used of someone who waters a field well. One of the clues to his success was multiple office-holding; he was not only a member of the cantonal general council but also a national minister of finance. People argue that because of multiple office-holding, all decisions are eventually made in Paris, the only way to influence them is through personal connections with a *personnalité*.

The Personnalités of Abriès
At present, Abriès has two aspiring personnalités. In order to understand their political careers – both are migrants to the village – we must first explore the career of a third man, an indigenous powerholder.

The Allands
Abriès now has two orbits of patronage. One system is small-scale, deals with concrete and limited resources in the village, and links clients to an old Abriès family. The other system is large-scale, involves crucial subsistence resources and potential future resources, and places clients in a wider network of power relations.

After the Second World War, the Abrièsois elected a mayor who was a shopkeeper, butcher, and cultivator. Jean Alland was from an old Abriès family that took pride in education (he has inherited books from his ancestors dating from 1709). Although not wealthy himself, he had two brothers who had become very successful merchants in Toulon. He married a woman from a similar though wealthier background whose relatives had established themselves in Aix. Her grandfather had been mayor of Abriès for twenty years, and her uncle and later her aunt served as secretary to the mayor. Alland was considered well-qualified for the job because of these connections and because of his affable personality.

As mayor at the time of the reconstruction of the village and the agricultural pilot project, Alland was called on to handle many conflict situations, and he made many enemies. Furthermore, his wife's opposition to land reform alienated many poorer cultivators from giving him continued support. As reconstruction slowly unfolded but economic conditions did not improve, opposition to him grew. Many people argued that he was not educated enough to extract subsidies from the state and that his wife's influence was blocking agricultural development.

In the mayoral election of 1959, the director of the children's sanitorium announced his candidacy on a program of tourist expansion. Alland lost by three votes. He now attributes his defeat to his own weariness as well as to the glamour of an outsider who had a better education and no history of village conflicts. The new mayor plugged Abriès into tourist development. He made friends with a Grenoblois contractor who knew Abriès from his army days and was interested in building projects in the village. Eventually the contractor developed political ambitions of his own, ran for mayor in the next election (1966), and won.

When asked why no villager ran in the 1966 election between two outsiders, the Abrièsois are unanimous in saying that no villager had enough education to qualify. The preceding administrations had been able to handle the state bureaucracy because they were primarily concerned with processing pension and family-allowance forms. But the new demands of tourist development are considered complex and risky. No villager has expressed willingness to take responsibility for such ventures as SicaSport deficit-spending or new chalet developments.

Alland still lives in the village, as does his former secretary, his wife's aunt, Mme Belier. Both still operate as patrons to some villagers, although their roles are quite limited. They dispense resources in return for loyalty and prestige but have no wider political ambitions. They behave strictly as patrons and not as power-brokers. For example, most villagers still go to Mme Belier if they have problems with the national pension bureaucracy. (The present village secretary does not live in Abriès but commutes to the village three days a week. Villagers who feel uncomfortable asking this new secretary questions, often have the option of not doing so, having had a history of positive experience with Mme Belier.) They do not pay Mme Belier money for her assistance, but they express loyalty to her by shopping at her nephew's grocery, by accompanying her to church or choir practice, and by behaving in a deferential manner with her. Mme Belier acquires prestige and status in the exchange.

More material resources are involved in the case of Alland. He and his wife have a small clientele who share-crop their gardens. Other clients obtain credit at the Allands' store and in return may be called upon to loan a mule when it is time to plant potatoes or to perform small services such as haircutting. Such exchanges are always phrased in terms of 'being of service' and are considered an expression of friendship. But some exchanges go beyond friendship in the sense that they are consistently lop-sided (Kenny 1960).

Clients' loyalties are expressed by shopping at the Alland store and by taking the Allands' part in factional disputes, some of which go back twenty years to the period when Alland was mayor. His present-day clients supported him then and continue to support him now. His opponents shop at competing stores, sit far away from the Allands in church, and avoid them on the street.

We can consider this kind of patron-client relationship to lie within the realm of the 'politics of reputation' (Bailey 1971). Values are crucial in such a system, and the material stakes are low. Neither Mme Belier nor Alland exercises enough economic power to create complete dependence. This is the essential difference between them and the new mayor.

The New Mayor

The new mayor, François Lebrun, is a patron with significant material resources to dispense, and he is also a power broker who has access to even more important contacts. Alland and Mme Belier are patrons in the strict sense of the anthropological definition. Their resources are finite and well defined (Boissevain 1969). The power of the new mayor stems from the fact that he has *potential* access to a much vaster array of resources.

First, the new mayor dispenses direct patronage in the form of municipal jobs. Thus the garbage collector and the garde champêtre are his clients and express loyalty to him even though they are also cousins of the Allands. Second, since the mayor is a promoter of tourism, he is credited with providing tourist-related jobs to the villagers. Third and most significant is the possibility that Lebrun may eventually bring more important, better-paying jobs to Abriès. In this context he has allied to himself the anti-Alland faction which contains the two families with teen-age children who are being directed into building trades in the expectation that tourism will bring construction jobs. As a contractor, the mayor is in a position to dispense any such jobs within the village and to know about such work in the region. The promise of a future chalet development is very attractive to these households, and they in turn are very active in their support of tourism.

Cultivators in the village are not as eager in their support of the mayor and tourism. Moreover they have ties to the old patron system, especially to the services of Mme Belier. But they do not form an opposition faction. Most accept that agriculture is secondary to tourism and that if they want to continue as agriculturalists, they must work through the new mayor to get subsidies. Although the mayor is not a cultivator and is generally acknowledged to know nothing about farming, he is allied with the mayor of Ceillac, who is building a career on a platform of combining tourism and agriculture. Ceillac's mayor supports the mowing-cow scheme of paying subsidies to cow-owners to graze the slopes. Lebrun also supports the plan and is credited with having facilitated subsidies for two Abriès cultivators.

A final and crucial area of support for the mayor is the recent migrant community. The hotel owners and managers, the boutique owners, and the baker say they would generally support Lebrun over a village-born mayor because he is more sophisticated, more energetic, and more capable of promoting tourism than a villager could be. They argue that Alland was too narrow and provincial to promote large-scale tourism properly. Although this group disagrees about the shape that tourist expansion should take – some want to develop cross-country skiing, while others are in favour of expanding downhill facilities – all agree that essential to expansion are the promotional talents and political connections of the dynamic Jaubert of Ceillac and his client, the mayor of Abriès.

Jaubert is further advanced in the political system than Lebrun and has access to useful contacts. Jaubert has already promoted and built a chalet development in Ceillac. He has also encouraged such a development in Abriès; however, the project has been stalled in the courts because a Grenoble judge who hears expropriation cases has taken a very long time to review the Abriès situation. The mayor of Abriès claims that the judge is a political enemy of Jaubert's. If Jaubert cannot overcome the judge's opposition and get the chalet project off the ground, Lebrun may withdraw his support and find a new patron. Since nothing specific holds him to Abriès at this point, he may cut ties with the village and move on to develop his career elsewhere.

The Contenders

A man who is less flexible in his political options is Daniel Levesque, the mayor of Ristolas and a contender for local power. Levesque is much more committed to staying in Abriès because, although he was born in Marseilles, he is married to an Abriès woman; they live in her parents' house and have three children in the village.

Levesque has attempted to launch his political career as an independent. Although he is an outsider, he is not a parachute mayor in the strict sense of the word. Ristolas, a village of only eighty people, found itself with no one willing to take on the job of mayor. Levesque was familiar to villagers as the director of works for the Department of Bridges and Roads in the Queyras, and he decided to accept the office.

In 1973 Levesque ran for a seat on the cantonal general council. The government party was attempting to define the elections as strictly apolitical, just a matter of administration, since it feared a loss and did not want the party name identified with one. Many villagers also argue that the council operates for the most part as an advisory body, rubber-stamping the budget and never disagreeing with the prefect; only a strong personnalité, they say, could go against such a system.

Levesque lost the cantonal election after a very low-key campaign in which he did not identify with any political party or any major issues, but presented himself as being for 'modern' tourist expansion. His general stance was in opposition to Bouvier, the Queyrassin who won a third term in the office and who is considered in Abriès to be arrogant, incompetent, and perhaps crazy. A staunch party member, he is considered by some an embarrassment to the party because his views are often to the right of its stance and because he has been known to employ strong-arm tactics during an election campaign. The party has discouraged him from running for deputy, but he feels that another success at the cantonal level will put him in position to run for higher office.

Bouvier's cantonal campaign stressed the fact that he was a personnalité, had experience in office, and was a proven money-getter. He outlined a program of milk subsidies, road improvements, and subsidies to schoolchildren. He also portrayed himself as an insider – 'a true child of the Queyras' – and as someone equally in favour of agriculture and tourism. His campaign literature described him as an 'agriculturalist-hotel owner'.

Levesque lost the election because he was not as experienced a broker as Bouvier. He did not have as many contacts or as many clients. Even in Abriès, Levesque was able to pull only ten more votes than Bouvier. (Seven votes went to the communist candidate, the director of the vacation colony.) Levesque has not been able to tap the mayor's client network in Abriès, and his base of operation, Ristolas, is demographically too small to compensate.

Lebrun, the mayor of Abriès, did not actively co-operate with Levesque in this election; in fact, Lebrun was away from the village for most of the campaign. The two men are in potential competition. Both are allied with Jaubert, but the mayor of Abriès would have gained very little by supporting Levesque for a post that he might someday be interested in contesting himself. Abriès is too small for Levesque to set up a competing clientele, and Levesque has too few resources and contacts to attract clientele away from its mayor. Abriès may, however, see these two aspiring personnalités in open conflict if the department's attempt to amalgamate Ristolas and Abriès is successful.

Only one village-born Abrièsois has said that he might be interested in pursuing politics. Considered very ambitious by villagers, he is moving out of farming into tourism. He is a supporter of the mayor and on the municipal council, but whether he will develop a political career is uncertain. If he does not, it is doubtful that Abriès will ever again have a mayor with an agricultural background. This trend within the political system reinforces the dominance of tourist development over agriculture.

POLITICS AND ECONOMICS

The political arena reflects the fragmentation of social and economic life in Abriès. There are few connecting links between village households and few horizontal coalitions. Most political links are in the vertical, unequal dyadic chains characteristic of a patron-client network. This pattern is the opposite of what social scientists tell us should appear in a modern political system in which 'political authority ... may be defined as the institutionalization of political goal attainment' (Nettl 1967: 57).

Power flows through a patron-client network in Abriès but not because the Abrièsois are unfamiliar with modern politics. They have been integrated into national politics for a long time, so that the 'forced process of familiarization with politics' said to be necessary (ibid. 70) is not the issue in this village. In fact, the political parties themselves, whose job it is, in theory, to provide institutional channels, contribute to the perpetuation of personalistic political networks.

The Abrièsois think of themselves as living in a republic and a democracy. But their participation in that democratic system has very little impact on policy-making. When we compare the kind of leverage Abrièsois had in the ancien regime, through the escarton system, to the weak leverage they possess today, we can argue that they are more politically demobilized under the modern system than they were during the old regime. Their traditional political system was not based on 'parochial hierarchy and acquiescence' (Shils 1970b: 304), and the modern system in which they are involved shows very little 'system sensitivity' to the local-level politics (Eisenstadt 1973: 74). It was the 'traditional' Abrièsois who had lobbyists in Paris; the 'modern' ones have none.

The politics of Abriès is part of an overall process of underdevelopment in which localities lose control over decision-making. This loss of control has been part of the process of modernization, not a remnant from a traditional past. Blok (1974) describes a similar, though more violent, pattern in a Sicilian village, analysed over one hundred years. In both cases political underdevelopment is connected with the dependency relations created by the penetration of capitalism in the nineteenth century and the flourishing of entrepreneurial power-holders who stand between the village and the state. Economic underdevelopment and emigration discourage alliances against the patronage system. In Abriès villagers have responded by making a virtue out of the process – defining their political participation in terms of choosing among patrons. Thus even within a situation of structural dependency, they continue to struggle to have some control over their own lives.

Many of the trends that were developing in the nineteenth century have come into sharp focus in the modern era. The most significant feature is that Abriès has resources of interest to the supralocal level but Abrièsois cannot exploit them. Thus there has emerged a split between villagers and the resources which in theory they hold. Collectively held resources, such as forests and pastures, were loosened from village control by state intervention in the nineteenth century. Now non-villagers exploit these resources for profit, while the village receives only nominal payment for their use.

Only a few native Abrièsois are now able to draw profits from agriculture. Most villagers are too undercapitalized to exploit the resources beyond subsistence needs. The native Abriès economy presents the classic profile of underdevelopment: migration-remittance, transfer payments, and underemployment.

Yet the commune of Abriès is a big, potentially profitable piece of real estate which can easily be developed as a tourist resort without the participation of many Abrièsois. In fact, the quiet, park-like quality of a depopulated Abriès is very attractive to tourists and is promoted by tourism developers. Only a skeleton staff of locals are needed for avalanche management, and even this job could be done by others. Some villagers who wish to hold onto their fields for farming are seen as impediments to tourist development, and efforts are being made to expropriate their land. In most cases, however, expropriation is not necessary. Land speculation, out-migration, and the aging of the village population are effectively withdrawing land from production.

On the surface, it seems that only private capitalists will profit from the conversion of Abriès to a tourist resort. Yet the central government has an important stake in managing the direction of the village's economy. First, tourism brings in tax revenues. It impedes general depopulation by bringing in a young, replacement population that pays taxes and does not draw on the state welfare payments. Furthermore, land for commercial and building purposes is taxed at a higher rate than agricultural land. Second and structurally more significant is the fact that Abriès and hundreds of villages like it provide cheap, affordable vacations to the working class of the large industrial cities of the south. By turning the Queyras into a regional park and promoting tourism, the state has been able to offer its southern working class a share in the good life which was once available only to wealthier people. Such a trade-off is a shrewd political strategy which attempts to gain the loyalty of a large population of urban southerners at the expense of a very small, politically expendable population of montagnards.

9

The Ironies of History

The aim of this book has been to trace as explicitly as possible how the large-scale processes of state-making and the spread of capitalism were experienced by a single village because a concrete example can often capture a fragment of reality in a way no abstract formulation can. As we have seen, Abriès was not a stereotypical peasant village during the ancien régime. Its inhabitants were not ignorant or apolitical or poor; rather they were a feisty, politically engaged population with the resources and skills to construct, operate, and defend substantial economic and political institutions.

During the old regime peasant production, although involved in local markets, was not geared essentially towards profit, and the Abriè-sois were able as a community to exercise considerable control over their local economy. They policed their own market system, controlled weights, measures, and prices according to Queyrassin standards of fairness, implemented public health measures, and maintained internal levelling mechanisms that discouraged wealth accumulation by individuals or families. By old regime standards, Abriès was relatively egalitarian in terms of both gender and class. Women made wills, inherited wealth, and were heavily involved in production. There were no powerful landowners. In economic terms, the village had decision-making power over its own destiny. The community supported a large population and weathered the periodic crises caused by warfare and disease.

Although Abriès was geographically distant from Paris, it certainly was not remote from state interest or scrutiny. Abriès had actively inserted itself into the state's purview through the fourteenth-century negotiations which created the coalition of the escarton system. When the crown was weak, Briançonnais villages were able to excercise considerable leverage on the centre, but as the French state worked out its ' "convulsive" progression towards a centralized monarchical State' (Anderson 1974: 86), the tables turned.

As France pushed towards European ascendancy, it began to demand loyalty from its border regions. The Briançonnais, with its transalpine passes, became a key strategic arena. The message of seventeenth- and eighteenth-century state intentions is visible to this day in the Vauban-designed fortresses throughout the Briançonnais. Peasants all over France were squeezed for tax money and soldiers to fight seventeenth- and eighteenth-century wars (Porchnev 1963), but the people of the Briançonnais were often very successful in deflecting these demands. And here we see the importance of analysing such processes from the bottom up. The Briançonnais villages met these demands with quite refined negotiations. Dealings with representatives of the central government did not cow the peasants; in fact, they often went straight to the top and actually maintained lobbyists in Paris to plead their cause. The fact that they acted so effectively was certainly not seen by the state as completely outside the realm of political discourse. In fact, the old regime successes of Briançonnais villages aroused suspicion rather than disbelief. Whatever else was going on, it is clear that representatives of the state, from military engineers to intendants, were engaged in serious political dialogue with the villagers of Abriès and the Briançonnais. Supralocal power-holders dealt with peasant representatives without disdaining or romanticizing them, as did later bureaucrats.

The legal/political structural changes of the Revolutionary era demoted and isolated the villages of the Briançonnais. With the escarton system dismantled, each village had to defend its interests on its own and had to deal with the fact that internal village politics were being recast as matters under the control of central administration. Thus by the end of the nineteenth century we see Briançonnais cultivators being extolled for their simple peasant virtues and their lack of political engagement. As local autonomy and agency declined, the capacity for stereotyping increased.

By this time the representative and responsible features of the escarton system seem to have been forgotten at both the village level and the supralocal level, and the structures of personal patronage became normative for political discourse at all levels. The position of local power-holders/mediators was enhanced, and the ability of villagers to put the breaks on accumulation of power was weakened.

A contemporary observer characterized the lifting of decision-making power out of local hands in nineteenth-century France this way: 'Every common interest was straightaway severed from society, counterposed to it as a higher general interest snatched from the activity of society's members themselves and made the object of government activity, from a bridge, a schoolhouse and the communal property of a village to the railways, the national wealth and the national university of France' (Marx [1869] 1969: 170–1). The new political culture which emerged at this time was read backwards into history to generate an image of unchanging and apolitical peasant life.

This transformation of the nature of the political past was facilitated by the experiments in directed development acted out in the nineteenth century. The message that peasants were incompetent and needed external guidance was delivered by supralocal power-holders in a variety of ways. Admiration for the skills, literacy, and prosperity of villagers faded in the face of a barrage of advice from experts and bureaucrats on how to manage economic change. The Abrièsois responded with a mixture of compliance, resistance, and escape, phrasing their actions in terms of 'peasant diplomacy.'

The story we have seen unfolding in Abriès is certainly not unique; in fact, it is easily compared to some of the examples of disastrous development planning found in the world today. The particular case of nineteenth-century Abriès is unusual only in that we have records of so much of the detail of bureacratic misperceptions and heavy-handedness and our knowledge of the village can be contextualized in a long-term perspective. We can reach into the distant past and assess the antecedents to capitalist development and then move to the present to examine its consequences. What we learn is that the Abrièsois had managed their economy quite effectively before intervention from the supralocal level and that they are still struggling with the fallout from nineteenth-century planning.

Many villagers today see the nineteenth century as a time when those who were smart did well – especially those who migrated to South America. This mythology of success and betterment elsewhere is usually coupled with statements about the egalitarian nature of village life in the days when parents and grandparents were all poor but equal. (Some women are not totally satisfied with this view of an egalitarian past; they comment that although women worked just as hard as men in the old days, their work was not valued as much, particularly on corvées where the contributions of females – usually widows – were rated at half the contributions of males.)

Today long-time Abriès residents certainly do not see themselves as incompetent; in that sense external attempts to label them have been resisted. Many continue to regard themselves as political actors, shrewdly working through a maze of personalistic politics, which is what 'peasant diplomacy' has come to mean. Others think of themselves as old and tired and describe their lives as more boring and more isolated than 'before.' They do not feel that they themselves can do very much to change their living conditions, and they wonder what changes new migrants will bring to the village. Older cultivators appear to fit the stereotype of peasant uncooperativeness towards change, especially at public meetings with agricultural officials, where each side expresses disdain for the competence of the other. With some justice, older agriculturalists can point out that they have 'heard it all before.' Younger farmers and recent migrants express a more energetic confidence in the future – but one that will be very different from the immediate past.

REFLECTIONS ON CHANGE

In the summer of 1977 I visited Abriès briefly and found signs of this tourist-oriented future. In the central square stood a small kiosk displaying wares of the usual alpine kitsch – everything from pressed edelweiss to miniature mountain scenes encased in clear plastic globes that fill with snow sprinkles when inverted. I had seen such generic mountain souvenirs in village stores before. What were new were tee-shirts and bumper stickers trumpeting the name Abriès in a variety of colours and designs.

Around me was the new Abriès, the one being merchandized. There were giant construction cranes, cement mixers, and half-constructed buildings all over the commune. One billboard for one project announced that its Vietnamese architect was building authentic alpine chalets. Another company – Agence Neige et Soleil – urged buyers to contemplate the 'construction traditionelle' of its electrically heated condominium apartments.

An Abriès friend told me that these new residences were being built by Algerian and Turkish construction workers, who were housed in wooden caravans at the edge of the town. 'Mon dieu, je pensais que c'était la cirque. Mais non, c'était un Turque' (My God, when I saw one of those Turks, I thought the circus had come to town), he quipped. But he went on to say that he found these chaps serious and hard-working and had invited some over for an occasional Sunday dinner because he could see that they were lonely.

I discussed with Abrièsois some of the history presented in this book, and they shared with me their view of history. Many have heard that the Queyras was once allied with four other valleys in a 'little republic.' Every summer some Abrièsois climb up to the pass fronting the border to meet with Italian villagers. The groups from both sides of the mountain, speaking exactly the same patois, enjoy a picnic which celebrates a startling sense of solidarity with the ancient escarton system.

Because population figures are the stuff of political controversy in Abriès, most of the current inhabitants know that the village had a population of 2000 some time in the past. They also know the name Berthelot, partly because descendants of that family maintain a summer house in Abriès. But today's villagers think of the Berthelots as having been aristocrats whose powers were swept away by the Revolution of 1789.

Many of today's Abrièsois cultivators realize that some of their present agricultural practices are very ancient; they adopt the metaphor of a golden age to describe their happy, hard-working, non-materialistic past and to express pride in the continuity of its practices. Recent migrants to the village point to the same continuities as proof that peasants are hidebound and resistant to change and, therefore, incapable of seeing the virtues of tourist development. These competing perceptions are irreconcilable and would likely continue even if the 'true' story of Abriès were suddenly understood by both sides.

Politics in the village today draws on these representations of the past to explain and support changes or refusals to change in the present. In this sensibility the modern Abrièsois are not unlike generations of past bureaucrats, priests, army officers, agronomists, gendarmes, and tax collectors, who saw what they saw through lenses that reflected their own interests and status in the social, political, and economic systems of their moment in history. Could an eighteenth-century army engineer have foreseen the mass out-migration of Abrièsois in the nineteenth century? Do twentieth-century agricultural experts who suggest that the Abrièsois raise sheep and develop more collectivist practices know that nineteenth-century Forest Administration officials advocated just the opposite?

Villagers do not hold the full sweep of evolutionary, devolutionary, and involutionary transformations in their consciousness as they deal with various immediate political and economic issues. It is not just the 'true' past that is not known and not knowable; it is also the 'true' present. Decisions made around the world influence life in Abriès but the Abrièsois have no control over them. The policies of the European Economic Community are not negotiated with villages; neither are the budgets of multinational corporations such as Nestlé. The vote does not touch these institutions. The institutions it does touch are rarely relevant to the village as a unit; rather they deal with the Abrièsois in terms of categories that are regional (the poor south) or national (farmers or tourism developers). State machinery is not geared to generating a dialogue with every village in France.

The political economy analysis used in this study has permitted us to explore some of the multiple levels of historical change by seeing villagers as agents in the dialectical construction of transformations – agents not always operating within circumstances of their own choosing but active participants under even the most stressful of circumstances.

One area of the history of Abriès which remains unexplored is how and why so much of these past struggles, achievements, and failures have been erased from villagers' memories and from official histories. Certainly the Abrièsois have not suffered any concerted conspiracy to strip them of historical memory – there has been no official censorship or banning of books. What then are the mechanisms which fragment and disperse understandings of change? I can only mention some of the more obvious ones. Certainly, the massive out-migrations that started in the mid-nineteenth century were a factor in reordering peoples' understandings. How the diaspora interpreted what was happening we do not yet know. Neither do we know very much about how those who remained explained their decisions to themselves. An analysis of surviving letters, diaries, and other texts of this era would certainly allow us to enter a dimension of ethnohistorical interpretation not tapped by political economy analysis.

Another influence on the way villagers and officials interpret Abriès's past and its present situation is the fact that change in this village has almost always been what Rosa Luxemberg terms 'peaceful,' rather than proceeding by violent confrontation. The negotiated world of Abriès's history has a paucity of symbols of resistance. The silent crises of economic, demographic, and political transformations generated no memorializing symbols: no plaques referencing last stands, no statues of named martyrs, no songs eulogizing heroes and heroines.

Of course, these concerns are not often at the forefront of the Abrièsois's consciousness. Villagers must still cope with day-to-day economic and interpersonal problems. Yet there is an awareness of the enormous forces which constrain people's life decisions. Within such boundaries people still struggle to give shape and direction to their lives, to guide their children, and to communicate with God. Although underdevelopment is a reality of village life, it has not created despair among the population. But there is a sense of irrevocable loss, which villagers express in different ways. Some speak of the fact that their young people have no future in Abriès and must migrate out. Some talk about the loss of ambiance and fun – the boredom of village life. Some mention the loss of game animals and birds. One cultivator explained to me the rarity of eagles: with the decline of agricultural production, the field rodents and other agricultural pests which were the prey of eagles also disappeared. 'Today, we see no eagles soaring over the mountains of Abriès ... we have no more eagles.'

Sources

Archival sources are identified in the text, using the following abbreviations:

ADHA   Archives Départementales des Hautes-Alpes
ADI   Archives Départementales de l'Isère
AMA   Archives Municipal d'Abriès
AN   Archives Nationales
DDA   Direction Départementale d'Agriculture, Hautes-Alpes
DGFV   Dépôt Général de Fortifications, Vincennes

Albert, Antoine. 1783. *Histoire naturelle, ecclésiastique et civile du diocèse d'Embrun*. 2 vols. Paris: Bachelier (Typescript version issued by Association des Hautes-Alpes de Toulon et du Var, 1959)

Albert, Aristide. 1889a. "Le Pays briançonnais: Les Queyrassins negociants.' *Bulletin de la Société d'Etudes des Hautes-Alpes* 8: 313-31

- 1889b. *Biographie-Bibliographie du Briançonnais, Vallée du Queyras, Canton d'Aiguilles*. Gap: Jouglard

Allier, C. 1882. 'Note sur le rôle économique des fruitières dans les Hautes-Alpes.' *Bulletin de la Société d'Etudes des Hautes-Alpes* 1: 115-30

Allix, André. 1928. *Un Pays de Haute Montagne, L'Oisans*. Paris: Armand Colin.

Almond, G., and G.B. Powell. 1965. *Comparative Politics: A Developmental Approach*. Boston: Little Brown

Almond, G., and S. Verba. 1963. *The Civic Culture*. Princeton: Princeton University Press

Anderson, Perry. 1974. *Lineages of the Absolutist State*. London: New Left Review Editions

Anderson, R.T., and B.G. Anderson. 1964. *The Vanishing Village: A Danish Maritime Community*. Cambridge: Harvard University Press

Arensberg, C.M., and S.T. Kimball. 1940. *Family and Community in Ireland*. Cambridge: Harvard University Press

Aron, Jean-Paul, Paul Dumont, and Emmanuel Le Roy Ladurie. 1972. *Anthropologie du conscrit français d'après les comptes numériques et sommaires du recrutement de l'armée, 1819–1826*. Paris: Mouton

Aston, Trevor, ed. 1967. *Crisis in Europe, 1560–1660*. Garden City, New York: Anchor

Aubert, Bernard. 1959. 'Etude d'une haute vallée alpestre: le Queyras.' Thesis, Institut d'Urbanisme de l'Université de Paris

Bailey, F.G. 1969. *Stratagems and Spoils: A Social Anthropology of Politics*. Oxford: Basil Blackwell

Balandier, Georges. 1970. *Political Anthropology*. New York: Pantheon

Barnes, J.A. 1972. *Social Networks*. Addison-Wesley Module in Anthropology 26. Reading, Mass.: Addison-Wesley

Bee, Robert L. 1974. *Patterns and Processes: An Introduction to Anthropological Strategies for the Study of Sociocultural Change*. New York: The Free Press

Bendix, Reinhard. 1964. *Nation-Building and Citizenship: Studies of Our Changing Social Order*. New York: Wiley

Berge, Abbé. ca 1920. 'Histoire du Queyras.' Manuscript, Abriès Archives

Berger, John, and Jean Mohr. 1975. *A Seventh Man*. Harmondsworth, England: Penguin

Berger, Suzanne. 1972. *Peasants against Politics: Rural Organization in Brittany, 1911–1967*. Harvard University Press

Blache, Jean. 1923. 'L'Essartage, ancienne pratique culturale dans les Alpes dauphinoises.' *Revue de Géographie Alpine* 11: 572-3

Black, C.E. 1966. *The Dynamics of Modernization*. New York: Harper Torchbooks

Blanchard, Camille. 1933. *Une Famille queyrassine: Notes sur les Berthelots*. Bergerac: Imprimerie Générale du Sud-Ouest

Blanchard, Raoul. 1922. 'Aiguilles.' *Revue de Géographie Alpine* 10: 127-65

- 1950. *Les grandes Alpes françaises du Sud*. vol. 5 of *Les Alpes occidentales*. Grenoble, Paris: Arthaud

Blaxter, Lorraine. 1971. 'Rendre Service and Jalousie.' In *Gifts and Poison*, edited by F.G. Bailey. Oxford: Basil Blackwell

Blet, H., E. Esmonin, and G. Letonnelier. 1936. *Le Dauphiné: Recueil de textes historiques*. Grenoble: Arthaud

Bloch, Marc. 1961. *Feudal Society.* 2 vols. Chicago: University of Chicago Press
- 1966. *French Rural History.* Berkeley: University of California Press
Blok, Anton. 1969. 'Variations in Patronage.' *Sociologische GIDS* 16(6): 365-78
- 1974. *The Mafia of a Sicilian Village, 1860–1960: A Study of Violent Peasant Entrepreneurs.* New York: Harper Torchbooks
Boissevain, Jeremy. 1966. 'Patronage in Sicily.' *Man* 1: 18-33
- 1969. 'Patrons as Brokers.' *Sociologische GIDS* 16(6): 379-91
- 1974. *Friends of Friends: Networks, Manipulators, and Coalitions.* Oxford: Blackwells
Bonafous, Maurice. 1957. 'Introduction.' In *L'Evolution de l'agriculture de montagne: l'example des Hautes-Alpes,* edited by Comité Départemental de la Vulgarization et du Progrès Agricole, Hautes-Alpes Gap: Direction des Service Agricole
Brenner, Robert. 1982. 'Symposium: Agrarian Class Structure and Economic Development in Pre-Industrial Europe.' *Past and Present,* no. 67 (November): 16-113
Briot, F. 1881. *Etude sur l'économie pastorale des Hautes-Alpes.* Paris: Bureau de la Revue des Eaux et Forêts
- 1907. *Les Alpes Françaises.* Paris: Berger-Levrault
Burns, Robert K., Jr. 1961. 'The Ecological Basis of French Alpine Communities in the Dauphiné.' *Anthropological Quarterly* 34 (1): 19-35
- 1963. 'The Circum-Alpine Culture Area: A Preliminary View.' *Anthropological Quarterly* 36(3): 130-55
Cameron, Rondo. 1966. *France and the Economic Development of Europe, 1800–1914.* Chicago: Rand McNally
Campbell, John K. 1964. *Honour, Family and Patronage: A Study of Institutions and Moral Values in a Greek Mountain Community.* Oxford: Calendon Press
Canac, Roger. 1968. *La Montagne.* Paris: Seuil
Chabrand, Dr. 1888. *Briançon administré par ses consuls.* Paris: A. Delahaye
Chauvet, Pierre. 1954. 'Remarques sur deux plans d'amenagement: le bassin de la Durance et la zone-témoin du Queyras.' Speech given at meeting of *Centre de Hautes Etudes Administrative,* Gap, 12 June. Photocopy. DDA
- 1970. 'Définition d'une politique de renovation rurale dans les Alpes du Sud.' *Espace,* no. 9
Chomel, Vital. 1970. 'Mélanges: Pareries et frérèches en Dauphiné d'après

quelques textes inédits (vers 1250-1346).' *Cahiers d'Histoire* 15(3): 301-19

Clarke, John. 1965. *Population Geography.* Oxford: Pergamon Press

Cobban, Alfred. 1962. *A History of Modern France.* Vol. 1, *1715-1799.* London: Pelican

Cole, John, and E.R. Wolf. 1974. *The Hidden Frontier: Ecology and Ethnicity in an Alpine Valley.* New York: Academic Press

Comité Départemental de la Vulgarisation et du Progrès Agricole [Hautes-Alpes]. 1957. *L'Evolution de l'agriculture de montagne: l'example des Hautes-Alpes.* Gap: Direction des Services Agricole

Crubellier, Maurice. 1948. 'Le Briançonnais à la fin de l'ancien régime: Notes de géographie historique.' *Revue de Géographie Alpine* 36: 259-99, 335-71

Daumard, A., and F. Furet. 1961. *Structures et relations sociales à Paris au milieu du XVIIIe siècle.* Paris: Armand Colin

Davis, Natalie Zemon. 1977. 'Ghosts, Kin, and Progeny: Some Features of Family Life in Early Modern France.' *Daedalus* 106(2): 87-114

DCG. See *Délibérations du Conseil Général* [Hautes-Alpes]

de Beer, Gavin. 1967. *Hannibal's March.* London: Sidgwick and Jackson

Delafont, Pierre. 1838. 'Ceillac: Un village des Hautes-Alpes.' *Revue du Dauphiné* 1

Délibérations du Conseil Général [Hautes-Alpes]. 1889-91. Gap: Carnot

Deperraz, A., and L. Schultz. 1956. 'Une agriculture "affermie": l'example du Queyras.' Gap: Direction des Services Agricole. Photocopy

de Rochas, Albert, ed. 1882. 'Le Briançonnais au commencement du XVIIIe siècle.' *Bulletin de la Société d'Etudes des Hautes-Alpes* 1

Deutsch, Karl. 1961. 'Social Mobilization and Political Development.' *American Political Science Review* 55: 493-508

Devos, Roger, ed. 1973. 'Manuscrit inédit par Abbé Jacques Gondret. Moeurs et coutumes des habitants du Queyras au XIXe siècle.' *Le Monde Alpin et Rhodien: Révue Régionale d'Ethnologie,* no. 3, 4

Duhamel, Henry, ed. 1902. *Voyage d'inspection de la frontière des Alpes en 1752 par le Marquis de Paulmy.* Grenoble: Falque et Perrin

Duley, Margaret, and Mary Edwards, eds., 1986. *A Cross-Cultural Study of Women: A Comprehensive Guide.* New York: The Feminist Press

Eisenstadt, S.N. 1973. *Tradition, Change, and Modernity.* New York: Wiley

Essai sur la population des taillabilités du Dauphiné d'après les mémoires des Intendants, 1698-1762. 1912. Valence: Jules Céas et Fils

Estienne, Pierre. 1970. 'Démographie ancienne d'une paroisse haut-alpine, 1629-1822 (Ceillac).' *Cahiers d'Histoire* 15(3): 217-28

Fauché-Prunelle, André-Alexandre. 1856-7. *Essai sur les anciennes institutions autonomes ou populaires des Alpes-Cottiennes-Briançonnaises.* 2 vols. Grenoble: C. Vellot

Faure, Léon. ca 1881. *Etude comparative sur le lait de vache dans les Hautes-Alpes.* Gap: Imprimerie des Alpes Republicaines

Foster, George. 1965. 'Peasant Society and the Image of Limited Good.' *American Anthropologist* 67: 293-315

Fourastié, J. 1959. *Le Grand espoir du siècle.* Paris: PUF

- [1959] 1972. 'From the Traditional to the "Tertiary" Life Cycle.' In *Readings in Population,* edited by William Petersen. New York: Macmillan

Fourchy, P. 1944. 'Rémarques sur la question du déboisement des Alpes.' *Revue de Géographie Alpine* 32: 113-28

Frank, André Gunder. 1967. *Capitalism and Underdevelopment in Latin America: Historical Studies of Chile and Brazil.* New York: Monthly Review Press

Franklin, S.H. 1969. *The European Peasantry: The Final Phase.* London: Methuen

Friedl, Ernestine. 1959. 'Dowry and Inheritance in Modern Greece.' *Transactions of the New York Academy of Science* 22: 49-54

Friedmann, Harriet. 1978. 'World Market, State and Family Farm: Social Basis of Household Production in the Era of Wage Labour.' *Comparative Studies in Society and History* 20(4): 545-86

Froud, Nina, and Charlotte Turgeon, eds. 1976. *Larousse Gastronomique.* London: Hamlyn

Galjart, Benno. 1964. 'Class and "Following" in Rural Brazil.' *American Latina* 7(2)

Garreau, Gerrard. 1977. *L'Agrobusiness.* France: Calmann-Levy

Geisendorf, Paul-F. 1961. 'Recherches sur les conséquences démographiques de la révocation de l'Edit de Nantes en Dauphiné.' *Cahiers d'Histoire* 6(3): 245-64

Gellner, Ernest. 1970. 'Democracy and Industrialization.' In *Readings in Social Evolution and Development,* edited by S.N. Eisenstadt. Oxford, New York: Pergamon Press

George, Susan, ed., 1985. *How the Other Half Dies: The Real Reasons for World Hunger.* Harmondsworth, England: Penguin

Gill, Richard T. 1967. *Economic Development: Past and Present.* Englewood Cliffs, NJ: Prentice-Hall

Godechot, Jacques. 1968. *Les Institutions de la France sous la Révolution et l'Empire*. Paris: PUF

Godelier, Maurice. 1966. *Rationalité et irrationalité en économie*. Paris: François Maspero

Golaz, A. 1971. *Fort Queyras*. Gap: Société d'Etudes des Hautes-Alpes

Goodman, David, and Michael Redclift. 1981. *From Peasant to Proletarian: Capitalist Development and Agrarian Transitions*. Oxford: Basil Blackwell

Goubert, Pierre. 1952. 'En Beauvaisis: problèmes démographiques de XVIIe siècle.' *Annales* 7(4)

- 1960. *Beauvais et le Beauvaisis de 1600 à 1730*. 2 vols. Paris: SEVPEN
- 1969. *L'Ancien Régime*. Vol. 1, *La Société*. Paris: Armand Colin
- 1971. 'Local History,' *Daedalus* 100(1): 113-27

Guicherd, Jean. 1933. *L'Agriculture du département des Hautes-Alpes*. Dijon: Bernigaud et Privat

Guillaume, A. 1968. *Le Queyras*. Gap: Société d'Etudes des Hautes-Alpes

Guillaume, P., ed. 1890. 'Transitions de Molines-en-Queyras: Mémoires de Pierre Ebren de Fontgillarde (1577-1775).' *Bulletin de Société d'Études des Hautes-Alpes* 10: 401-20

- 1901. 'L'Industrie laitière dans les Hautes-Alpes d'après les anciens documents.' *Annales des Alpes* 5: 235-82

Guillaume, Pierre, and Jean-Pierre Pousson. 1970. *Démographie historique*. Paris: Armand Colin

Guillemin, P., ed., 1892. 'Le Briançonnais en 1754, par Jean Brunet, Seigneur de l'Argentière.' *Annuaire de la Société des Touristes du Dauphiné* 18: 326-62

Guitton, H. 1951. 'Les fluctuations économique.' *Traité d'Economie Politique* 12

Habermas, Jurgen. 1973. *Legitimation Crisis*. Boston: Beacon Press

Halpern, Manfred. 1971. 'A Redefinition of the Revolutionary Situation.' In *National Liberation*, edited by Norman Miller and Roderick Aya. New York: The Free Press

Harrisson, Pierre. 1982. *L'empire Nestlé: faits et méfaits d'une transnationale en Amérique Latine*, Switzerland: Favre

Heilbroner, Robert L. 1962. *The Making of Economic Society*. Englewood Cliffs, NJ: Prentice-Hall

Henry, Louis, 1970. *Manuel de démographie historique*, 2nd ed. Geneva, Paris: Droz

Hobsbawm, E.J. 1962. *The Age of Revolution, 1789-1848* New York: Mentor

Huizer, Gerrit. 1969. 'The Role of Patronage in the Peasant Political Struggle in Latin America.' *Sociologische GIDS* 6(6): 16–27

International Union of Food and Allied Workers' Associations. 1968. *Nestlé*. Switzerland: IUF Publications

Jessop, Bob. 1977. 'Recent Theories of the Capitalist State.' *Cambridge Journal of Economics* 1: 353–73

Judt, Tony. 1979. *Socialism in Provence, 1871–1914: A Study in the Origins of the Modern French Left*. New York: Cambridge University Press

Kenny, Michael. 1960. 'Patterns of Patronage in Spain.' *Anthropological Quarterly* 33(1): 14–23

- 1962. *A Spanish Tapestry: Town and Country in Castile*. Bloomington: University of Indiana Press

Laclau, Ernesto. 1979. 'Feudalism and Capitalism in Latin America.' In *Politics and Ideology in Marxist Theory*, edited by Ernesto Laclau. London: Verso Editions

Leeds, Anthony. 1973. 'Locality Power in Relation to Supralocal Power Institutions.' In *Urban Anthropology*, edited by Aidan Southall. London: Oxford University Press

Lenoble, F. 1923. 'La légende de déboisement des Alpes.' *Revue de Géographie Alpine* 21: 5–113

Léon, Pierre. 1958. *La Naissance de la grande industrie en Dauphiné*. Paris: PUF

Lerner, David. 1958. *The Passing of Traditional Society*. New York: Free Press

Le Roy Ladurie, Emmanuel. 1966. *Les paysans de Languedoc*. 2 vols. Paris: SEVPEN

- 1975. *Montaillou, village occitan de 1294 à 1324*. France: Editions Gallimard Flammarion

Leutrat, Paul. 1966. *Les Vaudois*. Paris: Editions sociales

Lucas, Colin. 1973. *The Structure of the Terror*. Oxford: Oxford University Press

Luxemburg, Rosa. [1913] 1968. *The Accumulation of Capital*. New York: Modern Reader

McPhee, Peter. 1981. 'Social Change and Political Conflict in Mediterranean France: Canet in the Nineteenth Century.' *French Historical Studies* 12 (1, Spring): 68–97

Mandel, Ernest. 1971. *Marxist Economic Theory*. London: Merlin

Margadant, Ted W. 1980. *French Peasants in Revolt: The Insurrection of 1851*. Princeton, NJ: Princeton University Press

Marion, Marcel. 1969. *Dictionnaire des institutions de la France aux XVIIᵉ et XVIIIᵉ siècles.* Paris: Picard

Marx, Karl. [1869] 1969. 'The Eighteen Brumaire of Louis Bonaparte.' New York: International Publishers

Mayer, Adrian. 1966. 'The Significance of Quasi-Groups in the Study of Complex Societies.' In *The Social Anthropology of Complex Societies*, edited by M. Banton. ASA monograph no. 4. London: Tavistock

- 1967. 'Patrons and Brokers: Rural Leadership in Four Overseas Indian Communities.' In *Social Organization: Essays Presented to Raymond Firth*, edited by M. Freedman. London: Frank Cass

Meillassoux, Claude. 1972. 'From Reproduction to Production: A Marxist Approach to Economic Anthropology.' *Economy and Society* 1: 93–105

Merriman, John. 1975. 'The *Demoiselles* of the Ariège, 1829–1831.' In *1830 in France*, edited by John Merriman. New York: New Viewpoints

- 1977. *The Agony of the Republic: The Repression of the Left in Revolutionary France, 1848–1851.* New Haven: Yale University Press

Ministère de l'Agriculture [France]. 1903. *Enquête sur l'industrie laitière*, vol. 1. Office de Renseignements Agricole, Service des Etudes Techniques. Paris: Imprimerie Nationale

Moore, Barrington, Jr. 1966. *Social Origins of Dictatorship and Democracy: Lord and Peasant in the Making of the Modern World.* Boston: Beacon Press

Moskowitz, Milton, Michael Katz, and Robert Levering. 1980. *Everybody's Business: An Almanac.* San Francisco: Harper and Row

Müller, Robert, and Ch.-P. Péguy. 1944. 'Contributions à l'étude humaine des Alpes briançonnaises.' *Revue de Géographie Alpine* 32: 59–98

Mus, P. 1952. *Viêt-nam, Sociologie d'une guerre.* Paris: Seuil

Netting, Robert McC. 1981. *Balancing on an Alp.* Cambridge: Cambridge University Press

Nettl, Peter. 1967. *Political Mobilization.* London: Faber and Faber

O'Brien, Donal Cruise. 1972. 'Modernization, Order, and the Erosion of a Democratic Ideal: American Political Science 1960–1970.' *Journal of Development Studies* 8(4): 351–78

Opperman, Alfred, ed., 1926. *Le Mouvement économique: l'industrie.* Vol. 8 of *Les Bouche-du-Rhône: Encyclopédie Départementale*, edited by Paul Masson. Paris: Champion

Paine, Robert. 1971. 'A Theory of Patronage and Brokerage.' In *Patrons and Brokers in the East Arctic*, edited by Robert Paine. Newfoundland Social and Economic Papers no. 2. Toronto: University of Toronto Press

Pecaut, Henri. 1907. *Etudes sur le droit privé des hautes vallées alpines de Provence et de Dauphiné au moyenage.* Paris: Larose et Tenin

Peristiany, J.G., ed. 1965. 'Introduction.' In *Honor and Shame: The Values of Mediterranean Society*, edited by J.G. Peristiany. New York and London: Columbia University Press

Pitt-Rivers, Julian. 1954. *The People of the Sierra*. New York: Criterion Books

Polanyi, Karl. 1957. *The Great Transformation: The Political and Economic Origins of Our Time*. Boston: Beacon Press

Pons, Paul. [n.d.] 'Un Famille Queyrassine: Les Toye-Riont. Manuscript. Gap

Porchnev, Boris F. 1963. *Les soulèvements populaires en France de 1623 à 1648*. Paris: SEVPEN

Portes, Alejandro. 1978. 'Migration and Underdevelopment.' *Politics and Society* 8: 1–48

Reiter, Rayna R. 1975. 'Men and Women in the South of France: Public and Private Domains.' In *Toward an Anthropology of Women*, edited by R. Reiter. New York: Monthly Review Press

Rémy, Pierre. 1972. 'Le Gaullisme et les paysans.' In *L'Univers Politique des Paysans*, edited by Pierre Rémy. Paris: Seuil

Roche, C. 1898. 'Nécrologie: Marius Toye-Riont.' *Bulletin de la Société d'Etudes des Hautes-Alpes* 17: 363–5

Rodney, Walter. 1972. *How Europe Underdeveloped Africa*. Dar Es Salaam: Tanzania Publishing House

Rogie, J.-P. 1957. 'L'Evolution de la production laitière dans le département des Hautes-Alpes.' *Bulletin de la Fédération Française d'Economie Alpestre*, no. 8, pp. 299–306

Roman, J. 1892. 'Statistique du Briançonnais en 1747 par Roux-La-Croix.' *Bulletin de la Société d'Etudes des Hautes-Alpes* 11: 343–65

Rosenberg, Harriet. 1976. 'Coutume du Pays: Women in an 18th Century French Alpine Village.' Paper presented at Third Annual Berkshire Conference on Women's History, Bryn Mawr College, Penn., June

Rosenberg, Harriet, R.B. Reiter, and R.R. Reiter. 1973. 'Peasants Working in French Alpine Tourism: Whose Development?' *Studies in European Society* (1): 21–38

Rostow, W.W. 1960. *The Stages of Economic Growth: A Non-Communist Manifesto*. Cambridge: Cambridge University Press

Routier, Jacqueline. ca 1970. *Petite Histoire de Briançon et des Briançonnais*. Grenoble: Editions des Cahiers de l'Alpe

Schneider, Jane. 1971. 'Of Vigilance and Virgins: Honor, Shame and Access to Resources in Mediterranean Societies,' *Ethnology* 10(1): 1–24

Schneider, Peter, Jane Schneider, and Edward Hansen. 1972. 'Modernization and Development: the Role of Regional Elites and Non-Corporate

Groups in the European Mediterranean.' *Comparative Studies in Society and History* 14(3): 328–50

Servolin, Claude. 1972. 'L'absorption de l'agriculture dans le mode de production capitaliste.' In *L'Univers politique des paysans*, edited by Y. Tavernier, M. Gervais, and C. Servolin. Paris: Armand Colin

Shils, Edward. 1962. *Political Development and New States*. The Hague: Mouton

‒ 1970a. 'Political Development in New States ‒ Alternative Courses of Political Development.' In *Readings in Social Evolution and Development*, edited by S.N. Eisenstadt. Oxford and New York: Pergamon Press

‒ 1970b. 'Political Development in New States ‒ The Will to Be Modern.' In *Readings in Social Evolution and Development*, edited by S.N. Eisenstadt. Oxford and New York: Pergamon Press

Silver, Judith. 1980. 'French Peasant Demands for Popular Leadership in the Vendomois (Loir-et-Cher), 1852–1870.' *Journal of Social History* 14 (2, Winter): 277–94

Silverman, Sydel F. 1968. 'Patronage and Community-Nation Relationship in Central Italy.' In *Peasant Society*, edited by Jack M. Potter, M. Diaz, and G. Foster. Boston: Little Brown

‒ 1974. 'Bailey's Politics.' *Journal of Peasant Studies* 2(1): 111–20

‒ 1978. 'Review of E. Weber's *Peasants into Frenchmen*.' *Ethnohistory* 25 (3, Summer): 295–7

Slicher van Bath, B.H. 1963. *The Agrarian History of Western Europe, A.D. 500–1550*. London: Arnold

Surell, A. [1841] 1870. *Etude sur les torrents des Hautes-Alpes*. 2 vols. 2nd ed. Paris: Revue des Eaux et Forêts

Terrisse, Michel. 1971. 'Proletariat flottant et migrations temporaires à Marseilles.' *Bulletin d'Information, Société de Démographie Historique*, pp. 2–7

Thivot, Henry. 1971. *La Vie publique dans les Hautes-Alpes vers le milieu du XIXᵉ siècle*. Grenoble: Editions des Cahiers de l'Alpe

Tilly, Charles. 1964. *The Vendée: A Sociological Analysis of the Counterrevolution of 1793*. New York: Wiley

‒ 1975. 'Reflections on the History of European State-Making.' In *The Formation of National States in Western Europe*, edited by Charles Tilly. Princeton, NJ: Princeton University Press

Tipps, Dean C. 1973. 'Modernization Theory and the Comparative Study of Societies: A Critical Perspective.' *Comparative Studies in Society and History* 15(2): 199–226

Tivollier, Jean. 1938. *Le Queyras*. 2 vols. Gap: Louis Jean

Toye-Riont, Maurice. 1932. 'L'Avenir économique du département des Hautes-Alpes.' Paper presented to Société des Enfants des Alpes de Marseille, Marseilles

Van de Walle, Etienne. 1974. *The Female Population of France in the Nineteenth Century: A Reconstruction of 82 Départements*. Princeton, NJ: Princeton University Press

Van Gennep, Arnold. 1946. *Le Folklore des Hautes-Alpes*. Paris: Maisonneuve

Veyret, Germaine. 1952. 'Les régimes démographiques dans les Alpes françaises: leur évolution.' *Bulletin de la Section de Géographie* 65: 149-58

Vezin, Charles. 1957. 'Groupement de Productivite,' In *L'Evolution de l'agriculture de montagne: l'example des Hautes-Alpes*, edited by Comité Départemental de la Vulgarization et du Progrès Agricole [Hautes-Alpes] Gap: Direction des Services Agricole.

Vigier, Philippe. 1963. *La Seconde République dans la région alpine*. 2 vols. Paris: PUF

Wallerstein, Immanuel. 1974. *The Modern World-System: Capitalist Agriculture and the Origins of the European World-Economy in the Sixteenth Century*. New York: Academic Press

Weber, Eugen. 1976. *Peasants into Frenchmen: The Modernization of Rural France, 1870-1914*. Stanford, Calif.: Stanford University Press

- 1980. 'The Second Republic, Politics and the Peasant.' *French Historical Studies* 11 (4, Fall): 521-50

- 1982. 'Comment la Politique Vint aux Paysans: A Second Look at Peasant Politicization.' *The American Historical Review* 87 (2, April): 357-89

Wiegandt, Ellen B. 1977. 'Communalism and Conflict in the Swiss Alps' PhD dissertation, University of Michigan

Wolf, Eric R. 1956. 'Aspects of Group Relations in a Complex Society: Mexico.' *American Anthropologist* 58(6)

- 1966a. *Peasants*. Englewood Cliffs, NJ: Prentice-Hall

- 1966b. 'Kinship Friendship and Patron-Client Relationships in Complex Societies.' In *The Sociology of Complex Societies*, edited by M. Banton. ASA Monographs. London: Tavistock

- 1969. *Peasant Wars of the Twentieth Century*. New York: Harper and Row

- 1982. *Europe and the People without History*. Berkeley, Los Angeles, and London: University of California Press

Wolfe, Alan. 1974. 'New Directions in the Marxist Theory of Politics.' *Politics and Society*, Winter: 131–59

Wolfisberg, Hans J. 1966. *A Century of Global Operations: The Flavorful World of Nestlé*. New York: The Newcomer Society

Wood, Ellen M. 1981. 'The Separation of the Economic and the Political in Capitalism.' *New Left Review*, no. 127 (May-June): 66–95

Wrigley, E.A. 1969. *Population and History*. Toronto and New York: McGraw-Hill

Index

Abriès: ancien régime, importance of, 12; architecture, as expression of centrality, 12; commune of, 10-11 (map); daily life in old regime, 29-30; description, 1970s, 167-8; economy, dependence on transfer payments, 168; economy, importance of stock raising in, nineteenth century, 97; economy, pre-capitalistic, 97; economy, unimproved by tourism, 188; household composition, 1970s, 179-81, 183-6; interest in past, xv, 6; literacy, 6; location, 1, 7, 2, 8 (map); records extant, 6, 210; resident-tourist interaction, 170-1; see also Demography
agricultural crisis: of 1760-66, 37; of 1846-47, 114; twentieth century, 209
agricultural experts, 162-4; Abrièsois scepticism of, 182-3; Guicherd (1933), 128; see also Forest Administration experts: Collective institutions, pasturing of stock
agricultural year, 15, 168-72

agriculturalists, dependence on transfer payments, 181
agriculture: ancien régime, 13-15; capitalization of, 116-20; mechanization of 162-3; multi-crop, as protection from potato blight, 114; peasant production under capitalism, 5, 45; perception of failure as reason for tourism development, 165; remodelling along industrial lines, 4; removal of forests from village economy, 172; stock raising, importance of, 97; subsidies to grazing animals, 176; subsistence crops, 97-8; transition to monopoly capitalism, 116-26; under direction of state experts, 116-25; 162-5, 182-3; undercapitalization of, 203; vaine pâture, resistance to abolition of, 129; war, effect on, 14; withdrawal of land from, 204; see also Crop failure; Crop rotation; Cultivators; Development; Forest Administration
Americains, mythologized in modern Abriès, 139-40
amusements and games, 30